680046518X

CW00537201

/3.00

IMPERIAL BRITAIN

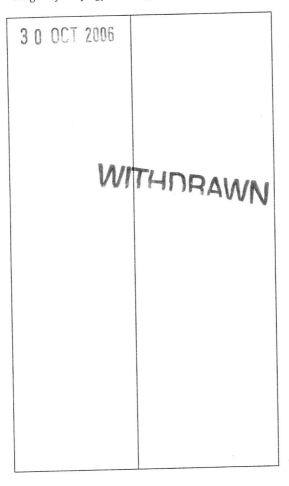

University of Wales Lampeter
Prifysgol Cymru Llambed

Library ~ Llyfrgell

Duration of Loan : On or before the latest date
stamped below. **N.B.** : Books may be recalled early
if wanted by another reader.
Cyfnod y Benthyciad : Ddim yn hwy na'r dyddiad
diweddaraf isod. **Sylwer** : bod llyfrau yn medru cael
eu galw yn ôl yn gynnar ar gyfer darllenwyr eraill.

Imperial Britain
The Empire in British Politics, *c.* 1880–1932

Andrew S. Thompson

An imprint of **Pearson Education**

Harlow, England · London · New York · Reading, Massachusetts · San Francisco
Toronto · Don Mills, Ontario · Sydney · Tokyo · Singapore · Hong Kong · Seoul
Taipei · Cape Town · Madrid · Mexico City · Amsterdam · Munich · Paris · Milan

Pearson Education Limited
Edinburgh Gate
Harlow
Essex CM20 2JE
England

and Associated Companies throughout the world

Visit us on the world wide web at:
www.pearsoneduc.com

First published 2000

ISBN 0-582-31920-X CSD
ISBN 0-582-31921-8 PPR

British Library Cataloguing-in-Publication Data
A catalogue record for this book is available from the British Library

Library of Congress Cataloging-in-Publication Data
Thompson, Andrew S. (Andrew Stuart), 1968–
    Imperial Britain : the politics, economics, and ideology of
empire, c. 1880–1932 / Andrew S. Thompson.
        p.   cm.
    Includes bibliographical references and index.
    ISBN 0-582-31921-8 (paper). — ISBN 0-582-31920-X (case)
    1. Great Britain—Colonies—History—20th century.
2. Imperialism—Public opinion—Great Britain—History—20th
century.   3. Imperialism—Public opinion—Great Britain—
History—19th century.   4. Great Britain—Politics and
government—1901-1936.   5. Great Britain—Politics and
government—1837-1901.   6. Great Britain—Colonies—History—19th
century.   7. Great Britain—Colonies—Economic conditions.
I. Title.
DA18.T5   2000
941.08—dc21   99–36023
                                                                CIP
Set by 35 in 10/12 pt Bembo
Produced by Pearson Education Asia Pte Ltd.,

Transferred to digital print on demand, 2006

Printed and bound by CPI Antony Rowe, Eastbourne

For Mum and Dad

Contents

List of Figures

List of Tables

Preface

The publication of this book is timely. Historical interest in the implications of Britain's empire for its own 'domestic' history has grown considerably during recent years. To a large extent, we have the efforts of cultural historians to thank. More than anybody else, they have alerted us to the need to inject imperial history back into Britain. In particular, they have shown how the literature, popular entertainment and commercial advertising of the nineteenth and twentieth centuries were heavily influenced by the fact that Britain was an imperial power. Yet other facets of Britain's imperial experience remain largely unexplored, not least the effects of empire upon British political life.

What follows is a study of imperialism as a political movement and ideology in late-nineteenth and early-twentieth-century Britain. Space did not permit a 'total history' of imperial Britain, and the Empire's impact upon the nation's religious, literary and cultural life is touched upon only tangentially. But the subject of the book – 'imperial politics' – is very broadly conceived. It embraces wider intellectual, demographic and economic influences upon Britain's political process, and involves an analysis of each of the main political movements inspired by the Empire. Imperialists in Britain campaigned intensively on a wide range of issues which were close to the centre of national political debate. In discussing these issues – fiscal policy, naval defence and overseas migration – several perspectives on imperial political activity are opened up. Attention is paid to the attitudes of imperialists, to their concepts of empire, to the way they mobilised popular support, and to the propagation of their beliefs, in particular through the press. The period studied stretches from the early 1880s, when J.R. Seeley published *The Expansion of England*, to the signing of the Ottawa tariff agreements in 1932. The dates are approximate because the focus is not on particular governments or parliaments but on grass-roots political activism.

My concern with the 'white' Dominions should be explained. Since the 1960s, Anglo-Dominion relations have been a somewhat unfashionable area of imperial history. Scholars exploring the manifestations of empire in British culture have faithfully reflected this trend, focusing on India and tropical Africa, and neglecting Canada, Australia, New Zealand and, to a lesser extent, South Africa. Yet, as I argue, this approach is profoundly problematic when studying imperialism as a domestic political phenomenon. Before the 1920s, not even India gave rise to any major organised political campaign regarding the Empire. Rather, it was the self-governing areas of that empire which had the highest political profile; and the dependent empire was not widely debated, despite the protests of men like Lord Curzon and the Earls of Cromer and Meath.

Ireland is only touched on briefly. In view of the complexity of Anglo-Irish relations, imperial history has long tended to treat them as separate from the rest of the British Empire. Moreover, Ireland's position was in many ways paradoxical for it was both a 'colonised' and an 'imperial' power. Irish nationalists identified with anti-colonial movements in Egypt and India; but many of the Irish participated in empire-building as well. Finally, Ireland was unlike any other areas of empire in that it was directly represented at Westminster. To have included Ireland would therefore have raised the problem of 'internal colonialism' within the United Kingdom, requiring at least another chapter in the book.

(Throughout this book, the place of publication is London, unless otherwise stated.)

Acknowledgements

While writing this book I have incurred many debts, and made many friends. In Oxford, Nuffield and Corpus Christi Colleges provided stimulating research and teaching environments, and I am grateful to both institutions for their support. More recently, a lectureship in Modern British History at the University of Leeds has provided me with the space to finish writing and to revise the manuscript. I would also like to thank the staff of the Bodleian Library, Oxford; Nuffield College Library; Birmingham University Library; the Brotherton Library, Leeds; Sheffield University Library; the Institute of Commonwealth Studies; the House of Lords Record Office; and the Northumberland Record Office for their help, as well as the Sea Cadet Association for allowing me to consult the records of the Navy League.

Individual chapters of the book were read by Jacky Beaumont, John Beeler, Peter Cain, Kent Fedorowich, Alex May and Alan Sykes. I benefited tremendously from their knowledge and constructive criticisms. The draft manuscript in its entirety was read by a number of colleagues. Paul Laity wielded his editorial pen, and shared his ideas on extra-parliamentary political cultures. David Omissi engaged me in stimulating debate about many issues, and his encouragement was greatly valued. Brian Harrison and Iain Smith read the manuscript at a late stage in the day, and offered some very valuable advice. Authors rely heavily on the generosity of such individuals, and I am very grateful to each for their help. As commissioning editors, Andrew MacLennan and Hilary Shaw eased the manuscript along at key stages, and applied just the right amount of pressure as the deadline for its submission approached. Sarah Bury copy-edited the manuscript with great care, and Verina Pettigrew oversaw the desk-editing sympathetically and efficiently. Others had an input into the making of this book which is less easy to measure. Thomas Charles Edwards was a brilliant colleague at Corpus Christi College, and Brian Harrison a marvellous 'room mate'. Richard Grayson not only read various drafts of the manuscript, but applied for the same jobs, attended the same interviews and became a close and unfailing friend. David Eastwood has been a trusted adviser ever since I began graduate work, equally liberal in sharing his wine and his ideas about the writing of political history. John Darwin has also been very supportive. As an undergraduate tutor and postgraduate supervisor he kindled my interest in imperial history. Since then, he has made many shrewd suggestions about this work, and been a kind mentor.

Finally, without a family writing a book would be a lot more difficult and a lot less fun. My parents have been extremely generous in supporting me through university and beyond. Most of all my wife, Sarah, has shared the ups and downs of academic life, and helped in so many ways to see this project through to completion. The biggest thanks of all therefore go to her.

AST
March 1999
University of Leeds

Abbreviations

ANZAC	Australian and New Zealand army corps
BIHR	*Bulletin of the Institute of Historical Research*
BWEA	British Women's Emigration Association
BWNL	British Workers' National League
CDC	Colonial Defence Committee
CES	Child Emigration Society
CID	Committee of Imperial Defence
CHR	*Canadian Historical Review*
CCO	Conservative Central Office
CO	Colonial Office
CUWFA	Conservative and Unionist Women's Franchise Association
DRC	Dominions Royal Commission
EC	Emigration Committee of the Royal Colonial Institute
EcHR	*Economic History Review*
EHR	*English Historical Review*
EIA	Empire Industries Association
EIO	Emigration Information Office
ELSC	Empire Land Settlement Committee
EMB	Empire Marketing Board
EPU	Empire Press Union
ER	*Empire Review*
FMCES	Female Middle Class Emigration Society
FO	Foreign Office
FTU	Free Trade Union
HJ	*Historical Journal*
HWJ	*History Workshop Journal*
ICS	Indian Civil Service
IFDC	Imperial Federation Defence Committee
IFL	Imperial Federation League
IHR	*International History Review*
IML	Imperial Maritime League

ISAA	Imperial South Africa Association
IWC	Imperial War Cabinet
JBS	*Journal of British Studies*
JCH	*Journal of Contemporary History*
JCPS	*Journal of Commonwealth Political Studies*
JEH	*Journal of Economic History*
JICH	*Journal of Imperial and Commonwealth History*
JMH	*Journal of Modern History*
JSAS	*Journal of South African Studies*
NFTL	National Fair Trade League
NL	Navy League
NLF	National Liberal Federation
NLJ	*Navy League Journal*
NMEL	Naval and Military Emigration League
NUCCA	National Union of Conservative and Constitutional Associations
P&P	*Past and Present*
RCI	Royal Colonial Institute
RCS	Royal Commonwealth Society
SACS	South African Colonisation Society
TCBH	*Twentieth Century British History*
TRHS	*Transactions of the Royal Historical Society*
TRL	Tariff Reform League
TUTRA	Trade Union Tariff Reform Association
UFTs	Unionist Free Traders
WAUTRA	Women's Amalgamated Unionist and Tariff Reform Association

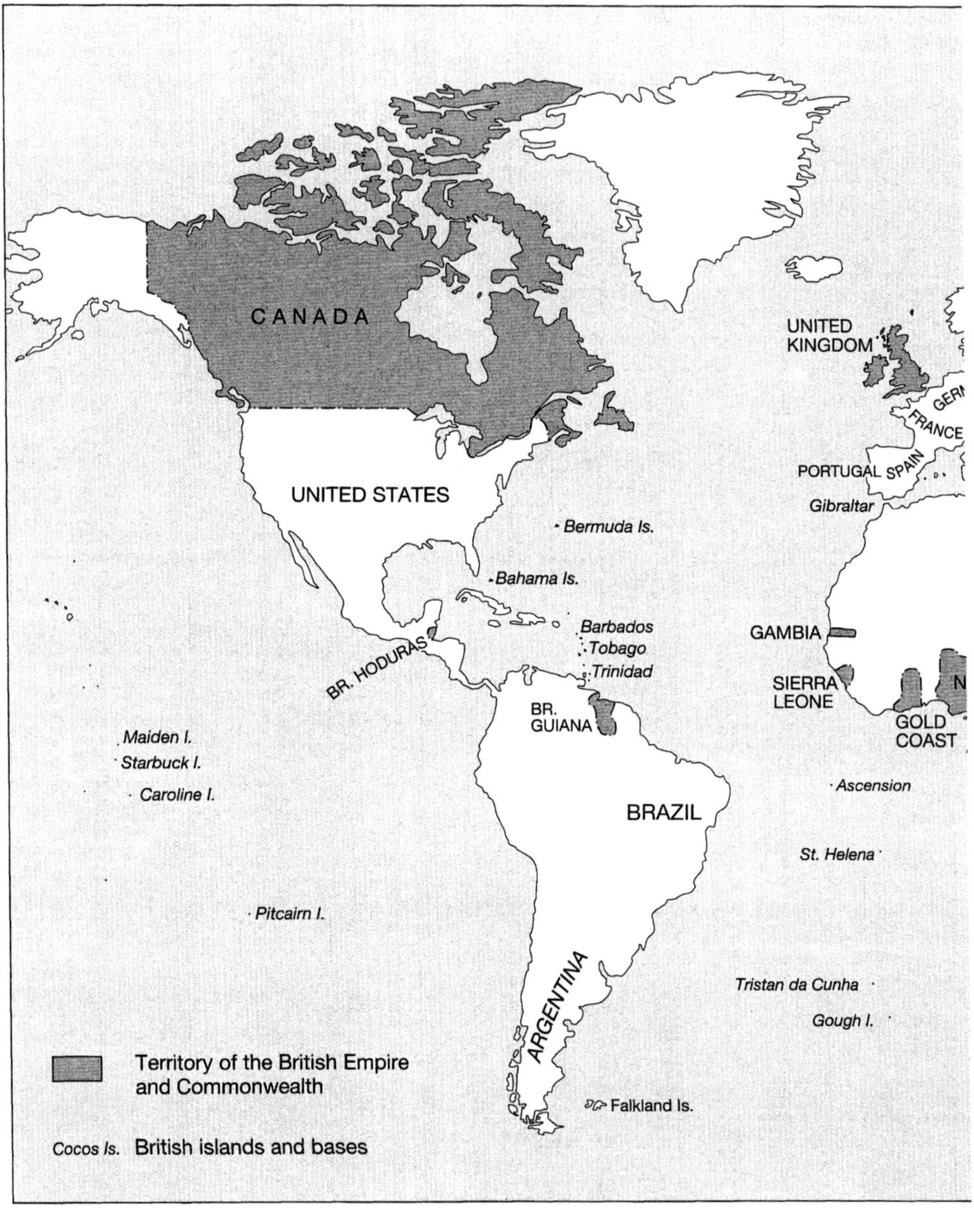
CANADA
UNITED KINGDOM
GERM
FRANCE
PORTUGAL
SPAIN
Gibraltar
UNITED STATES
Bermuda Is.
Bahama Is.
Barbados
Tobago
Trinidad
BR. HODURAS
GAMBIA
SIERRA LEONE
GOLD COAST
BR. GUIANA
Maiden I.
Starbuck I.
Caroline I.
Ascension
BRAZIL
St. Helena
Pitcairn I.
ARGENTINA
Tristan da Cunha
Gough I.
Territory of the British Empire and Commonwealth
Falkland Is.
Cocos Is. British islands and bases

The Empire in 1920

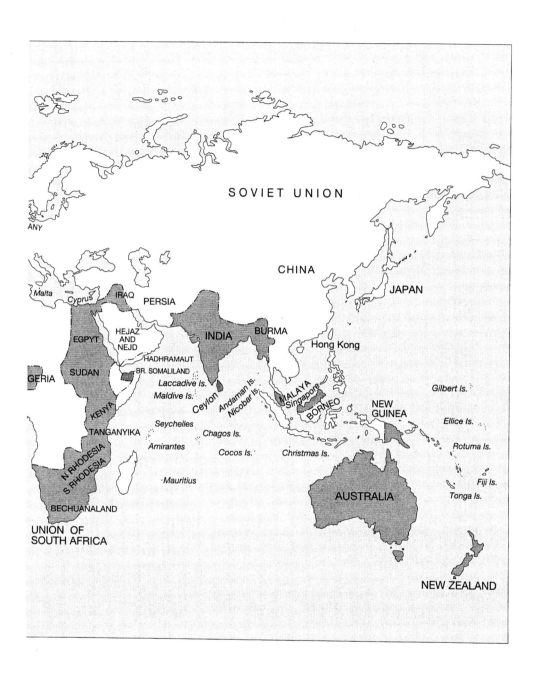

ANY

SOVIET UNION

CHINA

JAPAN

Malta

Cyprus

IRAQ

PERSIA

INDIA

BURMA

Hong Kong

EGPYT

HEJAZ AND NEJD

HADHRAMAUT

GERIA

SUDAN

BR. SOMALILAND

Laccadive Is.

Maldive Is.

Ceylon

Andaman Is.

Nicobar Is.

Gilbert Is.

KENYA

MALAYA

Singapore

BORNEO

NEW GUINEA

Ellice Is.

TANGANYIKA

Seychelles

Chagos Is.

Rotuma Is.

Amirantes

Cocos Is.

Christmas Is.

N RHODESIA

S.RHODESIA

Mauritius

Fiji Is.

AUSTRALIA

Tonga Is.

BECHUANALAND

UNION OF SOUTH AFRICA

NEW ZEALAND

Introduction

Historical writing about the British Empire has recently shown a new lease of life. Invigorating new perspectives on Britain's long imperial involvement have been provided by studies of the Empire's impact at home. For many years this subject was largely ignored. Captivated by the causes of British expansion, the structures of colonial rule, and the process of decolonisation, historians rarely stopped to ask what the Empire had done to Britain and its people. In the last ten years or so all this has changed, and scholars are now actively challenging insular and inward-looking approaches to the writing of British history. Moves towards closer European integration, the transfer of Hong Kong to China, Scottish and Welsh devolution, and the peace process in Northern Ireland – all these have undermined the idea that the Britain we know today is simply the creation of forces from within 'little England'. Thus in just the same way as historians have recently set the development of the British Conservative party in a broader continental European context,[1] so too they are recognising the need to inject Commonwealth-Imperial history back into the domestic history of modern Britain.[2]

This 'repatriation' of the Empire is something of a growth industry. In exploring the effects of the Empire within Britain itself, economic and cultural historians have been especially active. What is, however, conspicuously lacking in this new historiography is a study of the imperial impact on the domestic political scene. This is a major gap. Ruling an empire was inextricably linked to key questions in British politics like the allocation of resources and the decision to go to war. Hence no government could commit itself to a major initiative in imperial policy without taking into account how it would play at home. Yet the implications of Britain's role as an imperial power for its own internal political development remain unclear. Historians exploring this relationship have tended to focus either on particular aspects of imperial politics

1 E.H.H. Green, *The Crisis of Conservatism. The Politics, Economics and Ideology of the British Conservative Party, 1880–1914* (1995), pp.319–33.
2 S. Marks, 'History, the Nation and the Empire: Sniping from the Periphery', *HWJ* (1990), p.113; M. Daunton, 'Home and Colonial', *TCBH* (1995), p.344.

or to offer very generalised models of the Empire's political repercussions. The specialised studies fall into two main categories. First, there are investigations of intra-party factions, right-wing ideologies and parts of the press.[3] Second, there are biographies of leading journalists, officials and statesmen who were involved in public debate about empire.[4] While many of these works provide interesting insights, they fail to confront the bigger question of how British politics as a whole was influenced and modified by its imperial involvement.

Other historians have dealt more broadly with the domestic politics of imperialism from both high and low political perspectives. There are two widely circulating if perhaps equally flawed stereotypes of the political significance of empire. The idea of an 'official' or 'collective' mind – a policy-making elite – suggests that organised opinion in Britain was of little importance in the making of colonial policy. It maintains that the key debates about British expansion went on within Whitehall, and that the ordinary voter was too self-absorbed to bother much about what happened abroad.[5] Even those groups which did take an interest in Britain's colonies are said to have done so mainly for partisan reasons. Their imperialism was skin deep; motivated by party advantage and propelled by factional rivalries rather than by any ideological commitment to empire.[6] Not surprisingly, several objections have been levelled against this 'black box' model of an official mind. But its apparent disregard for an array of external forces working upon government has come in for especially strong criticism. Many historians believe that it is simply unrealistic to imagine that politicians in London took decisions about empire without being influenced by the way that empire was comprehended and imagined by the 'organs' of public opinion.

The other model of imperial politics is the 'popular imperialism' stereotype. Here, rather than being indifferent to empire, public opinion is red in tooth and claw. The British public, it is argued, had a highly positive if very generalised attitude to empire, the result of an intensive propaganda campaign which began in the late-nineteenth century.[7] On closer inspection, however, this approach turns out to be no less problematic, not least because the motives lying behind imperial propaganda are not properly explored. Enthusiasm for empire is explained in terms of elite manipulation – imperialism provided an effective

3 For imperially-minded groups within the Liberal and Conservative parties, see H.C.G. Matthew, *The Liberal Imperialists. The Ideas and Politics of a Post-Gladstonian Elite* (Oxford, 1973), and M. Pugh's study of the Primrose League, *The Tories and the People, 1880–1935* (Oxford, 1985). On the Edwardian 'Radical Right' and the discourse of 'national efficiency', see F. Coetzee, *For Party or Country. Nationalism and the Dilemmas of Popular Conservatism in Edwardian England* (Oxford, 1990); R.J. Scally, *The Origins of the Lloyd George Coalition: The Politics of Social Imperialism* (Princeton, NJ, 1975); G.R. Searle, *The Quest for National Efficiency* (Oxford, 1971); and A. Sykes, 'The Radical Right and the Crisis of Conservatism before the First World War', *HJ* (1983). For the press and empire, see the references provided in Chapter 2.

4 For a sample of such biographies see the Select Bibliography.

5 R. Robinson and J. Gallagher, *Africa and the Victorians. The Official Mind of Imperialism* (2nd edn, Basingstoke, 1981), pp.19–26.

6 J. Gallagher, *The Decline, Revival and Fall of the British Empire. The Ford Lectures and Other Essays* (Cambridge, 1982), pp.75–81.

7 E. Boehmer, *Empire Writing. An Anthology of Colonial Literature 1870–1918* (Oxford, 1998).

system of social discipline, reinforced hierarchical views of British society, and propped up Establishment interests. Yet this emphasis upon the conservative if not authoritarian impulse lying behind imperial propaganda belongs largely to the realm of speculation. For just as political analyses of imperialism tend to neglect its wider cultural impact, so cultural histories of empire frequently fail to set imperial propaganda activity in any sort of meaningful political context. In short, the 'popular imperialism' model is far too vague as to what types of political group became involved in imperial propaganda activity and why they felt it necessary to propagandise.

What we lack therefore is an assessment of the overall political significance of empire for Britain, which links imperial political activity to ideas, values and assumptions which existed in the country at large. This, then, is what this book seeks to provide. It is a study of imperialism as a *political* movement and cause, and of its modes of organisation, campaigning, publicity and propaganda. In no sense does it try to reduce imperial sentiment and beliefs to organised political activity, or to suggest that imperialism did not exist beyond the parties and extra-parliamentary agitations. As we are about to see, something of 'Imperial Britain' is to be found in popular forms of entertainment, in the nation's literary and religious life, in various forms of women's voluntary work, and in public ceremony and festival. However, this book does suggest that our understanding of what the Empire did to Britain has been greatly impoverished by the neglect of the political sphere in recent historiography. It also emphasises the difficulty of separating the study of 'politics' from broader demographic, economic, military and idealistic influences. And it demonstrates the importance of political activity in raising awareness and forging a wider public consciousness of empire.

If the political impact of empire has not received adequate attention, the imperial legacy has for a long time been a significant strand of debates about Britain's economic 'decline' or even 'failure' after 1880. Until fairly recently much of this literature had a strongly polemical thrust, the blame for the supposedly adverse consequences of 'soft' or 'sheltered' markets, the 'flight' of capital from Britain, and an 'old-fashioned education system', all being laid squarely at the Empire's door. More recently, historians have attempted to produce solid quantitative evidence to support the claim that empire was an economic liability for Britain. In particular, Davis's and Huttenback's cost-benefit analysis of British imperialism has come close to corroborating one of the main tenets of anti-imperialist literature; that is to say that the economy as a whole did not benefit from overseas possessions even if individual investors almost certainly did.[8] Their argument is advanced by examining the volume

8 L.E. Davis and R.A. Huttenback, *Mammon and the Pursuit of Empire: The Political Economy of British Imperialism, 1860–1912* (Cambridge, 1986). For a sample of the reactions, see P.K. O'Brien, 'The Costs and Benefits of British Imperialism, 1846–1914', *P&P* (1988), and the response by P. Kennedy, 'Debate. The Costs and Benefits of British Imperialism, 1846–1914', *P&P* (1989); J. Foreman-Peck, 'Foreign Investment and Imperial Exploitation: Balance of Payments Reconstruction

and direction of indirect or 'portfolio' investment passing through the London money market; by looking at the relative rates of return for a sample of just under 500 companies operating at home, abroad and in the Empire; and by considering government revenues and expenditures regarding the Empire. A particularly provocative claim, which needs to be scrutinised a lot more carefully by historians, is that imperialism acted as a mechanism for transferring wealth from British middle-class taxpayers, who shouldered the largest share of Britain's 'subsidy' to the Empire, to the upper classes or elites, who reaped substantial returns on their colonial investments.

Another facet of 'Imperial Britain' is to be found in the manifestations of empire in British popular culture. The work of John Mackenzie, general editor of the influential Manchester University Press *Studies in Imperialism* series, is particularly important here. It claims that the 'imperial ideal' left an indelible impression upon a variety of social activities ranging from music halls and cinema, to children's literature and school textbooks, to exhibitions and parades.[9] Thus what primarily interests Mackenzie and other contributors to the series is how empire featured in the lives of ordinary people. Imperialism is seen not just as the passion of a vocal minority, but as a more popular 'habit of mind', propagated successfully by non-official or extra-parliamentary institutions in co-operation with government. Mackenzie himself argues that imperialism was a 'core ideology' in British society from the 1880s until as late as the 1950s. The appeal of this ideology is explained by a combination of factors including a pervasive sense of racial superiority, popular devotion to royalty, a heightened sense of international rivalry, and the widespread worship of imperial heroes.

Linked to, but not to be conflated with, the *Studies in Imperialism* series is the school of post-colonial studies, which has established a powerful grip upon English literature in recent years.[10] Most widely debated is Edward Said's theory of 'orientalism', which rests largely upon an analysis of European, and especially British, literary engagement with empire.[11] Like several other scholars, Said is at pains to emphasise the centrality of empire to British literary culture from the late-eighteenth century onwards. Others have drawn attention to the immense popularity if not literary worth of the genre of 'imperial fiction' – popular adventure novels set in an imperial context, such as Rudyard Kipling's *Kim*, and Henry Rider Haggard's *King Solomon's Mines*. Different

---

for Nineteenth-Century Britain and India', *EcHR* (1989); A. Porter, 'The Balance Sheet of Empire, 1850–1914', *HJ* (1988); and A. Offer, 'The British Empire, 1870–1914: A Waste of Money?', *EcHR* (1993).

9 See especially J.M. Mackenzie, *Propaganda and Empire. The Manipulation of British Public Opinion, 1880–1960* (Manchester, 1986) and Mackenzie's introduction to *Imperialism and Popular Culture* (Manchester, 1986). For a precursor to the *Studies in Imperialism* series, see H. John Field, *Toward a Programme of Imperial Life. The British Empire at the Turn of the Century* (Oxford, 1982), esp. Chapter 3.

10 For a brief but informative discussion of colonial literature and post-colonial scholarship, see the introduction to Boehmer, *Empire Writing*, pp.xv–xxxvi.

11 E.W. Said, *Orientalism* (1978) and *Culture and Imperialism* (1993).

levels of significance have been attached to this type of writing. On the one hand, it can be argued that in view of the powerful hold of these authors over the public imagination, the experiences of empire they related were of crucial significance in forming popular perceptions of what Indian and Southern African societies were actually like. But it is also claimed that works of imperial fiction were themselves involved in the processes of empire; that Kipling and Rider Haggard were public spokesmen for empire who, through their writing, played a key role in justifying and legitimising British imperial rule.

It is therefore now widely asserted that British economic and cultural history cannot be divorced from the nation's imperial experience. Beyond this, there is a lively debate about the critics of imperialism. Historians, or more accurately certain types of historian, have always been drawn to studying dissent, and the history of the British Empire is no exception. Indeed it can be argued that the amount of attention devoted to the enemies of empire is disproportionate to their actual historical significance, and that this is part of the reason why enthusiasm for empire has not received sufficient attention. The allure of 'anti-imperialism' remains, however. Historians continue to reflect upon what inspired men and women to criticise colonial policy, and what sort of case they mounted against it, especially in the case of opposition to the South African (or second Anglo-Boer) War. The vociferous and well-known critics of this war have been closely scrutinised; individually, in the case of J.A. Hobson,[12] and collectively, in the case of the various 'pro-Boer' pressure groups.[13] The issue of how anti-imperialism was organised and articulated is also addressed by historians of the later-Victorian and Edwardian Liberal and Labour parties. Too many to mention in full, such studies include attempts to connect the doctrine of free trade to British imperialism;[14] as well as accounts of the highly disruptive impact of the South African War upon the various strands of the Edwardian Labour movement.[15] Finally, several historians proffer more general explanatory frameworks for understanding anti-imperialism.[16] Most recently, a major new study of anti-colonialism in twentieth-century British politics has surveyed the years before 1914, rightly emphasising how anti-imperialism was a limited and conditional stance which did not call for the dismantling of empire, but opposed the acquisition of additional colonies

12 See P.J. Cain, 'J.A. Hobson, Cobdenism and the Radical Theory of Economic Imperialism, 1898–1914', *EcHR* (1978); 'Hobson's Developing Theory of Imperialism', *EcHR* (1981); and 'J.A. Hobson, Finance Capitalism and Imperialism in Late Victorian and Edwardian England', *JICH* (1985).
13 For an overview of the pro-Boer movement, see S. Koss, *The Anatomy of an Anti-War Movement. The Pro-Boers* (1973). But the best study remains that by Arthur Davey, *The British Pro-Boers 1877–1902* (Cape Town, 1978).
14 A. Howe, *Free Trade and Liberal England, 1846–1946* (Oxford, 1997).
15 See M. Crick, *The History of the Social Democratic Federation* (Keele, 1994); A.M. McBriar, *Fabian Socialism and English Politics, 1884–1918* (Cambridge, 1962); and (on Trade Unions) D. Newton, *British Labour, European Socialism and the Struggle for Peace, 1889–1914* (Oxford, 1985).
16 A.P. Thornton, *An Imperial Idea and its Enemies* (1959); B. Porter, *Critics of Empire: British Radical Attitudes to Colonialism in Africa, 1895–1914* (1968); M. Taylor, 'Imperium et Libertas? Rethinking the Radical Critique of Imperialism during the Nineteenth Century', *JICH* (1991).

and argued for a more responsible and just administration of Britain's existing possessions.[17]

Beyond these critics and dissenters, there are three other main areas in which historians have explored the effects of empire upon British society: missionary activity; gender; and the monarchy. Missionary activity offers a compelling case study of the repercussions of empire for metropolitan Britain.[18] Although the field for missionaries was by no means exclusively imperial, the possession of an empire provided a strong stimulus to missionary work and, arguably, vice versa. Recent research on missionary societies has established their importance in Victorian religious life. They grew spectacularly, involved the mobilisation of large numbers of men and women, and raised substantial sums of money.[19] While we await a full-scale study of these societies, it is clear that they helped to draw together Christians of different denominations, to promote the position of lay people within the British churches, and to create a new reading public for the Empire (through widely-circulating missionary magazines). Moreover, the profile and prestige of missionaries rose considerably in the second half of the nineteenth century, not least because of the linkage between missionary work and exploration. David Livingstone's journeys into Central Africa in the 1850s generated huge public interest in the 'dark continent'. They also sustained a major biographical industry and led to the building of numerous public memorials. After his death, Livingstone was turned into a missionary 'martyr' and 'hero'.[20]

In the last two decades or so, feminist historians have begun to open up a long-overdue gender perspective upon the Empire's impact on metropolitan culture.[21] It is well recognised that British suffragism owed much to the backing, precedents and personnel from suffrage movements in Australia and New Zealand, where women gained the vote in 1902 and 1893 respectively. But British women themselves became caught up in the process of overseas expansion: as migrants, travellers, nurses, critics and colonial reformers. A common thread of debate which is implicit or explicit in many studies of gender and imperialism is how far women were the 'victims' of empire. There are different approaches on offer. Some see imperialism as being responsible for shaping culturally-repressive ideologies of motherhood, which confined the vast majority of British women to the roles of child-bearing and child-rearing.[22]

17 S. Howe, *Anti-Colonialism in British Politics: The Left and the End of Empire, 1918–1964* (Oxford, 1993), Chapter 2.
18 The word 'metropole' or 'metropolitan' is widely used by Commonwealth/Imperial historians to refer to the heart of the Empire – Britain itself.
19 A. Porter, 'Religion and Empire in the Long Nineteenth Century, 1780–1914', *JICH* (1992) and '"Cultural Imperialism" and Protestant Missionary Enterprise, 1780–1914', *JICH* (1997); B. Stanley, *The Bible and the Flag. Protestant Missions and British Imperialism in the Nineteenth and Twentieth Centuries* (1990) and *The History of the Baptist Missionary Society* (1992).
20 J.M. Mackenzie, *David Livingstone and the Victorian Encounter with Africa* (1996), Chapter 6.
21 See here the recent addition to the *Studies in Imperialism* series, *Gender and Imperialism* (Manchester, 1998), edited by Clare Midgley. Of particular interest is the historiographical overview provided by Midgley in the introduction.
22 See, in particular, A. Davin, 'Imperialism and Motherhood', *HWJ* (1978).

However, shifting the focus of enquiry to middle- and upper-class feminists – such as Josephine Butler, Mary Carpenter, Eleanor Rathbone and Margaret Cousins – others have pointed to the possibility of empire heightening women's political consciousness. In particular, much attention has been paid to the motivations of women who became involved in campaigns for Indian social reform (the ending of child marriage; the repeal of the Contagious Diseases Acts; women's education and health).[23] Taking up the 'white women's burden', it is argued, was not just a question of improving the plight of Indian women. Feminists in Britain were also struggling for recognition and equality at home, determined to demonstrate their fitness for citizenship and the vote.

The 'imperialising' of the British monarchy has likewise become a fashionable subject of study. In a pathfinding essay, David Cannadine suggested that there was a fundamental change in the image of the monarchy in the second half of the nineteenth century.[24] As the Crown retired from active politics, so its ceremonial duties expanded. This, in turn, led to the monarchy becoming more closely identified with the Empire. Not only was Queen Victoria proclaimed Empress of India in Delhi in 1877, but her golden (1887) and diamond jubilees (1897) were also pre-eminently imperial celebrations. A recent study of the public discussion of the monarchy in the reign of Queen Victoria reinforces the argument that the Crown benefited from its association with empire and vice versa.[25] The development of empire is seen as a defining characteristic of Victoria's reign. By 1901, the monarchy had been turned into a powerful symbol of imperial unity and authority, while the expansion of empire had come to epitomise the progress made during the later-Victorian era.

Despite this expanding historiography of 'Imperial Britain', there have been very few unifying studies which attempt to draw together the fields of economic, social and cultural history. Peter Cain's and A.G. Hopkins's concept of 'gentlemanly capitalism' is one of these.[26] Their two-volume reinterpretation of the British Empire turns our attention back to the metropole and the relationship between finance and imperialism. It presents the rapid rise of a service sector (banking, shipping, insurance) as the central fact of nineteenth-century British economic development and of British overseas expansion. This dynamic service sector provided the backbone of a new class of 'gentlemanly capitalists' – a fusion of the interlocking elites of government, finance, merchants and large landowners, based mainly in the south-east of England. These 'gentlemanly capitalists' had their own distinctive social ethos; a combination of the

23 A. Burton, *Burdens of History. British Feminists, Indian Women and Imperial Culture, 1865–1915* (Chapel Hill, NC, 1994); B.N. Ramusack, 'Catalysts or Helpers? British Feminists, Indian Women's Rights, and Indian Independence', in G. Minault (ed.), *The Extended Family. Women and Political Participation in India and Pakistan* (Delhi, 1981).
24 D. Cannadine, 'The Context, Performance and Meaning of Ritual: The British Monarchy and the Invention of Tradition, *c.* 1820–1977', in E. Hobsbawm and T. Ranger (eds), *The Invention of Tradition* (Cambridge, 1983), esp. pp.120–5.
25 R. Williams, *The Contentious Crown. Public Discussion of the British Monarchy in the Reign of Queen Victoria* (1997), Chapter 6.
26 P.J. Cain and A.G. Hopkins, *British Imperialism. Vol. I: Innovation and Expansion, 1688–1914* (Harlow, 1993), esp. Chapter 1.

social obligations of rank, Christian codes of honour, a renewed reverence for royalty, the pursuit of a leisured lifestyle, and a deeply-ingrained paternalism. Such values were asserted all the more vigorously in the colonies in order to put a protective barrier between British officials and the 'alien' environment in which they worked. Thus the 'gentlemanly capitalist' theory would appear to add weight to the view that the Empire was integral to British state and society, and not just an adjunct to it.

It is, then, widely argued that the Empire left a deep imprint on British society. However, in a string of incisive and imaginative articles investigating the 'elusive history of imperial Britain', Peter Marshall sounds a necessary note of caution.[27] While Marshall accepts that the history of Britain and the history of the British Empire cannot be easily separated, he prefers to see Britain's imperial experience as complementing rather than running counter to the main currents of its domestic history. The Empire, it is suggested, reflected and reinforced trends in British society, but did not push it in new directions. This proposition is fleshed out in discussions of the evolution of major British institutions and of the British middle class. Surveying the British parliament, armed forces, educational system and bureaucracy (exceptions are made for the monarchy and churches), scepticism is shown towards the claim that imperial expansion reshaped the British state, which, we are told, developed its own trajectory, to a large degree independent of what happened in the Empire. Doubt is also cast on the Empire's capacity to shift the main contours of British society. In particular, employment in the colonies is rejected as a sufficient explanation for the emergence of a professional middle class in Britain. In summary, while Britain's imperial enterprise is recognised to have been central to main currents of British history, its role is presented as a 'reflexive' rather than 'transforming' one.

Often referred to as an 'Age of High Imperialism', the later-Victorian and Edwardian era is now recognised as a period when empire was a pervasive and popular discourse. The growing strength of imperial themes in British political debate was already evident in the 1870s as Disraeli invoked the Empire in a direct appeal to the political nation.[28] From then on, it became increasingly difficult for politicians to run away from empire, though political feeling on the subject differed markedly within and between the parties. In the late 1890s, Britain's fight for supremacy in Southern Africa thrust the issue of imperialism to the forefront of the political stage. After the turn of the century, problems on the periphery and initiatives from the metropole – especially the issue of Chinese indentured labour and Joseph Chamberlain's tariff reform

27 P.J. Marshall, 'No Fatal Impact? The Elusive History of Imperial Britain', *Times Literary Supplement*, 12/3/1993, pp.8–10; 'Imperial Britain', *JICH* (1995); and a different essay under the same title, 'Imperial Britain', in Marshall (ed.), *The Cambridge Illustrated History of the British Empire* (Cambridge, 1996).
28 A. Hawkins, *British Party Politics, 1852–1886* (Basingstoke, 1998), pp.275–6.

campaign – ensured that imperialism remained firmly on the political agenda. Moreover, imperialism continued to be a significant strand of British political debate into the 1920s, as recent work on the longevity of the 'Dominion idea' in British politics, and the place of empire in the public doctrine of Stanley Baldwin, has affirmed.[29] Thus the problem when writing about the domestic politics of imperialism is not to show that the Empire was politically salient. Rather it is to establish precisely what empire meant for the development of political activity, and to determine how radically or fundamentally it changed patterns of political allegiance, alignment and debate.

Chapter 1 inspects the relationship between imperialism and late-nineteenth and early-twentieth-century political consciousness. It discusses the sorts of imperial-mindedness which emerged in British politics during this period. Here it is necessary to consider the fashioning of different imperial languages as well as the process of constructing imperial identities. States of mind, memory and consciousness are now highly fashionable themes among historians, who have become increasingly concerned with the roots of Britishness and increasingly preoccupied with who the British actually were (and are). It is now widely believed that empire significantly inflected what it meant to be British. From 1780 to 1830, the idea of Britain as a Christian 'Roman Empire' is thought to have been crucial to the development of British nationalism.[30] Historians of the late-eighteenth and early-nineteenth centuries also argue that a British identity was constructed negatively from notions of racial difference, the British people defining themselves 'in conscious opposition to the colonial "other" '.[31] The Victorian and Edwardian years receive similar treatment. Shula Marks asserts that it is impossible to understand the British nation outside the imperial and post-imperial experience, drawing attention to a 'corroding and pervasive racism' within British society.[32] Others point to nearly two centuries of successful Scottish participation in the Empire, suggesting that imperialism may not always have led to the suppression of regional and ethnic identities.[33]

Notwithstanding this growing body of scholarship, there remains much to learn about how Britain's role in the wider world affected the construction of British national identities. What is at issue here is not just the strength of public belonging to empire, but the very nature of that belonging. In order to tackle this question it is vital to get at the meanings of empire inside British politics. In a recent article I considered what late-Victorian and Edwardian

---

29 J. Darwin, 'The Third British Empire. The Dominion Idea in Imperial Politics, 1918–1965', in *The Oxford History of the British Empire* (forthcoming); P. Williamson, 'The Doctrinal Politics of Stanley Baldwin', in M. Bentley (ed.), *Public and Private Doctrine. Essays in British History presented to Maurice Cowling* (Cambridge, 1993).
30 C.A. Bayly, *Imperial Meridian. The British Empire and the World, 1780–1830* (Harlow, 1989), pp.11, 15.
31 L. Colley, 'Britishness and Otherness', *JBS* (1992).
32 Marks, 'History, the Nation and the Empire', pp.113, 117.
33 J.M. Mackenzie, 'Empire and National Identities: The Case of Scotland', *TRHS* (1998).

politicians meant when they spoke of empire, and the extent to which its meaning varied between different political groups.[34] But Chapter 1 takes the analysis further, connecting the new histories of identity, language and culture with an older political history of Anglo-Dominion relations. It argues that a key dimension of the British people's sense of themselves as an imperial race – often missing from, or passed over with embarrassment in, the existing literature – was consciousness of a 'Greater Britain'. From the mid-1880s until at least the late-1920s it was a widely held belief among British politicians that the chief hope for the preservation of Britain's great power status and its social structure lay in closer relations with the English-speaking Empire. Chapter 1 explores the origins and implications of this deeply-ingrained sense of a worldwide British identity.

In attempting to situate empire in Britain's larger political landscape, it is also necessary to consider the organisational side of imperialism. Where did the impetus for imperial campaigning come from? How was imperial sentiment marshalled into an organised form of politics? Which groups in Britain attempted to construct a national political agenda around the Empire? What sort of constituencies did they carry? And how did they try to make imperial issues interesting and intelligible to a wider public? The problem with much imperial history-writing is that it still tends to be history from above.[35] Histories of imperialism heavily weighted towards the 'official mind' – their 'politics' often very narrowly defined – suggest that imperial issues were rarely at the centre of national political controversy.[36] However, British politics is not solely Westminster, nor its government solely Whitehall, and the mainsprings of imperial campaigning are to be found not in party or parliamentary structures but in extra-parliamentary activism and press agitation. Chapters 2 and 3 explain why this was the case. But here it is worth pausing briefly to reflect upon how imperialism interlocked with the party structures, and to ask why the parties struggled to contain imperial interests and enthusiasms at this time. The issue is complex because it involves the attitudes of party managers towards imperial questions; the development of the modern party caucus, and its implications for parliamentary debate; and the different motivations for and purposes of extra-parliamentary activism.

In trying to make the Empire a guiding principle of government, imperialists met with a lot of resistance from party officials who believed that colonial policy was best left to the experts and mandarins in Whitehall. The problem of securing a satisfactory forum for imperial debate was exacerbated by improvements in party organisation at Westminster. By the end of the nineteenth century parties had much more control over parliamentary business, and pressure groups seeking to impinge directly on the legislative process were thus more likely to be disappointed.

---

34 A.S. Thompson, 'The Language of Imperialism and the Meanings of Empire: Imperial Discourse in British Politics, 1895–1914', *JBS* (1997).
35 Marks, 'History, the Nation and the Empire', p.112.
36 Gallagher and Robinson, *Africa and the Victorians*, pp.19–26.

Weaknesses of party organisation are also vitally important in understanding why imperialism did not sit comfortably within existing political structures. Take, for instance, the various societies, clubs and pressure groups spawned by Joseph Chamberlain's tariff reform campaign. Their aim was to overhaul and modernise the Unionist party's organisation. The Tariff Reform League led the way here, gaining control of parts of the party's propaganda machinery, but failing to capture the Conservative Central Office. In other instances, the impetus for the formation of imperial movements came from antipathy to the party system; an important but frequently misunderstood feature of later-Victorian and Edwardian politics. For some imperialists this antipathy to party arose from a belief that the crude polarity of two-party confrontation made for dangerous discontinuities in imperial policy. This attitude was particularly influential among defence experts. But other extra-parliamentary groups were not interested in generating debates about specific aspects of imperial policy. Their concern was to foster a more general attachment to empire among ordinary working people by making them feel proud of it, and by promoting various festivals and ceremonies to celebrate it. This emphasis on the social side of political organisation is characteristic of a popular movement like the Primrose League and of women's imperial societies like the Victoria League.

Others simply felt ambivalent about party; it was viewed as politically necessary, but not, perhaps, sufficient. A discussion group and intellectual gathering like the Co-efficients is a case in point. Here the aim was to fashion a programme of social and imperial reconstruction by drawing together men with different types of knowledge and expertise regardless of their party affiliation – 'a brains trust with a definite political object' was how one contemporary described it. Other organisations, mainly on the left, came into being either because they felt that the prominence of imperial issues had led to the neglect of matters closer to home, or because they felt that the party leadership was failing to criticise policies which were damaging both Britain and its colonies. This was especially true of the pro-Boer protest groups formed after 1899. Finally, a pro-imperial propaganda body like the Imperial South Africa Association, though strongly connected to the Unionist party, insisted upon formal party neutrality. This can be explained partly by the strength of its overseas associations (with loyalist organisations in South Africa), and partly by the fact that independence from the party caucuses made it easier for the Association to conceal its connections with ministers and officials.

The Empire also shaped and structured intra-party allegiances and identities. Tensions between Liberal-Imperialists and Radical Liberals, splits within the Fabian Society and the Social Democratic Federation, argument about the fiscal question within the Edwardian Unionist party – all these are evidence of the disruptive effect of imperialism upon later-Victorian and Edwardian party politics. Imperial politics, then, was pre-eminently an extra-parliamentary activity; its centre of gravity lay not at Westminster or Whitehall but in the country at large. Historians, of course, have long agonised over the Empire's popularity. Yet it was widely believed at the time that invoking empire was a good way of winning popular support. Public interest in empire was recognised to have been stimulated by royal ceremonial and public festivals; by exciting wars reported in the provincial and national press; by relatives and friends who had settled there; by exploration and missionary work in the tropics; and by the discovery of minerals such as diamonds and gold. Hence imperialists were confident that pro-imperialist sentiment was part of the fabric of British society, and anxious to direct it towards a clear political goal. What follows, therefore, is not a top-down study of empire, focused exclusively on elite political attitudes. But neither is it a blinkered study from below. Rather the book emphasises the indivisibility of pressure group and press agitation, party activity, parliamentary debate and official thinking. In so doing, it seeks to connect 'high' politics with imperial ideas and interests in the rest of the country.

Chapters 4, 5 and 6 move on from political identities and structures to take a more down-to-earth interest in the specific policy debates surrounding the Empire. What were the principal political issues which imperialists championed? Can they be counted among the major topics of the day? How did thinking about these issues relate to official deliberations and the policy-making process? Although debates about empire were multi-faceted, and encompassed a range of concerns, it will be suggested that questions of trade, defence and population were particularly prominent. Here it is important to emphasise that the study of 'economics' in this book centres on contemporary debate and not on later historical controversies regarding the Empire's benefits and costs. While the end of Chapter 4 (which discusses trade within the Empire, and its potential for future growth) and the middle sections of Chapter 5 (which discuss Britain's defence budget, and the possibility of extracting contributions from the colonies) do touch indirectly upon the Davis and Huttenback debate, the overall emphasis is upon how politicians at the time related empire to the performance of the British economy.

Doctrines of imperial defence are analysed with reference to the navy and not the army. The justification for this is not that the army was not culturally affected by the experience of empire. Arguably it was, and especially by India. Regimental days commemorated colonial battles; regimental mascots and mementoes were taken from the colonies; and regimental friendships were forged with troops like the Gurkhas.[37] The language of soldiers also betrayed the army's imperial involvement, as the famous Anglo-Indian dictionary – *Hobson–Jobson* – testifies. The army slang 'Blighty', for instance, was a telling corruption of an Urdu word meaning 'a country far away'.[38] Nor should we ignore the part played by colonial warfare in bolstering the military's reputation after 1850.[39] Nonetheless, as Chapter 5 explains, before 1914 it was generally

37 B. Farwell, *For Queen and Country. A Social History of the Victorian and Edwardian Army* (1981), Chapter 3.
38 I am grateful to David Omissi for supplying this reference.
39 J.M. Mackenzie (ed.), *Popular Imperialism and the Military, 1850–1950* (Manchester, 1992); E.M. Spiers, *The Late Victorian Army, 1868–1902* (Manchester, 1992), Chapter 10.

thought that the essence of imperial security was naval and not military. After the withdrawal from colonial garrisons championed by Cardwell, the army's imperial role was restricted to defending India and fighting in minor colonial wars, whereas without naval supremacy the whole fabric of empire was thought to be at risk. Even the Haldane reforms, urged by the experience of the South African War, appear to have had Europe as much as the Empire in mind. Only after the First World War was this situation reversed. Expansion in the Middle East, and nationalist uprisings elsewhere in the Empire, hugely increased the responsibilities of the army, while spending on the navy was drastically curtailed in the 1920s. These developments are discussed in Chapter 7.

Chapters 4–6 reconstruct later-Victorian and Edwardian ideologies of empire. It has often been said that imperialists were not interested in ideas. Left-wing critics of empire, in particular, have tended to conceive of imperial activism in extremely negative terms. Most famous of all, J.A. Hobson maintained that imperialism was not a genuinely popular emotion but something which was foisted upon the British public by interested parties and by a jingoistic press. Much writing about imperialism has adopted a broadly Hobsonian position in the sense that it has reduced political support for empire to the various vested interests which are understood to have profited from it. It is this assumption about the sectionality of imperial politics which has repeatedly stood in the way of scholars acknowledging ideology as an important influence upon its development.

Yet ideas about empire were important. Often progressive and forward-looking, these ideas identified the nation's imperial 'mission' as a spur to economic and political progress, not only for Britain's colonies but for Britain itself. Moreover, imperial beliefs were significant in the way they intersected with a number of other issues which were central to the politics of the period: the alleviation of urban poverty and unemployment; the adequacy of Britain's institutions in the face of intensifying international economic and military rivalries; the growth of class politics; and the acceptable limits of government interference. Thus, the patterns of political thought surrounding the Empire were far more complex than most historians are apt to allow. Far from being a unified or consistent political doctrine, there were varieties of imperial activism, to be distinguished in terms of their different philosophical underpinnings, and in terms of the sorts of state structure which they espoused. Imperial ideology, therefore, was fragmented. Chapter 4 (on tariff reform) examines the doctrine of constructive imperialism; Chapter 5 (on naval defence), the doctrine of free trade imperialism; and Chapter 6, a 'third way', as represented by the ideas of the empire migration movement.

Finally, whereas many studies of British politics and/or British imperialism end in 1914, Chapter 7 considers what happened to imperial politics during and after the First World War. Did the War strengthen or weaken the hands of imperialists? How far did the fact that Britain had to draw heavily upon the resources of its Empire – in India and tropical Africa as well as the 'white'

Dominions – push the politics of imperialism in new directions? It is still sometimes argued that imperialism ceased to be a fashionable political creed after the suffering and slaughter experienced between 1914 and 1918. Recent writing, however, has emphasised that the War did not put an end to the British public's interest in empire. Chapter 7 reinforces this view. Two of the political causes studied in this book – imperial preference and empire migration – received a considerable fillip from the First World War. The War also led to the incorporation of Milner and many of his supporters into Lloyd George's administration, and produced a new piece of governmental machinery, in the form of the Imperial War Cabinet. In reality, therefore, the strength of the imperial factor in British political thinking did not suddenly subside in 1918. Imperialism continued to structure and shape aspects of Britain's political process well into the inter-war period.

CHAPTER 1

Imperial Languages, Identities and Beliefs

A curious blindness seems to beset the average educated Briton when he is asked to picture to himself our colonial Empire. Almost instinctively he visualises Canada, Australia, and only quite recently South Africa – the rest he virtually ignores. (J.A. Hobson, 1902)[1]

LANGUAGES OF IMPERIALISM

If we are to grasp the purposes and priorities of imperial agitation in Britain, it is vital to get to grips with the meaning of empire in contemporary political usage. Recent writing has emphasised the way in which core concepts like patriotism and imperialism were not only highly unstable, but frequently reshaped and redefined.[2] Moreover, the meaning of words like 'empire' and 'imperialism' did not change accidentally. However imperfectly, the vocabulary of politics reflected changes in society; while politicians themselves strove to bend such concepts to their will.

To the mid-Victorians the term imperialism was strongly associated with authoritarian methods of government, particularly those of Louis Napoleon. Part of the challenge facing later-Victorians and Edwardians therefore was to free the concept of imperialism from its uncongenial connotations of foreign, and especially, French rule.[3] This had previously been attempted by the school of colonial reformers at the time of the Durham report in 1839. Their concept of a 'Colonial Empire' revolved around the self-governing colonies and Britain's responsibilities towards them. It was, however, articulated by a small elite, and did not begin to gain a wider currency until the late-1860s. Of particular note here is Charles Dilke's travelogue, *Greater Britain*. Published in

---

1 J.A. Hobson, *Imperialism: A Study* (3rd edn, 1938), p.131.
2 D. Eastwood, 'Robert Southey and the Meanings of Patriotism', *JBS* (1992), pp.265–87; H. Cunningham, 'The Language of Patriotism, 1750–1914', *HWJ* (1981), pp.8–33.
3 The seminal study of imperial language, which charts the changing meanings of empire during the nineteenth and twentieth centuries, is that by R. Koebner and H.D. Schmidt, *Imperialism. The Story and Significance of a Political Word, 1840–1960* (Cambridge, 1964).

1868 after a two-year trip around the English-speaking world, the book made a lasting impression upon an educated reading public. Dilke's organising theme was the uniqueness of the English peoples and their superior civilisation. Yet no sooner had his idea of a 'Greater Britain' – or wider 'Anglo-Saxondom' – begun to catch on than it was temporarily eclipsed by Disraelian political rhetoric.

When Disraeli became Prime Minister in 1874 he did not claim any detailed knowledge of empire, nor did he offer any definite proposals for future imperial policy. He was, however, an enthusiast for Britain's Asiatic Empire, which he believed to have boosted the power and prestige of Britain and of the Conservative party.[4] Indeed, by closely associating British expansion with the affairs of the nation's greatest dependency – India – his speeches gave a new twist to imperial language.[5] Whereas Dilke had appealed strongly to affinities within the Anglo-Saxon race, Disraeli directed attention to the military aspects of empire, to Anglo-Russian rivalries in central Asia, and to England's providential destiny to bring its 'superior' civilisation to non-European peoples.[6] Through a series of actions – the purchase of shares in the Suez Canal Company (1875), the passage of the Royal Titles Act (1876), and the occupation of Cyprus (1878) – British paramountcy in the East was reaffirmed and reinforced. An indication of Disraeli's success in orientalising the Empire is given by the periodical press, which during the 1870s printed an unprecedented number of articles on Indian affairs.

In the 1880s and 1890s the language of imperialism was again refashioned as imperialists experimented with a variety of new names to describe the evolving relationship between Britain and its colonies of settlement – 'Greater Britain', 'British Commonwealth', 'Oceana', and 'Britannic realms', to name but a few.[7] Although we now live in an era when the word 'imperialism' is typically associated with the desire for territorial expansion, this was not the prevailing understanding of empire at the end of the nineteenth century. In the minds of most later-Victorian and Edwardian politicians, the true meaning and purpose of imperialism lay in the efficient organisation of the existing Empire, not its further extension. Thus talk of imperial reconstruction referred mainly to the Empire's English-speaking peoples. The concept of community was fundamental to this new imperial language. It, in turn, was predicated upon a deep-seated belief that emigration, not conquest, was the most genuine enlargement of British nationality. As young societies with short histories, the self-governing Dominions were widely referred to as 'sister

4 C.C. Eldridge, *England's Mission. Imperial Ideas in the Age of Gladstone and Disraeli, 1868–1880* (1973), Chapters 7, 8, and his more recent *Disraeli and the Rise of a New Imperialism* (Cardiff, 1996).
5 A. Hawkins, *British Party Politics, 1852–1886* (Basingstoke, 1998), pp.195–6.
6 Although the famous Crystal Palace speech of 1872 broached the question of reconstructing the 'Colonial Empire' with reference to tariffs, defence and a representative council, Disraeli subsequently showed little interest in the self-governing colonies: Eldridge, *England's Mission*, pp.175–6, 180, 231.
7 S.R. Mehrotra, 'On the Use of the Term "Commonwealth"', *JCPS* (1963), pp.4–5.

nations' of the 'mother country' which had grown up rapidly from 'childhood' through 'adolescence' to the maturity of self-government.[8] The question why the British Empire came to be envisaged in this way is addressed in the first two sections of this chapter. The third and fourth sections consider how imperialists planned to restructure the Empire, and how far their ideas were compatible with the national aspirations of the Dominions. A fifth and final section explores the difficulty of incorporating India into the idea of a British world, as well as changing attitudes in Britain towards that other home of the Anglo-Saxon race – the United States.

IMAGINING EMPIRE: THE IDEA OF A BRITISH WORLD

The idea of a British world was a popular way of imagining the late-Victorian and Edwardian empire. Conceived as an historical community of English-speaking states centred upon Britain, this new imperial identity had both social and political dimensions. The social dimension stemmed from the familiarity – real or imagined – of the overseas 'British' societies in the Empire. In a speech to the Royal Colonial Institute in 1897, Joseph Chamberlain remarked on a growing tendency to speak of those who lived in the self-governing colonies 'as part of ourselves'.[9] Many of Chamberlain's closest colleagues, including his 'Man Friday', Edward Goulding, were to play upon similar sentiments when campaigning for tariff reform:

> No friendship with foreign countries can compare with the precious gift of our brethren – just think any one of us can feel at home in every state in our vast Empire the moment he sets foot in it – though one's whole previous life may have been passed miles away. They are men of our blood, speaking our tongue, glorifying in our traditions, confident in our imperial destiny.[10]

The idea of a British world was given added piquancy by the use of the family metaphor, an extremely popular imperial idiom in this period. When speaking of the future of imperial unity, politicians like Milner drew heavily upon the language of kith and kin:

> the idea which lies at the root of [Imperial unity] is that the scattered communities, which all owe allegiance to the British Crown, should regard and treat one another not as strangers but as kinsmen, that, while each thinks first of his own interests, it should think next of the interests of the family, and of the rest of the world only after the family. . . . To my mind any

---

8 A.S. Thompson, 'The Language of Imperialism and the Meanings of Empire: Imperial Discourse in British Politics, 1895–1914', *JBS* (1997), p.175.

9 Speech by Joseph Chamberlain as Secretary of State for the Colonies at the annual dinner of the RCI, 31/3/1897, quoted in C.W. Boyd (ed.), *Mr. Chamberlain's Speeches*, Vol. II (1914), pp.1–6.

10 Handwritten speech notes on tariff reform, Edward Goulding (undated), *Wargrave papers*, 7/6.

weakening of that idea, any practical departure from it would be an incalculable loss to all of us.[11]

The Empire, then, was partly conceived as an English-speaking cultural community, sharing a common language, literature, and religion. But it was also envisaged as a political community of laws, ideals and institutions. Just as the Whig interpretation of history was fundamental to constructions of a British national identity, so it occupied a privileged place in thinking about the British Empire. The Empire was regularly referred to as the unique home of liberty, boasting a strongly indigenised tradition of parliamentary government, a profound respect for law and order, and a special aptitude for political organisation. Of particular note here is the Victorians' fondness for references to classical imperialism. In 1899, pro-war propagandists defended British military intervention in South Africa by likening the nation's imperial 'mission' to that of Periclean Athens – in both cases, mature democracies had taken it upon themselves to assist younger nations to reach full citizenship. Neither was this belief in the political wisdom of the British only held by those on the right of the political spectrum.[12] Despite his dislike of the 'new imperialism', J.A. Hobson was at pains to differentiate between 'Imperialism' and 'Colonialism'. Whereas the former implied 'political bondage' as far as the major processes of government were concerned, the latter was recognised to be a 'natural overflow of nationality' as emigrants established 'local self-government in close conformity with the political customs of the mother country'.[13]

This view of the Dominions as part of the very fabric of the British nation received its most powerful expression in Seeley's canonical text, *The Expansion of England*. Seeley occupied the chair in Modern History at Cambridge from 1869 to 1894. His book originated in a set of lectures given at the university in 1881–82. It enjoyed great public acclaim, selling 80,000 copies in its first two years, and staying in print until 1956.[14] Surveying the last two centuries of English history, Seeley took as his central unifying theme the rise of empire and spread of English-speaking peoples throughout the world. India hardly came into his reckoning. Rather, his concept of nationality was founded upon Britain's 'colonial brethren': 'our Empire is not an Empire at all in the ordinary sense of the word. It does not consist of a congeries of nations held together by force, but in the main one nation, as much as if it were no Empire but an ordinary state.'[15] Moreover, for Seeley history had a serious political function in that it was to guide the making of public policy. The overriding

11 'Tariff Reform', speech at Tunbridge Wells, 24/10/1907, in A. Milner, *Constructive Imperialism: Five Speeches* (1908), pp.20–1.
12 See S.D. Otter, *British Idealism and Social Explanation. A Study in Late Victorian Thought* (Oxford, 1996), p.50.
13 Hobson, *Imperialism: A Study*, pp.4–7, 120–1.
14 P. Burroughs, 'John Robert Seeley and British Imperial History', *JICH* (1973), p.192.
15 J.R. Seeley, *The Expansion of England*, edited and with an introduction by John Gross (reprint, 1971), p.44. See also pp.12–13, 38–45, 62–3, 147.

objective of government, he argued, was to reunite the scattered fragments of the English-speaking race. The recent development of Russia and America had proved that large-scale political unions were possible. British statesmen were urged to follow their example.

However influential in itself, *The Expansion of England* needs to be located within a wider cultural climate. If Seeley's intellectualising of empire was targeted at an informed and educated reading public, a heightened consciousness of a 'Greater Britain' was by no means confined to the universities or to the realm of high culture. It would seem likely that migration to the Dominions, which rose rapidly from 1901 to 1914, also had a significant impact upon public perceptions of empire. Certainly, many people at the time assumed that it did. An anonymous writer in a leading periodical remarked upon 'a widening of touch with life in the daughter states which comes from the constant growth in the number of home-staying families who have members or relatives settled in the Colonies'.[16] With half of British overseas migrants heading for the Empire by the early 1900s,[17] a sizeable segment of Edwardian society was directly linked by family ties to the settlers, missionaries and businessmen living and working in the 'white' Dominions.

Another important issue is how far return migration affected public attitudes to empire. Only very recently have demographic historians begun to study the movements of returning migrants. It is a crucial factor in the British case as approximately 40 per cent of those emigrating from England and Wales between 1860 and 1930 are thought to have subsequently come back to Britain.[18] Improvements in transportation facilitated this movement, and by the end of the nineteenth century many people who left Britain expected ultimately to return. Yet the wider implications of this process remain obscure. Some 'colonials' who came back to the mother country made important careers in journalism, finance and politics; and some of those who grew rich by farming brought their money back to Britain to purchase large country houses or grand London residences. Even so, it is very difficult to measure the effect of returning migrants upon how the colonial connection was viewed. Board of Trade figures for the years 1887–1900 reveal 10,000 people arriving annually in the United Kingdom from Australia and New Zealand (both British and Australian-born). Sadly, the majority of them are then lost to the historians' view. However, a recent study of return migration from Australia shows how the word 'home' was still being used by Australians to refer to Britain until at least the late-nineteenth century. It argues that this was partly the consequence of the vast improvement in communications at this time, but also stresses the importance of a 'new kind of imperial sentiment' – articulated by Chamberlain in Britain and Deakin in Australia – in making Australians

16 Unsigned, 'Domestic Parties and Imperial Government', *Quarterly Review* (July, 1900), p.260.
17 G.F. Plant, *Overseas Settlement. Migration from the United Kingdom to the Dominions* (Oxford, 1951), p.58.
18 D. Baines, *Emigration from Europe, 1861–1900* (Cambridge, 1991), p.39.

feel that they had two places which they could call home.[19] In similar vein, a leading historian of the First World War has suggested that the volume of migration from Britain to the colonies of white settlement and back again may well have helped to blur distinctions between local patriotisms and a belonging to empire.[20] Obviously, a lot more research is needed to support this thesis. But it could well be that return migration is a missing ingredient in the making and meaning of a British national identity in the 'long' nineteenth century.

So far we have been examining the sympathy and solidarity of people in Britain with relatives and friends elsewhere in the English-speaking Empire. However, when exploring popular experiences of empire historians have tended to focus on dependent territories, on ideas of racial difference, and upon friction between European and non-European peoples. In doing so they have posited very negative notions of a British imperial identity. There is not the space here for a systematic study of the place of the self-governing Dominions in the later-Victorian and Edwardian public imagination – literature, exhibitions, and colonial royal tours would all need to be taken in account. It is, however, possible to take some soundings by looking briefly at organised sport[21] and organised religion.

Often considered to be a golden age of English sport, the Edwardian era was a time when team games were followed, enjoyed and supported by a widening public. The importance of sporting competition as a unifying force within a white imperial fraternity has recently been emphasised by J.A. Mangan,[22] while Richard Holt has highlighted the contribution of rugby and cricket in reconciling Dominion national sentiment with wider membership of the Empire.[23] In New Zealand, for example, the success of the All Blacks reinforced a dominant culture of loyalty to the Empire yet without prejudicing national pride – witness the famous 1905 tour when the All Blacks took Britain by storm, winning thirty-one of their thirty-five matches, and drawing huge crowds to watch their superior skills. Turning to Australia, the focal point of sporting contact was the struggle for the Ashes.[24] Test matches, unofficial until 1903, afterwards organised by the MCC (Marylebone Cricket Club), attracted huge crowds, and figures like the Australian fast bowler, Fred

19 K.S. Inglis, '*Going Home*. Australians in England, 1870–1900', in D. Fitzpatrick (ed.), *Home or Away? Immigrants in Colonial Australia. Visible Immigrants*, Vol. 3 (Canberra, 1992), pp.106–7, 120.
20 J.M. Winter, 'British National Identity and the First World War', in S.J.D. Green and R.C. Whiting (eds), *The Boundaries of the State in Modern Britain* (Cambridge, 1996), p.265.
21 For the view that sport is a missing dimension in the historiography of imperialism, see J.A. Mangan, *The Cultural Bond. Sport, Empire, Society* (1992), esp. pp.1–9.
22 J.A. Mangan (ed.), *Pleasure, Profit and Proselytism. British Culture and Sport at Home and Abroad, 1700–1914* (1988). Of particular interest is Katharine Moore's study of the idea of a Pan-Britannic athletic festival, first floated in 1891 by J.A. Cooper, and received positively by the press. The idea eventually lapsed due to Cooper's initial suggestion of money prizes, and the failure to take any practical steps to advance the plan. See 'The Pan-Britannic Festival: A Tangible but Forlorn Expression of Imperial Unity', Chapter 8.
23 R. Holt, *Sport and the British. A Modern History* (Oxford, 1989), Chapter 4.
24 For the spreading of the 'gospel' of cricket by British migrants and missionaries among the colonies see, K.A. Sandiford, *Cricket and the Victorians* (1994), Chapter 8.

Spofforth, were respected and revered by the English press.[25] Cricket became a symbol of rivalry as well as friendship between the two countries during the English tours to Australia in 1894–95 and 1897–98. Indeed it was sometimes said that the best thing a visiting English eleven could do for imperial unity was to return home the losing team! The competitive atmosphere was no less intense when the Australian tourists came to England. Writing from Sydney in July 1899, the *Morning Post*'s correspondent Richard Jebb observed:

> The progress of the Australian cricket team in England is the absorbing interest of the man in the street. The success of their champions over 'All England' and in most of the provincial matches evokes a good deal of derision which finds expression even in the newspapers. . . . In future years the relation of England to Australia, and of the unity of the Empire, will be considerably affected by the question of *circenses* as well as *panis*. . . . We can at least retain their respect through *circenses*, but if we can't manage to keep beating them they will consider England a broken reed, and lend a ready ear to American bombast – which cannot be so readily probed in test matches.[26]

Yet if success at cricket boosted the Australians' self-esteem it was perhaps partly because it was proof that British society could flourish in the Antipodes. Cricket was certainly not the breeding ground of a nascent republicanism, nor did it foster separatist sentiment. On the contrary, the strength of Anglo-Australian ideals in these years is attested to by the fact that at least six cricketers played Tests for both sides from 1877 to 1900.

Admittedly, the popularity of cricket and rugby, and the attitudes they fostered, differed across the English-speaking Empire. In South Africa, for instance, test cricket was played enthusiastically by the loyalist English-speaking population in the major urban centres of Cape Town, Pietermaritzburg and Port Elizabeth. In New Zealand, cricket developed very slowly, and did not become a truly popular game until as late as the 1930s.[27] Cricket also had a chequered history in Canada, enjoying a high public profile until the 1880s but falling into decline thereafter, as the country came to adopt spectator sports from America and to develop its own games like ice hockey and lacrosse.[28] Neither was cricket just a white game. It gained a substantial following in India and the West Indies, despite the obstacles placed in the path of coloured players.[29] Nonetheless, across much of the English-speaking empire sporting competition did play a role in cementing imperial relations by fusing a deepening sense of nationality with a feeling of a shared Britishness. Reconciling these two tendencies lay at the heart of the task of reconstructing the Empire.

25 R. Cashman, 'Symbols of Imperial Unity. Anglo-Australian Cricketers, 1877–1900', in Mangan (ed.), *The Cultural Bond*, Chapter 6.
26 Sydney, 30/7/1899, *Jebb papers* B/2/3/20–21.
27 Sandiford, *Cricket and the Victorians*, p.147.
28 The Scots were more successful in encouraging sport in Canada, urging the adoption of golf, tennis and bowls, as well as the revival of curling. See D. Birley, *Land of Sport and Glory. Sport and British Society, 1887–1910* (Manchester, 1995), pp.158, 166.
29 Sandiford, *Cricket and the Victorians*, pp.153–6.

During the last third of the nineteenth century, an increasing consciousness of a 'Greater Britain' was likewise evident in the churches.[30] From 1867, in response to the undermining of its authority abroad, the Anglican church held decennial conferences at Lambeth, at which bishops from all over the globe gathered together. In 1897, a committee was convened to consider the duties of the Anglican church to the colonies.[31] It noted that in more recent years there had been a tendency to favour the claims of the 'heathen world' and to lose sight of the church's responsibilities to the Dominions. In order to sustain ties with the 'settler Empire', it was argued that the church must now prioritise its work there. Particular emphasis was placed on the need to stop relying upon voluntary effort to meet the spiritual needs of migrants, and for a corporate response to the problem of church-building in the self-governing colonies. The committee's recommendations were set out in a special report. They included a scheme for the service of young clergy in the Dominions; liberal financial support to colonial churches in their early stages and in times of distress; an extension of the episcopate; and a reaffirmation of the measures approved for the care of emigrants at the previous conference in 1887. In these ways, it was thought that religion might reinforce racial and economic ties with British settlers.

Among Wesleyan Methodists, enthusiasm for empire derived from their traditional outlook and from a strong missionary impulse.[32] The dynamic Rev. Hugh Price Hughes, editor of the *Methodist Times*, even believed that a 'Wesleyan Forward Movement' in Africa and Asia might halt the denomination's decline by giving it a new imperial 'mission'. Yet Wesleyan Methodists also looked to the new world, hoping to lay the foundations of an 'Anglo-Saxon federation' – an imperial ecclesiastical organisation stretching across the entire English-speaking world. This sense of brotherhood with other parts of the Anglo-Saxon race was present in other Nonconformist churches too. The Baptist leader and well-known Free Churchman, John Clifford, is a case in point. Clifford castigated the 'false imperialism' of the South African War as a 'senseless vaunting of mere bigness',[33] and happily accepted the presidency of the militant Stop-the-War Committee. But whatever Clifford's misgivings about the war, he firmly believed in the positive side to empire.[34] He was the author of *God's Greater Britain*, an account of a journey around the Dominions in 1897, which celebrated the contribution of the Anglo-Saxon race in 'opening the gates of the world for the entrance of civilisation'.[35] Nor was the importance of the English-speaking world to nonconformity expressed only rhetorically. Although slower than the Anglican church to organise themselves

30 J. Wolffe, *God and Greater Britain. Religion and National Life in Britain and Ireland 1843–1945* (1994), p.220.
31 S. Dark, *The Lambeth Conferences: Their History and Their Significance* (1930), Chapter 3; R.T. Davidson, *The Five Lambeth Conferences* (1920), Chapters 3 and 5.
32 S. Koss, 'Wesleyanism and Empire', *HJ* (1975), pp.105–18.
33 J. Clifford, *Brotherhood and the War in South Africa* (1900), p.24.
34 Thompson, 'The Language of Imperialism', pp.167–8.
35 J. Clifford, *God's Greater Britain. Letters and Addresses by John Clifford* (1899), p.11.

internationally, the Free Churches made significant progress in this direction towards the end of the century.[36] Methodists held their first Ecumenical conference in 1881; Congregationalists organised an International Council a decade later (the suggestion having come from an Australian); and in 1905 the Baptist World Alliance was formed (with Clifford as its President).

In exploring the relationship between Christianity and imperialism, historians have written extensively about missionary activity and the work of the churches among the indigenous populations of the dependent empire. It is, however, less frequently acknowledged that the Anglo-Saxon world was an integral part of the consciousness of the British churches. Among Anglicans and Nonconformists, there developed during the second half of the nineteenth century a strong sense of the closeness of British society at home and the overseas British societies of the Empire, reflected in the organisational structures of these churches, and in the doctrine and discourse of their leading public spokesmen.

In the political sphere, the move of the Dominions to the centre of the imperial stage originated in part from anxieties arising from the consequences of granting self-government. The spectre of separation was of course long-standing, and had its roots in Britain's estrangement from the American colonies in the late-eighteenth century. In the mid-nineteenth century, separatist fears were provoked by a school of so-called 'anti-imperialists', who were accused of sowing the seeds of a conspiracy to dismember the Empire. Although these fears gradually subsided during the 1860s and 1870s, they resurfaced with a vengeance towards the turn of the century when the growth of Dominion nationalism again raised the possibility of the English-speaking empire 'breaking up into a mere meteoric shower'.[37]

Another major source of anxiety for later-Victorian and Edwardian imperialists was that of accelerating competition from other nation states. The end of the American Civil War in 1865, and the unification of Germany in 1871, prompted searching questions about British hegemony. In the 1850s, Britain had been the strongest naval power and most advanced capitalist economy in the world. But over the next three decades the gap with its rivals narrowed considerably. The growing economic power of the United States was partly to blame. Between 1875 and 1900 manufacturing production in America more than trebled; and it rose again by nearly a half between 1900 and 1910. Whereas in 1880 the economy of the United Kingdom accounted for 22.9 per cent of world manufacturing output, and that of America for 14.7 per cent, by 1900 the tables had turned – Britain's share stood at 18.5 per cent while America's had increased to 23.6 per cent.[38] This trend was reinforced by the First World

---

36 See J. Munson, *The Nonconformists. In Search of a Lost Culture* (1991), Chapter 7.
37 J.L. Garvin quoted in D. Ayerst, *Garvin of the* Observer (1985), p.52.
38 A. Orde, *The Eclipse of Great Britain. The United States and British Imperial Decline, 1895–1956* (1996), pp.1, 35.

War.[39] Britain's other major challenger was Germany. Between 1850 and 1869, Germany's output of pig iron increased more than six-fold, while from 1880 to 1913, its coal production rose from 47 million to 191 million tons. Whereas at the beginning of the 1880s, Germany's exports were valued at 2.9 billion marks, by 1913 the figure stood at 10 billion. As a result, German products began to displace those of Britain in the world market.[40]

These developments in the international economy produced a mood of uncertainty and apprehension about Britain's destiny, a mood intensified by the problems of military recruiting and the poor performance of the British army during the South African War. By the turn of the century, politicians from all parties were beginning to reassess Britain's place in the world.[41] Accepting that world leadership could not be retained by a small island off the north-west coast of Europe, imperialists argued that the British state could only compete with larger, land-based continental powers by organising itself on a bigger scale. This emphasis on state-building lay at the heart of the so-called 'social Darwinist' school of thinking. A lot has been written on the relevance of 'social Darwinism' to the public culture of later-Victorian and Edwardian Britain.[42] Yet in their obsession with attitudes towards race (and in particular eugenics), historians have frequently lost sight of social Darwinist conceptions of statehood, which had equal if not greater contemporary resonance. As well as classifying races into some sort of hierarchy, social theorists like Karl Pearson and Benjamin Kidd grappled tenaciously with the problem of how societies evolved, and what sort of state structures were necessary to allow peoples to develop and progress. In doing so, they arrived at a very predatory and pessimistic view of international affairs: states that were on the old scale of magnitude were considered to be insignificant, unsafe and essentially obsolete, or destined to become so.[43]

This feeling that the day of small nations was passing away and that the future lay with large aggregations of states (with the greatest area of natural resources and the largest populations at their disposal) contrasts sharply with our late-twentieth-century experience of disintegration and disaggregation. Yet at the turn of the century it was widely predicted that successful states would expand rather than contract. As the Fabian Sidney Webb opined: 'Twentieth century politics will not be based upon abstract rights of "nationalities"

39 P. Kennedy, 'British and German Reactions to the Rise of American Power', in R.J. Bullen, H. Pogge Von Strandmann and A.B. Polonsky (eds), *Ideas into Politics. Aspects of European History, 1880–1950* (1984), p.16.

40 V. Berghahn, *Imperial Germany 1871–1914. Economy, Society, Culture and Politics* (Oxford, 1994), pp.4–5.

41 W. Ross Johnston, *Great Britain. Great Empire. An Evaluation of the British Imperial Experience* (1981), p.99.

42 For one of the more rounded and subtle studies, see G. Jones, *Social Darwinism and English Thought. The Interaction between Biological and Social Theory* (Brighton, 1980).

43 C.H. Pearson, *National Life and Character. A Forecast* (1893), esp. pp.86–133, 180–226; and B. Kidd, *Social Evolution* (1895), pp.326–50.

but on concrete administrative necessities of definitely organised common-wealths.'[44] For Italy and Germany, nineteenth-century state-building took the form of powerful unification movements led by Cavour (from Piedmont) and Bismarck (from Prussia). For America, it took the form of an expansionist drive beyond the Appalachian mountains towards the Pacific coast, the taming of the great plains (or 'wild west'), and mass immigration from Europe. And for Russia, defeated by Britain and France in the Crimean War, and unable to expand further west, it involved the acquisition of territory in central Asia. Meanwhile for Britain, the opportunity of organising a 'commonwealth', and preserving a special status in the world, was understood to lie in drawing its colonies into a closer, more permanent relationship. As the geographer, Halford Mackinder, counselled: 'only by gathering together the several nations of the Empire can we cope in the international balance of power with newly-organised continental states'.[45] The several nations to which Mackinder referred were the self-governing Dominions. Half a century earlier the prevailing attitude towards these states had been essentially negative – they were regarded as burdens on the British state.[46] Now a new mood began to crystallise. The Anglo-Dominion relationship was perceived as a source of great strength, vital to Britain's ability to compete on equal terms with other great powers.

IMPERIAL REFORM

The challenge of reconstructing the later-Victorian and Edwardian Empire was essentially that of combining a strong sense of imperial unity with the fullest and freest assertion of local liberties. Certainly, imperialists recog-nised that a developing sense of colonial identity precluded any return to the old centralised imperial system of the eighteenth century – 'one free people could not govern another free people', as the Tory historian, James Froude, declared.[47] Thus although the consolidation of regional groupings of colonies through local unions or federations – Canada in 1865, Australia in 1901, and South Africa in 1910 – was welcomed, it was apparent that such constitution-building was only the first step towards a larger scheme of unity. The fact that Dominions wanted to be treated as Britain's equals, or at the very least to be assured of a future when they would be treated so, required imperialists to rethink completely the nature of imperial loyalty. Older concepts of colonial subordination had to be replaced by newer ideas of partnership, equality

44 Sidney Webb, *Twentieth Century Politics: A Policy of National Efficiency*, Fabian Society Tract, no. 108 (November 1901).
45 Quoted in W.H. Parker, *Mackinder. Geography as an Aid to Statecraft* (Oxford, 1982), p.68.
46 See here Froude's remarks in *Oceana or England and her Colonies* (1886), pp.6, 173–5, 336–7, and Seeley's in *The Expansion of England*, p.121.
47 Froude, *Oceana*, pp.2–3, 11.

and joint participation.[48] A few examples will have to suffice. The Duke of Marlborough spoke of a 'United Empire' in which Britain would be *primus inter pares* but nothing more.[49] George Parkin envisaged an 'Independence of Partnership', defined as the utmost freedom of action compatible with united strength. J.A. Spender looked forward to a 'true imperial union' as an alliance of equal states on equal terms.[50] And Leo Amery championed the principles of mutual support and joint responsibility, claiming that the Dominions would not be content with 'a maimed and mutilated British citizenship' and must be provided with a voice in the administration of the Empire.[51] In each case, British domination was rejected in favour of the principles of mutuality, reciprocity and co-operation.

The vast majority of imperialists were also highly conscious of the dangers of a premature tightening of the bonds of empire in the constitutional sphere. That is not to deny that the Empire's constitution was widely debated. The Imperial Federation League looked into the question of constitutional reform in the 1880s, so too did the Pollock Committee in the early 1900s,[52] and the Round Table was to revive the subject after 1910. Nonetheless, an older imperial historiography did us a great disservice in focusing on constitutional questions to such an extent that it failed to draw our attention to the many other and more important ways in which the goal of 'federation' was pursued.[53] In fact, most imperialists felt the idea of overhauling the Empire's governmental structures to be dangerous and divisive, for it was difficult to frame any such proposal without it being seen to threaten the colonies' independence from Westminster. Hence the word 'federation' was actually very broadly defined. It referred to any scheme for the strengthening of imperial unity, but especially those schemes which were felt to be pragmatic.

The notion of 'practical unity' took three main forms. Tariff reformers were adamant that closer economic relations were the master key to the problem of imperial federation, and a necessary first step towards reconstructing political relationships.[54] Admittedly, when Colonial Secretary, Joseph Chamberlain had taken an interest in the idea of an imperial council with limited executive powers, but the idea was rejected at the Colonial Conference of 1897. In 1902, Chamberlain tried for a purely consultative assembly, but the colonies

---

48 This point is pursued in Saul Dubow's interesting case study of Milner's political philosophy and its relationship to the ideas of the Kindergarten: 'Colonial Nationalism, the Milner Kindergarten and the Rise of "South Africanism", 1902–10', *HWJ* (1997), pp.53–85.
49 Duke of Marlborough, 'The Imperial Problem', *United Empire* (December, 1910), p.845.
50 J.D. Startt, *Journalists for Empire. The Imperial Debate in the Edwardian Stately Press, 1903–13* (Westport, CT, 1991), p.158.
51 L. Amery, *My Political Life. England before the Storm, 1896–1914*, Vol. I (1953), pp.302–4.
52 See pp.128–9.
53 From H.E. Egerton (in the early 1900s) to C.A. Bodelsen (in the 1940s), the grand narrative of imperial historians was usually to be found in Britain's constitutional relations with her colonies of settlement. See F. Madden and D.K. Fieldhouse (eds), *Oxford and the Idea of Commonwealth: Essays Presented to Sir Edgar Williams* (1982), pp.10–11.
54 Amery, *My Political Life*, Vol. I, p.52, and *Union and Strength. A Series of Papers on Imperial Questions* (1912), preface.

were again unenthusiastic, agreeing only to a regular meeting of the conference every four years.[55] By 1903, then, experience had taught Chamberlain that closer political relations would have to be preceded by some other form of co-operation. Chapter 4 discusses at greater length why tariff reform was regarded by constructive imperialists as the best strategy for uniting the Empire. But part of the attraction in developing the economies of the Dominions more rapidly was to make it possible for them to enter into a workable political partnership with Britain.

Those who put defence at the forefront of the argument for imperial unity also stressed the practicality of their proposals. It was thought to be self-evident that 'every British citizen who grasps the principles of sea power must be an advocate of imperial federation, in that he or she must desire the organised co-operation of the entire resources of the Empire towards the single end of victory in war'.[56] Without sea power, it was argued, the Empire would be unable to protect its trade or its communications; and in such a situation, Britain and its colonies would exist only as independent nations, entirely dependent on their own resources.[57] Exactly how greater co-operation in military affairs was to be achieved was the subject of some debate. There was a great deal of talk of a deliberative or advisory body to deal with matters of imperial defence and foreign policy. This body was to differ from a federal parliament in that it would not have executive powers and thus not require any changes to the machinery of ministerial responsibility in Britain or the Dominions. Unlike the Committee of Imperial Defence, however, the colonies were to have permanent membership, allowing them to be properly consulted on all major matters of defence strategy. In short, it was suggested that such a council would rapidly become an instrument of a newly recognised 'greater' British military unity, first ushered in by the South African War.[58]

Imperial migrationists argued that there was a pressing need for a more efficient distribution of population throughout the Empire. In a lecture to the Compatriots Club in 1905, the journalist, H.A. Gwynne, declared that while the Dominions were magnificent in territory they were nonetheless deficient in population. Without a more equal distribution of manpower within the Empire he suggested that other schemes of federation were unlikely to progress for the Dominions would not enter into a closer union – constitutional or otherwise – if it was seen to be unequal.[59] Moreover, by acting in concert over emigration policy, migrationists hoped to foster a spirit of accord between British and Dominion governments, and to improve their capacity for reaching agreement on major policy issues.

---

55 G. Martin, 'The Idea of "Imperial Federation" ', in R. Hyam and G. Martin (eds), *Reappraisals in British Imperial History* (1975), pp.131–2.
56 H. Wyatt, 'The Navy League Envoy', *NLJ* (October, 1904), p.257.
57 C. Bellairs, *A New System of Preference* (1912); C.W. Dilke and H. Spencer Wilkinson, *Imperial Defence* (1892), Chapters 1 and 11; G.R. Parkin, *Imperial Federation* (1892), Chapter 3.
58 See pp.127–30 and 171–5.
59 H.A. Gwynne, 'The Proper Distribution of the Population of the Empire', in J.L. Garvin (ed.), *Compatriots' Club Lectures*, First series (1905).

DOMINION NATIONALISM AND IMPERIAL INTEGRATION

It is often claimed that 'federation' was an aspiration or ideal imposed from outside the colonies and supported by no more than a handful of disloyal or misguided colonial subjects. A number of historians play down its importance for this very reason. L.E. Davis and R.A. Huttenback contend that Dominion intransigence makes it impossible to discover whether the quest for imperial unity had any substance at all;[60] Bernard Porter claims that the Empire was not federated chiefly because the colonies did not want to be;[61] and Geoffrey Searle asserts that projects for creating a 'Greater Britain' all foundered on the rock of colonial nationalism.[62] The problem with this view is the misleading polarity it posits between nationalism and imperialism. In reality, a great deal of public feeling in the colonies was not readily classifiable as either.[63] So much is evident from the opinions expressed by overseas delegates at the Imperial Press Conference (1909) on the nature of imperial loyalty. On the opening day of the conference, J.W. Kirwan spoke on behalf of the visitors. Kirwan was editor of the *Miner*, a Kalgoorlie paper of high standing, and a member of the Western Australian legislative council. He also contributed frequently to various English newspapers. Referring to the growing spirit of nationalism in the self-governing Dominions, he affirmed 'the spirit and pride of being an Australian, a Canadian, or a New Zealander – and determination to reserve all of their self-governing powers'. But he went on to identify a change coming over those states which 'felt that they were slowly but surely tending towards a period of nations in alliance', maintaining that 'the future would be something grander and greater than it had been in the past'.[64] It was in a similar vein that P.D. Ross spoke at a banquet given by the Corporation of Glasgow. Ross was the managing editor of *The Ottawa Journal*, who described himself as 'one of those Canadians who joined to a Canadian patriotism, in which they yielded to none, the fervent hope that the future of Canada would be part of the future of Great Britain'. His address forecast a future in which Britain and the Dominions would grow together as 'partners in a political alliance', the details of which could not presently be foreseen.[65] Thus an influential body of thought in the Dominion press regarded national self-consciousness and a wider imperial commitment as perfectly compatible ideals.

It would, of course, be wrong to think of the Dominions' attachment to empire entirely on a sentimental level. The Dominions were strategically dependent upon Britain. For Canada, empire offered an alternative to American

60 L.E. Davis and R.A. Huttenback, *Mammon and the Pursuit of Empire: The Political Economy of British Imperialism, 1860–1912* (Cambridge, 1986), p.302.
61 B. Porter, *The Lion's Share. A Short History of British Imperialism, 1850–1983* (2nd edn, Harlow, 1984), pp.138–9.
62 G.R. Searle, *The Quest for National Efficiency* (Oxford, 1971), p.71.
63 On this point see D. Cole, 'The Problem of "Nationalism" and "Imperialism" in British Settlement Colonies', *JBS* (1971), pp.160–82.
64 T.H. Hardman, *A Parliament of the Press. The First Imperial Press Conference, 1909* (1909), p.44.
65 Ibid., p.103.

domination. For South Africa, it stood as a guarantee of the peaceful progress of the Union, and of protection from other European powers. For Australia and New Zealand, it was a buffer against the rise of Japanese power. In each case, the imperial connection was valued for reasons of power as well as sentiment. Moreover, as the political bonds between Britain and the Dominions slackened, it is arguable that economic ties became stronger.[66] Britain provided an outlet for their exports, a steady flow of migrants, and a prime source of development capital. Thus when the Canadian Conservative leader, Robert Borden, campaigned against a trade reciprocity treaty with the United States in 1911, it was to the importance of the British market as much as English-speaking sentiment that he appealed. Borden followed faithfully in the footsteps of the 'Canada First' movement of the 1870s, which had supported close relations with the Empire, and whose conservative, loyalist wing had vigorously opposed any form of union with Canada's powerful neighbour.[67]

Neither should we overlook the fact that in two of the self-governing Dominions – Canada and South Africa – there was a substantial body of opinion suspicious of links with Britain. In Canada, suspicion came from an old-established French community, constituting four-fifths of the population of the province of Quebec; in South Africa, it came from parts of the Boer community, which formed a majority of the white population. If imperialists in Britain genuinely believed that 'Greater Britain' was to be something more than an English-dominated union, what sort of cultural fusion did they think might take place? And how did they respond to the feelings of French Canadians or Afrikaners, groups which emphatically did not think of themselves as Britons first and Canadians or South Africans second? This dilemma was raised very awkwardly for the Liberal Canadian prime minister, Wilfrid Laurier, at the time of the South African War. Laurier had to balance demands from English-speaking Canada to rally round the British flag with opposition from his French-speaking compatriots to the idea that Canadians should be sent to die in a British colonial war, particularly when a non-British racial group was fighting for its survival.

Some imperialists in Britain did confront the problem of non-English-speaking cultures within the Empire, though they tended to focus on Canada and South Africa in doing so. Very little mention was made of the Aborigines of Australia, or the Maoris of New Zealand, the indigenous inhabitants of the Dominions being pushed to the periphery of imperialists' political thinking just as firmly as coloured groups elsewhere in the Empire. Moreover, even with respect to the 'difficult cases' of Canada and South Africa, imperialists differed in their assessment of how far such a reconciliation of cultures could be achieved. The contrasting approaches of Amery and Milner are instructive here. Amery was an eternal optimist. By appealing to those ties not confined

66 P.J. Cain and A.G. Hopkins, *British Imperialism. Vol. I: Innovation and Expansion, 1688–1914* (Harlow, 1993), Chapter 8.
67 K. McNaught, *The Penguin History of Canada* (1988), pp.157–8; C. Berger, *The Sense of Power. Studies in the Ideas of Canadian Imperialism, 1867–1914* (Toronto, 1970), Chapters 2–3.

to the English-speaking parts of the Empire – principally its liberal parliamentary tradition – he was confident of persuading *Canadiens* and Afrikaners to embrace a 'wider patriotism, blended with and yet transcending our several national patriotisms'.[68]

Recent reassessments of Afrikaner politics suggest that Amery's hopes were not entirely unrealistic. Moti Tamarkin's work on the Cape Afrikaners argues that loyalty to the British Crown and the Empire was part and parcel of their political consciousness in the 1890s.[69] Similarly, some Afrikaner political leaders in the Transvaal embraced a wider imperial identity after the war. Smuts, for example, came to regard a gradual fusion of South Africa's two white populations – 'a grand racial aristocracy' as he put it – as essential to the survival of the Boers and the British, and therefore distanced himself from the more intransigent elements of the Afrikaner national movement.[70] Nor was Smuts the only Afrikaner to embrace a pluralistic future for white South Africa. Charles Fichardt, editor of the Bloemfontein *Friend* – mouthpiece of the Orangia Union party – spoke in very similar if more striking terms at the Imperial Press Conference in 1909. Fichardt had fought as a captain of the southern Boer commandos during the South African War, when he had been wounded and captured during a dramatic escape from Paardeberg. After an evening banquet in Sheffield, Fichardt responded on behalf of the visitors. His closing words were later recalled by P.D. Ross:

> I am a Boer. In that bloody and devastating war which swept over our country, you British overcame us. There was left a sullen anger among our ruined people ready to seize any opportunity of a new struggle. You conquered our troops, our lands, our bodies – but our hearts and our spirits – never! So we thought. Then came a day, a wonderful day, when the conqueror with open hand approached us, holding out to us freely that inestimable thing for which we had fought – that liberty for which so many of us had died – and from that moment, I think, we were really conquered, we joined hands with you, and if ever need arises there will speak for England on the wild and lonely veldt the unerring rifle of the Boer.[71]

Milner's assessment of the problem of reconciling local loyalties with a common imperial feeling was more pessimistic than Amery's. Imperial patriotism, he argued, might be developed in races of non-British origin but it was unlikely to be 'of a fervid type'.[72] Part of the problem, Milner felt, lay in the political and cultural primacy of England, and its implications for the

68 W.R. Louis, *In the Name of God, Go!: Leo Amery and the British Empire* (1992), p.32.
69 M. Tamarkin, 'Milner, the Cape Afrikaners, and the Outbreak of the South African War: From a Point of Return to a Dead End', *JICH* (1997).
70 I. Smith, 'Jan Smuts and the South African War', paper given at the 'Rethinking the South African War' conference, Unisa, Pretoria, 3–5 August 1998.
71 P.D. Ross, *Retrospects of a Newspaper Person* (Toronto, 1931), p.161.
72 'Empire Citizenship', speech to the Authors' Club, 2/12/1912, *The Nation and the Empire* (1913), p.492.

construction of a wider British identity. Because of England's wealth, power and population, and possibly because of its cultural diffuseness,[73] English consciousness and British consciousness were very closely entwined – hence the temptation to use the words 'English' and 'British' interchangeably. Population was a particularly important factor. The nineteenth century witnessed a big demographic shift within the British Isles towards England and away from Ireland and the 'Celtic fringes' more generally. From 1861 to 1911, the population of England and Wales increased from 20.1 million to 36.1 million, whereas Scotland's population increased only from 3.1 million to 4.8 million, and the population of Ireland actually decreased (from 5.8 million to 4.4 million).[74] Thus the English were expanding demographically within Britain.

Yet this does not mean that imperialists believed empire patriotism to be incapable of transcending a narrower English nationalism. Sensitivity was shown to the different national characters within the British Isles. For example, when addressing the University of Glasgow as its Chancellor in 1908, Rosebery was at pains to emphasise that Britishness was not a denial of other identities, and spoke at length about the Scots' stake in Britain's imperial enterprise. According to Rosebery, the 'impelling force' of the Scottish race was 'self-reliance'; the very same self-reliance that the British Empire was built upon.[75] Even Milner made some effort to dispel the impression that Englishness and Britishness were synonymous.[76] He used his public speeches to highlight the contribution of the Celtic fringe – and Scotland in particular – to the building of empire, while praising the imperial instincts of England's neighbours.[77] Both Rosebery and Milner were tapping a deep vein of Scottish culture. John Mackenzie has written powerfully about the way in which the 'imperial experience' helped to bind the Scots into the British state.[78] Scottish soldiers, administrators, entrepreneurs and missionaries earned their country a remarkable reputation for empire-building in this period. Scottish migrants formed a significant part of the populations of Canada and Australia: in 1901, Scots accounted for 15 per cent of the British-born population of Australia and 21 per cent of Canada's, whereas they formed 10 per cent of the United Kingdom's population.[79] And the Scots celebrated their imperial achievement through a variety of cultural forms – painting, public statues, exhibitions, and consumer commodities. Hence the cry of common allegiance to empire need not necessarily be dismissed as English aggrandizement. The

---

73 A point emphasised in K. Robbins, *Nineteenth-Century Britain. Integration and Diversity* (Oxford, 1995), pp.1–28, and in R. Colls and P. Dodd, *Englishness. Politics and Culture, 1880–1920* (1986), esp. pp.29–61.
74 Figures from C. Cook and J. Stevenson, *The Longman Handbook of Modern British History, 1714–1995* (Harlow, 1996), p.152.
75 Address delivered as Chancellor of the University of Glasgow, 12/6/1908 in Lord Rosebery, *Miscellanies. Literary and Historical*, Vol. II (1921), pp.149–50.
76 J.H. Grainger, *Patriotisms: Britain, 1900–39* (1986), pp.48–9.
77 Milner, *Constructive Imperialism*, pp.57–68.
78 J.M. Mackenzie, 'Essay and Reflection: On Scotland and the Empire', *IHR* (1993), pp.714–39, and 'Empire and National Identities: The Case of Scotland', *TRHS* (1998), pp.215–32.
79 K. Robbins, *Great Britain. Identities, Institutions and the Idea of Britishness* (1997), p.214.

Empire provided one of the few contexts in which the particular patriotisms of the Welsh and Scots could be successfully integrated with a wider British identity.[80]

No doubt there is a danger of exaggerating the Empire's capacity to forge a shared sense of Britishness. The Irish as a whole could not be induced or coerced into accepting a wider British identity (and the majority of imperialists were remarkably silent on this point). Neither was the loyalty of the Dominions to Britain based simply on racial characteristics. It was the economic and strategic attraction of a continuing imperial connection which provided the most compelling logic for Afrikaners and French Canadians not to reject empire. What might broadly be termed a 'Britannic culture' – constituted by liberal political ideals, respect for law and order, and a preference for self-government – was certainly a strong factor in UK and Dominion politics. But it did not foster as ecumenical or encompassing an imperial identity as many imperialists liked to imagine.

MARGINS OF EMPIRE: INDIA AND AMERICA

If the position of Afrikaners and French Canadians in a 'Greater Britain' was awkward, that of India and Britain's other dependencies was decidedly ambiguous. Imperial politics was premised upon the assumption that there were in fact two British empires: a liberal empire of settlement, created by overseas migration, and dedicated to the ideals of representative government and a large measure of freedom for its component nations; and an empire of authority, an aggregation of territories, constitutionally subordinate to Westminster, neither Christian, nor white, nor English in culture and speech. The greater unity for which imperialists were striving was a unity of the English-speaking Empire. It did not normally embrace India or any other of Britain's dependent colonies. In fact, as Seeley observed, a 'federal' relationship with these territories seemed absurd: regarded as 'alien' in terms of race, religion, custom, and in terms of their system of government, there was no obvious way of assimilating them into a 'Greater Britain'.[81]

There were, however, those who reacted against this conception of empire. On returning to Britain in 1905, Curzon pleaded for a more ecumenical approach to the task of imperial reconstruction. He was particularly vexed by the Chamberlain school's misplaced reliance upon the Dominions. According to Curzon, the politics of fiscal reform was symptomatic of a wider imperial malaise in that it ignored the tremendous military and economic benefits which

---

80 For the combination of Welsh patriotism and loyalty to empire, see John Grigg, *The Young Lloyd George* (1973), Chapter 10; G.A. Williams, *When Was Wales?* (1985), pp.180–1, 199, 201–3, 220–1; and K.O. Morgan, *Rebirth of a Nation: Wales 1880–1980* (Oxford), pp.30–1, 45.
81 Seeley, *The Expansion of England*, pp.14–15, 40–3, 132, 141, 148–51. See also S.R. Mehrotra's excellent study of the imperial federation movement as it affected India, 'Imperial Federation and India, 1868–1917', *JCPS* (1961), pp.29–40.

India bestowed upon the Empire.[82] Indeed, the ex-Viceroy claimed that the prevailing passion for imperial unity had tended to marginalise India, and to regard it as:

> lying somewhat outside the main congeries of States and communities that compose [the] Empire; to regard it, so to speak, as a magnificent jewelled pendant hanging from the Imperial collar, but capable of being detached there from without making any difference to its symmetry or strength.[83]

Up and down the country, Curzon argued vigorously for a true appreciation of India's role within the Empire and a fair treatment of India's interests. He was a powerful proponent of the view that any worthwhile refashioning of imperial relations had to retain a central place for India alongside the Dominions.[84] Yet as he himself realised, incorporating India into 'Greater Britain' required a complete rethinking of the precepts of imperial reform. Few imperialists showed any sympathy for such a project.

The Earl of Meath, originator of the Empire Day Movement, likewise objected to the narrowness of the ideal of imperial federation. Addressing a Delhi Durbar celebration in London in 1912, Meath emphasised the need to make India feel proud of her position in the Empire. Imperialism, he reflected, consisted of a bond of fellow feeling between the Empire's citizens. In the case of the Dominions there was the triple bond of blood, religion and language: 'the three great ties which served as a strong chain binding white man with white man'.[85] None of those ties existed in the case of India. The tendency, therefore, was for Englishmen to think a great deal more about strengthening relationships with their colonial brethren than of forging links with the Empire's Eastern subjects. Meath made a strong case but offered no practical proposals for remedying the situation.

After returning from Egypt as Consul-Egypt, Cromer too came to question the centrality of the self-governing Dominions to debates about the reorganisation of the Empire. Surveying British imperial policy in 1910 – in the wake of the Morley–Minto reforms – he spoke not of 'federation' as the great dilemma of the next generation, but of the extent to which 'some 350 millions of British subjects, who are aliens to us in race, religion, language, manners, and customs, are to govern themselves, or are to be governed by us'.[86] The Dominions were relegated to a secondary imperial role. The primary 'Imperial

---

82 Curzon was not the only statesman to criticise tariff reform on such grounds. Lord George Hamilton, Secretary of State for India (1895–1903), argued that if other parts of the Empire enjoyed the benefits of protection and preference these could not be denied to India. See the newspaper of the British Committee of the Indian National Congress, *India*, 13/11/1903, p.148.

83 G.N. Curzon, *The Place of India in the Empire. Address Delivered before the Philosophical Institute of Edinburgh, October 19th, 1909* (1909), p.8.

84 Here I benefited greatly from reading D. Blakeley's unpublished study of Curzon's imperial politics post-1903, 'India in the Debate over Empire, 1903–1919', delivered as a paper at the American Historical Association Meeting, 6/1/1996, Atlanta, Georgia.

85 The Earl of Meath's speech at the Delhi Durbar celebration in London, 12/12/1912, reported in *The Navy* (January, 1913).

86 Earl of Cromer, *Ancient and Modern Imperialism* (1910), p.18.

problem' was to secure the loyalty of those colonies whose inhabitants were not bound to Britain by cultural ties. In Cromer's view, the foundations of British imperial policy in the English-speaking Empire had already been laid – from the time of the Durham report (1839) these colonies had practically governed themselves. But the future of Britain's dependencies was not at all certain.

The neglect of India in contemporary political debate is all the more striking given the salience of the *Raj* in the popular literature of the period, such as the adventure stories of G.A. Henty and Rudyard Kipling. Part of the explanation lies in India's own history. The Indian National Congress was formed as early as 1885. However, it was not until the non-co-operation campaign of the early 1920s, and the mass protests organised by M.K. Gandhi, that the prospect of India separating from the Empire began to be contemplated seriously in Britain.[87] India's marginalisation in the political language of empire also resulted from the new status attained by the Dominions towards the end of the nineteenth century. Previously spoken of as a liability, burden or encumbrance, the self-governing colonies now came to be regarded as vital imperial assets. Why these societies should have been thought to be more valuable to Britain than its dependent territories, or its so-called informal empire in South America and China, is considered at greater length in Chapters 4–6. But it is worth drawing attention to the spectacular growth of Canada, Australasia and South Africa in the period covered by this book.

In the second half of the nineteenth century, the populations of these societies increased dramatically, as did the size of their leading cities, and the total value of their agricultural exports. Their economies experienced surging foreign investment, diversified out of primary production, and achieved levels of production in terms of manufactured goods per head which rivalled even those of Germany. Many imperialists were enthralled by these developments.[88] Milner was particularly forthright on the relative merits of the self-governing and dependent empire: 'If I had to choose between an effective union of the great self-governing states, and the retention of the dependent states accompanied by complete separation from the distant communities of our own blood and language, I should choose the former.'[89] While few of Milner's compatriots would have cared to speak so candidly, their view of the dependent empire was substantially the same. In other words, Seeley's verdict on the *Raj* was widely accepted. Having 'advanced beyond the limits of nationality', British rule in India was understood to be precarious and artificial.[90] To be sure, India could be supported as a responsibility which Britain had undertaken

87 See pp.163–5.
88 See, for example, the sequel to C.W. Dilke's *Greater Britain: A Record of Travel in English-speaking Countries during 1866 and 1867* (1868), *Problems of Greater Britain* (1890), which suggested that it was possible that the growth of Canada and Australasia might enable the British Empire not only to continue to rival the United States but to assert its supremacy on some points, p.3.
89 'The Two Empires', speech to the RCI, 16/6/1908, quoted in A. Milner, *The Nation and the Empire* (1913), p.293.
90 Seeley, *The Expansion of England*, p.40.

and could not responsibly throw off. But far from being a crown jewel, for many imperialists India seemed to have added to the dangers of a far-flung empire while providing Britain with few corresponding advantages.

Moreover, in the Dominions themselves attitudes were if anything more firmly set against the inclusion of India or any other of Britain's dependencies in the 'inner sanctum' of the Empire. This is apparent from debates about the rights of British imperial subjects to move from colony to colony. In theory everyone born within the Empire had identical rights, including the right of residence in another colony. However, under the British Nationality and Status of Aliens Act (1914) it was accepted that the Dominions would regulate immigration as they saw fit, even if this meant differentiating between different classes of imperial subject.[91] In particular, Australia's freedom to exclude Asiatic immigrants was neither challenged nor curtailed.

It is, however, worth remembering that for some imperialists the basis for a partnership of Britain and the Dominions lay partly in a joint guardianship or trusteeship of the dependencies. The Duke of Marlborough, a former Under-Secretary at the Colonial Office, was an especially strong advocate of co-operation in this field. Speaking to the RCI in 1910, he remarked upon a developing tendency towards disintegration in the 'administration of native races'. He proposed a meeting of the Empire's statesmen to exchange views on the question of the political rights of non-European races and their capacity for self-government.[92] In the meantime he suggested that the bureaucracy of the East African Protectorate should be put 'on a truly imperial basis' by assigning to the Dominions a proper quota of administrators. Noting the increased interest of the Australasians in the Pacific islands, Milner too expressed the hope that the exercise of trusteeship might eventually become 'a sentiment of great potency' in the self-governing empire.[93] He was supported by Leo Amery and Richard Jebb, both of whom argued forcefully for the appointment of colonials to the Indian Civil Service in the belief that such a measure would further stimulate the colonies' interest in the Empire.[94] This proposal was firmly rejected by the Viceroy Lord Minto, who reminded the Indian Secretary of State, John Morley, that appointments to the Indian Civil Service were by competition, and that any advantage given to colonial candidates would be extremely unpopular in India.[95]

Another dilemma facing imperialists was whether a reconstructed empire – an anglophone cultural community – could afford to exclude the United States.

91 P. Thane, 'The British National State and the Construction of National Identities', in B. Melman (ed.), *Borderlines: Genders and Identities in War and Peace, 1870–1930* (1998), pp.35–8.
92 Marlborough, 'The Imperial Problem', pp.841–2.
93 Milner later supported Canada's bid to take over the West Indies in 1916–17, despite the reluctance of the Colonial Office to relinquish any of its responsibilities. Canada's campaign continued after the War, but ran up against public opinion in the West Indies and the 'entrenched interests' of the United Fruit Company of Boston. See P.G. Wigley, *Canada and the Transition to Commonwealth. British–Canadian Relations, 1917–26* (Cambridge, 1977), pp.47–50.
94 Amery, *Union and Strength*, pp.26, 234–5.
95 Mehrotra, 'Imperial Federation and India', p.34.

Part of the British political establishment thought not, and was convinced of the potential for Anglo-American co-operation. For example, Dilke and Rosebery believed the English-speaking peoples of the British Empire and America to be essentially one. Dilke's book *Greater Britain* numbered America in its list of 'true colonies',[96] while Rosebery's objection to tariff reform derived partly from its exclusion of America, which he saw as a vital element of the union of the Anglo-Saxon race.[97] But not all imperialists believed in Anglo-Saxon kinship or looked so benevolently on American power. In 1895, the intervention of the Cleveland administration in a boundary dispute between Britain and Venezuela temporarily strained relations between the two countries.[98] Britain, of course, had good reason to stay on friendly terms with the United States in view of the actual and expected challenges to its imperial position from Germany, Russia and Japan. Yet the argument that the rise of American power was limited to areas where Britain's interests were not thought to be vital is hard to sustain. Negotiations between Canada and America over a possible Trade Reciprocity agreement during 1910–11 certainly alarmed many journalists and politicians in Britain. Chapter 4 shows how this episode shook many Unionist MPs out of their previously complacent acceptance of American imperialism.[99] Another index of the growing concern among imperialists with the rise of American power is provided by attitudes towards overseas migration. As early as 1886, Froude spoke of those migrants leaving for the United States as having renounced their British allegiance, whereas those destined for the Dominions were regarded as an element of strength for Britain.[100] Chapter 6 examines the reasons why individuals and organisations involved with this area of social policy felt that Britain had to stop populating foreign countries – in particular the United States.[101] What needs to be emphasised here is that by the beginning of the twentieth century the trans-Atlantic relationship was no longer on a par with the formal imperial connection. What had once been a loyal and friendly offshoot of Britain was now increasingly viewed by imperialists with a measure of jealousy and suspicion.

CONCLUSION

The argument of this chapter is two-fold. First, that imperial beliefs were both widespread and deeply-embedded in British society. The excitement, adventure and spectacle of empire captured the public imagination in a variety of ways: through travel literature and historical writing; through relatives who had emigrated to, and settled in, the colonies (and who increasingly returned);

96 Dilke, *Greater Britain*, Chapters 15 and 28.
97 H.C.G. Matthew, *The Liberal Imperialists. The Ideas and Politics of a Post-Gladstonian Elite* (Oxford, 1973), pp.165–6.
98 Orde, *The Eclipse of Great Britain*, pp.10–11.
99 See pp.96–7.
100 Froude, *Oceana*, p.11.
101 See pp.135–8.

through international sporting competition; through missionary activity; through public ceremony and festival (Chapter 2); and through the reporting of colonial wars (Chapter 3). There was, in short, plenty of imperialist feeling for politicians to marshall and mobilise. The problem was not so much to whip up such sentiment as to harness it securely to a practical political programme.

Second, the chapter has emphasised how the white, English-speaking colonies came to hold a special place in imperialists' affections. Indeed, the political discourse of the later-Victorian and Edwardian era often leaves one with the impression that empire consisted of little else but the self-governing Dominions. There was at this time a profound transformation in the language of imperialism as the nature of imperial loyalty was reconceptualised, antiquated notions of colonial inferiority and subservience were abandoned, and a new agenda was constructed around the idea of a 'Greater Britain'. In the words of one historian, by the turn of the century 'all politicians, no matter of what party, had at least to address the issue of union, if they wished to play a useful role in the ongoing debate over the future of the empire'.[102] At the centre of that debate lay the assumption that the strengthening of Anglo-Dominion relations was a *sine qua non* of imperial reorganisation.

Yet despite broad agreement on the underlying precepts of reforming the Empire, imperialists most definitely did not constitute a unified movement. Collectively they expressed confidence in the public's pride in the Dominions and the popularity of their cause. But if imperial unity was a fashionable cry, it was far from being a single policy or programme. In the aftermath of the South African War, a range of strategies emerged for unifying and consolidating the Empire. In theory it was possible to pursue some or all of them simultaneously; in practice there was little co-ordination of imperial activity. Joseph Chamberlain summed up the situation in 1909 when he remarked that other extra-parliamentary campaigns were a distraction from the work of tariff reform and should wait their turn until the question of imperial preference had been settled.[103] Chapters 2 and 3 show how imperial movements competed with each other for members, for money, and for the attention of party leaders and the press. Chapters 4–6 argue that there were also significant ideological tensions between them. These tensions reflected more than a difference of opinion over the fiscal question; they were political and philosophical as well as economic in nature, arising in part from deep-seated disagreements about the proper limits of state action.

---

102 J. Kendle, *Ireland and the Federal Solution. The Debate over the United Kingdom Constitution 1870–1921* (Kingston, 1989), p.235.
103 J. Chamberlain to E. Goulding, 27/7/1909, *Wargrave papers*, 2/30.

CHAPTER 2

Mobilising Imperialists

THE MAINSPRINGS OF IMPERIAL POLITICS

When writing about imperialism as a domestic political phenomenon, historians have usually adopted parliament or party as their frame of reference, not the extra-parliamentary sphere.[1] There has also been a strong tendency to portray imperialism as an elitist, paternalist and even regressive form of political activity. In particular, the attitudes of the Empire's 'proconsuls' – its most powerful and prominent officials – are produced as proof that imperialists were authoritarian in their outlook, either avoiding popular politics altogether, or being dragged into it against their will.[2] This chapter contends with both schools of thought. It argues that the progress of imperialism as a political cause owed a great deal more to popular agitation and press campaigning than to conventional party politics. It also questions the notion that imperialism was (partly) responsible for the lack of a strong participatory tradition in British politics. On the contrary, those who wished to construct a national political agenda around the Empire often had to move beyond the confines of the party caucus in order to forge new political structures. These structures were more open and more inclusive than is commonly thought.

In speaking of imperialism as a 'popular' political movement it is important to make it clear at the outset in what sense this term is being used. The word 'popular' is not intended to imply that imperial politics was predominantly a working-class activity. Such a claim would not only be extravagant, it would be anachronistic too. As with other extra-parliamentary movements of the period, the involvement of working men in Victorian and Edwardian imperial campaigning was limited, even if it was greater than their involvement in the

---

1 For examples, see J.R.M. Butler, 'Imperial Questions in British Politics 1868–1880' and R.E. Robinson, 'Imperial Problems in British Politics, 1880–1895', in E.A. Benians, J. Butler and C.E. Carrington (eds), *The Cambridge History of the British Empire* (Cambridge, 1959); A.P. Thornton, *The Imperial Idea and its Enemies* (1959); M. Beloff, *Britain's Liberal Empire, 1897–1921* (1969); C.C. Eldridge, *England's Mission. Imperial Ideas in the Age of Gladstone and Disraeli, 1868–1880* (1973); R. Shannon, *The Crisis of Imperialism, 1865–1915* (1974).
2 R. Faber, *The Vision and the Need. The Late Victorian Imperialist Aims* (1966), pp.78–85.

party caucuses. Rather imperialism will be presented as a broadly-based and participatory movement in the sense that it appealed to a wide spectrum of social groups, drew in people of differing political persuasions, penetrated the grass roots of British politics, and promoted the involvement of middle- and upper-class women.

Britain's imperial involvement gave rise to many agitations, but three in particular stand out. They dealt with the issues of tariff reform, naval supremacy and empire migration. It is these agitations which form the focus of this book. Their significance stems from the fact that they grappled more effectively and more persistently than any other section of the political nation with the question of Britain's role and responsibilities as an imperial power. It was also largely due to their influence that wider public interest in empire was carried beyond the purely rhetorical sphere and translated into specific policy debates.

EXTRA-PARLIAMENTARY AGITATION AND EMPIRE

Extra-parliamentary agitation, or 'the politics of pressure', is an integral part of Britain's political heritage. Beginning with the anti-slavery crusade led by Wilberforce in the 1790s, it encompasses the Anti-Corn Law League lobbying of the 1840s, the popular evangelical campaigns of mid-Victorian Liberalism, the militant suffragism of Edwardian women, and, more recently, the direct action protests of the environmental lobby. For two centuries of British history, this type of political activity has provided people with a passion with an opportunity of registering their opinion and making their voices heard. Between the mid-1880s and late-1920s imperial politics was increasingly to conform to this pattern.

In the 1860s and 1870s the preponderance of pressure groups moved within the orbit of Gladstonian Liberalism; their impact on the Conservative party was relatively weak.[3] Later-Victorian and Edwardian political life saw an important shift in pressure politics. With the growth of the Liberal party machine, the room for extra-parliamentary activity on the left was restricted.[4] Meanwhile, on the right of British politics, pressure groups began to proliferate. Historians of modern Britain have lagged behind European historians in exploring the extra-parliamentary right.[5] Until very recently, studies of nationalist and imperialist pressure groups were mainly psephological.[6] Accounts of the general

3 E.J. Feuchtwanger, *Disraeli, Democracy and the Tory Party. Conservative Leadership and Organisation after the Second Reform Bill* (Oxford, 1968), pp.191, 212–15.
4 P. Auspos, 'Radicalism, Pressure Groups and Party Politics: from the National Education League to the National Liberal Federation', *JBS* (1980), pp.199–201.
5 The historiography on Wilhelmine Germany boasts a sophisticated literature on nationalist associations. See G. Eley, *Reshaping the German Right. Radical Nationalism and Political Change after Bismarck* (1980); R. Chickering, *We Men Who Feel Most German: A Cultural Study of the Pan-German League, 1886–1914* (1984); M.S. Coetzee, *The German Army League: Popular Nationalism in Wilhelmine Germany* (Oxford, 1990).
6 But see Anne Summers' essay, 'The Character of Edwardian Nationalism: Three Popular Leagues', in P. Kennedy and A. Nicholls (eds), *Nationalist and Racialist Movements in Britain and Germany before 1914* (Oxford, 1981).

elections of 1906 and 1910 revealed an upsurge in pressure group activity in general, and offered brief accounts of groups such as the Tariff Reform League, National Service League, Navy League, Liberty and Property Defence Association, and Imperial South Africa Association.[7] Fresh perspectives on nationalist and imperialist agitation have come from new approaches to the writing of the history of Conservatism.[8] Focusing on grass-roots political activism, this scholarship has deepened our understanding of the organisational basis and ideology of a whole range of Edwardian pressure groups. However, in presenting the extra-parliamentary right as functionally dependent upon the Tory party, it serves only to reinforce the time-honoured view of imperialism as Conservative in terms of its intellectual origins, organisational basis and electoral significance.

This chapter argues that it is simply not possible to sandwich a history of imperial politics between 'blue' covers. The majority of the movements inspired by the Empire operated outside party structures, and mobilised support across the political spectrum. They also frequently came into conflict with party officials. The growing impatience of imperial enthusiasts with Establishment politics first expressed itself in 1884 with the foundation of the Imperial Federation League. The IFL was dissolved in 1893, owing to a schism between proponents of a 'kriegsverein' (defence union) and 'zollverein' (customs union),[9] but tensions between imperialists and party managers remained. For their part, party officials preferred not to allow imperial questions to intrude into domestic politics: 'The whole art of party management lay not just in the selection of issues to be played up but also in the equally careful judgement of which issues to play down or bury altogether. Rightly or wrongly, party managers on all sides . . . saw little profit in playing up imperial issues and every reason to reduce their discussion to a barest dignified minimum.'[10] In the view of the political parties, therefore, empire existed to serve party, not the other way around.

The perspective of imperialists was very different. They felt that the parties were failing to articulate clear and convincing colonial policies, and stifling public discussion of imperial affairs. Only by developing a new kind of imperial politics did it seem possible to prevent the Empire from becoming a pawn in the party game. Thus the emergence of preferential tariffs, naval defence, and state-aided migration as subjects of national political debate relied upon the fashioning of alternative structures of political action. For this reason,

---

7 A.K. Russell, *Liberal Landslide: The General Election of 1906* (Newton Abbot, 1973), pp.64, 128–30; N. Blewett, *The Peers, the Parties and the People. The General Elections of 1910* (1972), pp.330–9.

8 F. Coetzee, *For Party or Country. Nationalism and the Dilemmas of Popular Conservatism in Edwardian England* (Oxford, 1990); M. Fforde, *Conservatism and Collectivism, 1886–1914* (Edinburgh, 1990).

9 The best account of the IFL remains that by C.A. Bodelsen, *Studies in Mid-Victorian Imperialism* (1953).

10 J. Darwin, 'The Fear of Falling. British Politics and Imperial Decline since 1900', *TRHS*, 5th series (1986), pp.40–1.

imperialism is best approached not as an offshoot of late-Victorian or Edwardian Conservatism, but as a series of single-issue campaigns, organisationally distinct from the parties, and described at the time as 'leagues', 'movements', and 'causes'. The language is important, for it was intended to convey that imperial political activity was not motivated by self-interest but by a genuine belief in the need for far-reaching imperial reform. Furthermore, from the pressure groups' point of view, being non-party had the advantage of extending some hope that support would be attracted from all parties rather than from one.

This chapter does not provide detailed organisational histories of each of these movements. It is, however, necessary to discuss briefly their origins, organisation and propaganda techniques, before moving on to consider the ways in which they conceptualised and negotiated their relationships with the political parties, and their views of how the political nation should be defined.

THE TARIFF REFORM LEAGUE

Just as one individual – Richard Cobden – is now synonymous with the repeal of the Corn Laws so another – Joseph Chamberlain – is identified with the campaign for tariff reform. Radical Joe began his political life as a great municipal reformer, played a key part in building the National Liberal Federation, and then parted company with the Liberal party over the issue of Irish Home Rule in 1886. From 1895 to 1903, Chamberlain served as the Colonial Secretary in the Unionist governments of Salisbury and Balfour. At first his attention turned to the possibility of developing Africa's tropical estates. Thwarted by the Treasury, he then looked to a reform of fiscal policy to promote closer unity within the English-speaking empire. Speaking in his Birmingham constituency in May 1903, he praised the self-governing Dominions for rallying to Britain's side during the South African War, and argued that it was Britain's duty to cement this mutual affection with its kinsfolk by expanding imperial trade.[11] Few other statesmen could have opened up in the course of a single evening a debate which would dominate British politics for nearly a decade. Chamberlain, however, was among the greatest platform orators of the day. Leo Amery best captured the impact of the Birmingham speech by comparing its challenge to free trade orthodoxy to the theses which Luther had nailed to the church door at Wittenburg.[12] Implicit in the analogy was a recognition that Chamberlain's radical instincts had not been abandoned during his move from the Liberal party to the Conservative party. What had changed was the idiom – after the turn of the century, Chamberlain's radicalism was expressed in terms of economic policy rather than institutional reform.

The second stage in the tariff reform campaign followed Chamberlain's resignation as Colonial Secretary in September. Keynote speeches were delivered

11 The initial phase of Chamberlain's tariff reform campaign is carefully documented by J. Amery in *Joseph Chamberlain and the Tariff Reform Campaign*, Vol. 5 (1969), esp. pp.184–95, 283–320.
12 L. Amery, *My Political Life. Vol. I: England before the Storm, 1896–1914* (1953), p.236.

41

in the major industrial and commercial centres of the United Kingdom, and attention was turned to the problem of building an effective organisational structure. The Tariff Reform League was inaugurated at a meeting at Stafford House on 21 July 1903. Drawing upon the enthusiasm and expertise of figures from the press, the universities, the literary world and parliament,[13] the League rapidly established itself as the driving force behind the tariff reform campaign. Its mandate was to 'advocate the employment of the tariff with a view to consolidate and develop the resources of the Empire, and to defend the industries of the U.K.'. The issue of imperial unity was central to its mission. Speaking at the first annual meeting in July 1904, Chamberlain told those present that they had to rise above the level of domestic controversies to address the salient subject of the day:

> There is a growing appreciation on the part of every Briton that it is given to this generation to solve the great problem of a United Empire – (cheers) – that if we do not solve it disaster is certain; that what not I, but every statesman who deals with the subject, sees is true – that the time has come to draw closer to our kinsfolk, or we shall certainly drift apart. (hear, hear.)[14]

What Chamberlain described as 'the magnificent conception of a federated Empire' fired the imaginations of the men and women who took up the cause of fiscal reform after 1906. Indeed, it was the combination of imperial patriotism and organisational crusading zeal which made the Tariff Reform League such a politically formidable organisation. The League's total membership is very difficult to determine with precision.[15] What we do know is that there were over six hundred local branches by 1910, grouped together into nineteen regional federations, which oversaw the work of organising lectures, canvassing constituents and distributing literature. Typically individual branches numbered a few hundred members. But some were larger: Aberdeen counted a thousand members in 1906, and Bristol four thousand in 1907. Of the federations, the most significant covered metropolitan London, South Wales, and Lancashire, Cheshire & the North-West Counties.[16] There was a clutch of medium-sized federations in Kent, Hertfordshire, and the Western Counties; and smaller federations in Hampshire, Lincolnshire, Middlesex, Devonshire, Dorset, Cambridgeshire and Oxfordshire. In Scotland, there were two divisions of the TRL. The East of Scotland branch had a presence in Dundee, Hawick & Galashiels, Kircaldy, Dumferline, Aberdeen, Inverness, Fort William and Edinburgh, although it often worked through existing 'local Imperial

13 See Appendix for biographical details.
14 Quoted in *Monthly Notes on Tariff Reform* [hereafter *Monthly Notes*] (August, 1904), p.86.
15 Information on the membership levels and branch structure of the TRL is mainly culled from its journal, *Monthly Notes on Tariff Reform*, the short run of minute books covering the years 1911–13 [deposited at the library of the London School of Economics], and the memoirs and private papers of the most regular attenders of its executive.
16 When Henry Page Croft became Chairman of the Lancashire, Cheshire and North-West Counties Federation of the TRL in 1913 it claimed over 50,000 supporters.

Unions'. In order to reach more remote areas, a caravan was purchased by its executive committee.[17] The West of Scotland branch staged mass meetings, distributed literature and endeavoured to form branches among Glasgow's working men.[18] The two divisions were amalgamated in 1908 into the Scottish Tariff Reform League which claimed a total of 157 branches by 1909.[19]

The TRL was amply funded. When attempts were made to secure Milner as its Chairman in 1906, a salary of £2,000 per annum was discussed. Nobody flinched at the mention of this considerable sum. The main sources of the League's income were member subscriptions, donations from wealthy benefactors, and revenue raised from the sale of its journal, *Monthly Notes on Tariff Reform*. In 1908, for instance, £8,400 was raised from subscriptions, £2,100 from donations, £215 from literature, making a combined annual income of nearly £11,000 (equivalent to £650,000 in 1997 prices). In the pre-election year of 1909 this figure increased to £42,000. Looking back over the period from 1903 to 1910, T.W.A. Bagley, the League's Secretary, estimated that nearly £160,000 had been raised (equivalent to roughly £9.5 million in 1997 prices).

The TRL's evangelical, crusading approach to politics was partly dependent upon the extraordinary success of this fund-raising. Few other extraparliamentary organisations were able to produce propaganda on the same scale. In 1908, for example, the League's literature department recorded the distribution of 38,500 copies of its *Speaker's Handbook*, 120,500 copies of *Monthly Notes*, 23,400 new sheets for press editors, and a staggering 6,034,000 leaflets, posters and pamphlets. The following year, in the run-up to the general election, its propaganda output rivalled that of the major parties.[20] A similar story is told by the League's schedule of public meetings. Its second annual report noted that some 2,600 meetings had been held across the country, with an estimated attendance of 925,000 people. Moreover, the TRL was successful in penetrating rural as well as urban areas. For instance, in the autumn of 1906, the Kent branch ran special trains from the countryside to a mass meeting in Canterbury at which Austen Chamberlain addressed a crowd of six and a half thousand people.

Another major strength of the League was its pioneering grasp of new forms of political campaigning. Arthur Pearson, in particular, had a theatrical eye for the striking gesture. At the beginning of the campaign, he hired an actress and supporting chorus of artisans to spout Chamberlain's monologues from the back of a lorry. Later, through the offices of the *Daily Express*, he organised a 'Fiscal Parrot Show'. Prizes were awarded to parrots which could repeat the phrase 'your food will cost you more' – ridiculing the free trade slogan! In effect, the TRL became Joseph Chamberlain's new caucus. In the same way as he had used the National Liberal Federation to establish his

---

17 East of Scotland annual meeting, 5/12/1904, *Monthly Notes* (December, 1904), p.289.
18 Second annual meeting of the Glasgow and West of Scotland division, *Monthly Notes* (March, 1906), p.161.
19 *Monthly Notes* (October, 1908), p.311; *Monthly Notes* (May, 1909), p.424.
20 Blewett, *The Peers, the Parties and the People*, p.332.

ascendancy over the radical wing of the Liberal party, so the League was turned into a vehicle for establishing the tariff reform programme, and the constructive imperialist ideology which underpinned it, as the dominant voice in British Conservatism.

THE NAVY LEAGUE

The Navy League was founded in December 1894 by a small group of defence enthusiasts brought together by Henry Cust, a flamboyant Conservative MP and editor of the *Pall Mall Gazette* (1892–96). Its aim was to promote the command of the sea as 'the primary object of national policy', and to 'preserve the maritime supremacy of the Empire'.[21] Unlike the TRL, the NL did not attract a political leader of national stature. Its long-serving President was Robert Yerburgh,[22] the Unionist MP for Chester (1886–1906, 1910–16). Yerburgh's political interests were skewed towards agriculture and a concern to get people back on to the land. He was a leading spirit in the Agricultural Organisation Society, formed by landowners in 1901 to help farmers create co-operative groups; Vice-President of the Soldiers' Land Settlement Association; and part of a deputation on the food supply question which met with Balfour in 1903. Yerburgh was assisted as President by a sizeable group of backbenchers, drawn from both parties, and by a small circle of retired naval officers and distinguished defence journalists and authors (see the Appendix for biographical details).

The Navy League was not a service organisation. In fact, its relationship to the Admiralty was fraught with difficulty.[23] As a result of the wide-ranging reforms introduced by the energetic and outspoken John Arbuthnot Fisher (First Sea Lord, 1904–10), attitudes in the Admiralty polarised into two opposing camps – the Fisherites and the anti-Fisherites. Fisher was responsible for four major schemes of change: the wholesale scrapping of obsolete warships (many of which were stationed on the 'outer margins of empire'); the reorganisation of the reserve fleet; the strategic redistribution of fleets and squadrons (which led to their withdrawal from the Pacific and then Mediterranean waters); and the introduction of a new type of capital ship – the dreadnought – of unprecedented speed and fire power. In pushing through these changes, Fisher was able to outmanoeuvre his adversaries by use of the press and through the manipulation of promotions and appointments to bring his own supporters into positions of power. One critic, however, refused to be silenced. Charles William Beresford, the Commander of the Mediterranean (1905–7) and Channel

21 A six-point statement of the NL's aims, *The Objects of the Navy League*, is contained in the papers of Patrick Hannon.
22 The NL's first president was Admiral Sir Geoffrey Phipps-Hornby, a highly respected officer of the fleet, who died within a month of the League's foundation. Phipps-Hornby was succeeded by the Earl of Drogheda in March 1896. Yerburgh became president in October 1900.
23 W.M. Hamilton, 'The "New Navalism" and the British Navy League, 1895–1914', *Mariner's Mirror* (1978), p.40.

fleets (1907–9), was equally adept at manipulating opinion outside the Service, and publicly denounced Fisher's reforms as 'a fraud upon the public and a danger to the Empire'. This polarisation of opinion between pro- and anti-Fisher camps was reflected in the Navy League. In 1908, the League actually split, when a small group of activists led by Harold Wyatt and Lionel Horton Smith broke away to form a rival Imperial Maritime League.

Thus, like the Navy League in Germany, the British Navy League was a political organisation which reflected a growing public concern with the state of the nation's maritime defences. The navy first became a lively political issue during the scare of 1884. W.T. Stead's revelations of defensive weakness, published in the *Pall Mall Gazette*, ignited a press campaign for the renovation and modernisation of the navy. So successful was Stead that the Gladstone government was forced to spend an extra £3.1 million on warships and £2.4 million on naval ordnance and coaling stations in that year alone.[24] Hard on the heels of the 1884 agitation came a number of tracts proclaiming the necessity of naval supremacy. This new wave of navalist writing culminated in the publication of the historical studies of the hitherto unknown American naval captain, Alfred Thayar Mahan. Mahan's *The Influence of Sea Power in History* (1890), and its two-volume sequel *The Influence of Sea Power upon the French Revolution* (1892), had a tremendous impact. Along with the Colomb brothers, Philip and John, Mahan became a leading exponent of a new 'blue water' school of naval historiography, explicitly linking the growth and prosperity of nations to sea power. The British Empire, it was argued, was primarily a naval power; thus the navy, not the army, had the greatest claim upon the nation's resources. This insistence that it was sea power and not land power which guaranteed the stability and security of the Empire constituted a powerful challenge to the army credo. It was powerfully expressed in Charles Dilke and Henry Spenser Wilkinson's celebrated short study, *Imperial Defence* (1892), which warned of a loss of individual British colonies if Britain relinquished superiority at sea.[25]

A heightened public awareness of the navy is also revealed by the populist 'hurrah trips' around the English coast in the 1890s; by greater press coverage, reaching a crescendo in June 1897 when the fleet assembled at Spithead to celebrate Queen Victoria's Diamond Jubilee; by the growing number of 'tombstone' biographies of naval officers, in addition to various plays and poetry dealing with nautical themes; and by the German invasion literature which flourished in the early 1900s.[26] It is in this context of a navy-conscious nation that we must set the strategy of the Navy League. The League aimed to educate public opinion (distilling the message of men like Mahan into pamphlets, leaflets and other forms of propaganda suitable for a mass audience), and to

24 P. Kennedy, *The Rise and Fall of British Naval Mastery* (1976), p.178.
25 C.W. Dilke and H. Spenser Wilkinson, *Imperial Defence* (1892), pp.36–63.
26 A.J. Marder, *The Anatomy of Sea Power: A History of British Naval Policy in the Pre-Dreadnought Era, 1880–1905* (1964), pp.205, 281; A.J. Marder, *From the Dreadnought to Scapa Flow: The Royal Navy in the Fisher Era, 1904–19* (Oxford, 1978), pp.4, 45–56.

harness popular pride in Britain's naval heritage to its campaign for faster naval expansion. The high point in its public calendar was the commemoration of Trafalgar Day. This event was intended to link the idea of sea power to a great naval victory and an emotive part of the national memory. For most of the nineteenth century the anniversary had been marked only by the Admiralty. After the formation of the Navy League in 1895, it became more widely recognised. The League made the celebration of Trafalgar Day (21 October) a key part of its public ritual. At the League's instigation, Nelson's column was festooned with flowers, municipalities were encouraged to hoist flags on public buildings, and a grand commemorative dinner was held in London at which addresses were given by Dominion statesmen as well as by Admirals of the Fleet. By the centenary celebration of Trafalgar Day in 1905, the programme included prayers, the reciting of Kipling's 'Recessional', the playing of the reveille, and the singing of the national anthem. Over 20,000 men and women gathered for the event, with the queue of people wishing to see Nelson's column stretching some three miles in length.[27]

Another aspect of the NL's drive to mobilise popular naval sentiment was its nationwide branch organisation. Branches first flourished in towns and cities with a strong naval heritage where there was a significant mercantile and shipping interest, such as Liverpool and Bristol. Other large branch organisations were formed in Glasgow (1,700 members in 1914), Newcastle (1,000 members in 1910), Hertfordshire (7,600 members in 1912), south Oxfordshire (1,100 members in 1910) and central London (1,000 members in 1914). By 1912, the number of branches totalled 133 – seventy-one in the United Kingdom, twenty-nine in public schools, and thirty-three in the colonies.[28] Although some of these branches fell into decay, others met regularly, helping to distribute literature, organise mass meetings, and secure invitations for League lecturers to speak at a variety of non-governmental organisations, including friendly societies, working men's clubs, teacher training colleges, and habitations of the Primrose League. Leaflets, pamphlets, postcards and maps of the Empire were supplied to the branches by Head Office. Print runs of pamphlets and leaflets frequently ran into five figures. In addition, the League published a journal, *The Navy League Journal*, later *The Navy*, which claimed a circulation of approximately 20,000 copies per month by 1911.

THE EMIGRATION COMMITTEE OF THE ROYAL COLONIAL INSTITUTE

In April 1910 an Emigration Committee was formed under the auspices of the Royal Colonial Institute. It co-ordinated the work of some forty-nine voluntary emigration societies, and put pressure on the British government

27 Programme for The Nelson Centenary, *NLJ* (October, 1905), p.246; 'The Navy League and Trafalgar Day', *NLJ* (November, 1905), p.273.
28 A thorough study of the NL's branch structure is provided by Coetzee in *For Party or Country*, esp. Chapter 1.

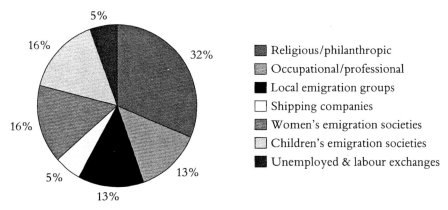

5%

16%

32%

16%

5%

13%

13%

- ■ Religious/philanthropic
- ▨ Occupational/professional
- ■ Local emigration groups
- □ Shipping companies
- ▨ Women's emigration societies
- ▨ Children's emigration societies
- ■ Unemployed & labour exchanges

Figure 1   The character of the voluntary societies affiliated to the Emigration Committee of the Royal Colonial Institute

to redirect migrants to the Empire. The RCI was mainly an educational body for promoting the study and knowledge of empire.[29] It was not very wealthy, but the Emigration Committee benefited from its expertise and reputation, and rapidly established itself as the leading forum for debates on overseas migration.

The voluntary emigration societies which the EC represented encompassed a broad range of interests and enthusiasms, classified in Figure 1 in seven categories.[30] By the turn of the century these societies were playing a bigger part in organising overseas migration than ever before. From 1901 to 1911, for example, the Self-Help Emigration Society assisted 5,317 migrants; the Church Emigration Society 4,327; the British Women's Emigration Association 7,118; and the Charity Organisation Society 17,631.[31] The main services they offered were the provision of information and advice to intending migrants, supervision on board ship, and reception in the Dominions. They also occasionally helped out with the cost of purchasing tickets.[32]

The formation of the Emigration Committee was the culmination of a growing grass-roots concern with the issue of overseas settlement and its importance in consolidating and developing the Empire. Heightened public interest in empire migration was expressed in the 1880s during the campaign of the National Association for Promoting State Colonisation.[33] This interest re-emerged in the aftermath of the South African War as Milner made the

29 T.R. Reese, *The History of the Royal Commonwealth Society* (Oxford, 1968).
30 For a full list of the societies, see 'The Emigration Conference', *United Empire*, Vol. 1 (July, 1910), pp.510–21.
31 W.A. Carrothers, *Emigration from the British Isles. With Special Reference to the Development of Overseas Dominions* (1929), pp.228, 252, 321.
32 S. Constantine 'Empire Migration and Social Reform, 1880–1950', in C.G. Pooley and I.D. Whyte (eds), *Migrants, Emigrants and Immigrants. A Social History of Migration* (1991), p.168.
33 H.L. Malchow, *Population Pressures: Emigration and Government in Late Nineteenth Century Britain* (California, 1979), pp.9–10.

settlement of rural areas a priority of his reconstruction programme.[34] More-over, opportunities for migration were heavily publicised at the White City series of exhibitions (1908–14) and at provincial exhibitions in Bradford, Wolverhampton and Glasgow, the official programmes of these events going to great lengths to reinforce the Empire's appeal in preference to other foreign countries (especially the United States).[35] The impact of this campaigning cannot be measured precisely. But a recent demographic study suggests that working-class enthusiasm for emigration had reached unprecedented levels by the early 1900s, and that many misgivings about migration – especially to the white colonies – had by then disappeared.[36]

The idea for the Committee came from the conference of voluntary emigra-tion societies organised by the Royal Colonial Institute. The conference was one of the rare occasions when the majority of agencies at work in this field were gathered together.[37] Earlier efforts to form a grand alliance of emigra-tion societies had come to nothing, and the EC's aim was to bring order to a highly disorganised area of social policy. With forty-nine affiliated voluntary organisations, the Committee did not need to construct a branch network. Freed from this task, it directed its energies to the preparation of specific schemes of emigration and land settlement. These were discussed in detail by separate sub-committees, the reports of which were then circulated among the relevant government departments in Britain, the various emigration agencies in the Dominions, and the British press. These reports drew heavily upon the practical experience which the Emigration Committee's members had of work-ing alongside government officials – some served as Poor Law Guardians, others as unpaid staff of Whitehall's Emigration Information Office. Further-more, the societies which members of the Committee represented were fre-quently called upon to deal with individual cases of migration in preference to the state.[38]

The government body which had the greatest impact on the develop-ment of the emigration movement was the Dominions Royal Commission (appointed in April 1912). The DRC's mandate was to investigate the natural resources of the Dominions and their development. Prevented from making recommendations concerning fiscal policy, it was to devote much of its time to the issue of emigration. Evidence was gathered from the Dominions during visits to Australia and New Zealand in 1913, and to Canada, Newfoundland

34 A.S. Thompson, 'The Language of Imperialism and the Meanings of Empire: Imperial Dis-course in British Politics, 1895–1914', *JBS* (1997), pp.152–5.
35 J.M. MacKenzie, *Propaganda and Empire. The Manipulation of British Public Opinion, 1880–1960* (Manchester, 1986), p.107; P. Greenhalgh, *Ephemeral Vistas. The Expositions Universelles, Great Exhibitions and World's Fairs, 1851–1939* (Manchester, 1988), pp.52–81.
36 N.L. Tranter, *Population and Society, 1750–1940. Contrasts in Population Growth* (1985), p.132.
37 'Editorial notes and comments', *United Empire* (April, 1910); 'The Emigration Conference', *United Empire* (July, 1910), pp.510–18.
38 This point is made effectively by K.I. Williams in *The British State, Social Imperialism and Emigration from Britain, 1900–22: The Ideology and Antecedents of the Empire Settlement Act*, Univer-sity of London PhD (1985), pp.23–4.

and South Africa in 1914. Many of the voluntary emigration societies affiliated to the Emigration Committee submitted evidence to the DRC, and several of its leading members were interviewed on questions relating to specific types of migration and possible forms of government assistance. The DRC's recommendations on emigration were drafted by Sir Henry Rider Haggard. Haggard had a long-standing interest in land settlement as a solution to the problem of rural depopulation. In 1916, he visited all of the Dominions as a representative of the RCI in order to investigate the question of settling demobilised soldiers. Haggard's recommendations to the DRC owed a great deal to the evidence and experience of the Edwardian migration movement.

THE POLITICAL STATUS OF IMPERIAL CAMPAIGNS

Extra-parliamentary campaigns have always claimed non-party status. In theory, at least, looseness of party connection makes it possible for them to play off one party against another, or to mobilise support across the political spectrum. It is also true, however, that each of the major political movements inspired by the Empire had its own distinctive reasons for operating outside party structures.

Before the policy of imperial preference could be adopted, Chamberlain and his supporters needed to silence the enemies of tariff reform – the Unionist Free Traders. The UFTs were subject to fierce attacks from local branches of the Tariff Reform League[39] and from a secret society called the Confederacy.[40] These activities brought tariff reformers into repeated conflict with Conservative Central Office, which accused them of drawing funds and members away from local Conservative associations and setting up a rival source of authority within the party. The Tariff Reform League, however, baldly declared that 'there were interests transcending those of party', and warned party managers that it would not be deterred from agitating on any aspect of the fiscal issue.[41] It also lambasted the party's 'patrician' leadership for being out of touch with grass-roots opinion.[42] For the party to prosper, it argued, the existing organisational machinery would have to be overhauled.

The Navy League's claim to non-party status had a very different basis from that of the tariff reform movement. Inter-party co-operation on naval policy was not uncommon.[43] The navy secured the country against invasion,

39 The fierce antagonism which often existed between branches of the TRL and local Conservative Associations is described by H. Page Croft in his autobiography *My Life of Strife* (1949), pp.41–2, and by Lord Robert Cecil in 'The Attack on Unionist Free Trade Seats', quoted in A. Sykes, *Tariff Reform and British Politics 1903–13* (Oxford, 1979), pp.90–1.
40 There appears to have been a substantial overlap between members of the Confederacy and the TRL executive. The best account of the Confederacy is provided by A. Sykes, 'The Confederacy and the Purge of the Unionist Free Traders, 1906–10', *HJ* (1975), pp.349–66.
41 *The Times*, 22/07/1903, p.7.
42 Joseph Chamberlain to Ridley, 6/2/1906, *Ridley papers* ZRI 25/99; D. Dutton, *His Majesty's Loyal Opposition. The Unionist Party in Opposition 1905–15* (Liverpool, 1992), pp.126–7.
43 B. Semmel, *Liberalism and Naval Strategy* (1986), pp.1–8; G.L. Bernstein, *Liberalism and Liberal Politics in Edwardian England* (1986), pp.167, 175–8.

protected its overseas trade, and played a vital role in suppressing the slave trade. It also removed the need for conscription and a large standing army. Maintaining a strong navy was therefore just as important to the Liberals as the Conservatives. For example, during the 1906 parliament, many aspects of naval policy were supported by party leaders on both sides of the House of Commons,[44] and this bi-partisan approach was also adopted by navalists beyond Westminster. Maintaining that it 'knew no politics', the Navy League argued for a suspension of party conflict in regard to matters of national defence. During the January 1910 election campaign a typical poster proclaimed, 'Drop Party For Once And Vote For A Supreme Fleet And The Navy League Programme Which Is Two-Keels-To-One'.[45] Admittedly, not all Navy Leaguers were happy with the organisation's political 'neutrality'. However, the President, Yerburgh, refused to let the Navy League fall into the hands of the party faithful. Thus although the composition of the League's executive and parliamentary committees was biased towards the Conservative party, a significant Liberal presence was preserved on both bodies.

Of all aspects of imperial policy, the issue of empire migration had the greatest potential to unify people of disparate social, religious and political backgrounds. In the 1880s the movement for state-aided migration had attracted strong support from organised labour, metropolitan clergy, middle-class professionals and the landed aristocracy. When in 1910 migration re-emerged as a form of organised politics it continued to cut across party and denominational lines, although the trade unions no longer had a place. The Emigration Committee contained diverse political perspectives. Clement Kinloch-Cooke, chairman of the Central Emigration Board, was a Conservative MP and a strong supporter of tariff reform, while Walter Hazell sat as a Liberal MP for Leicester (1894–1900), and later became Treasurer and Chairman of the Peace Society. The religious consciences of its members were very varied too. The Church Emigration Society was affiliated to the Committee, and two of its more regular attenders were devout Anglicans – the Rev. R.L. Gwynne and Lady Knightley of Fawsley. However, Walter Hazell was a Congregationalist, while Lady Edmund Talbot was a leading light of the Catholic Social Union to whom she lectured on settlement work. Likewise, in social terms, the EC reflected different tendencies. Philanthropic organisations, especially those dealing with child welfare, affiliated in large numbers. But the moving spirit behind the Committee during the First World War was E.T. Scammel, a member of the Naval and Military Emigration League, which was exclusively concerned with soldier settlement.

In accounting for the non-party status of imperial campaigns it is necessary, therefore, to pay attention to their particular aims and motivations. Yet to

44 R. Williams, 'Arthur Balfour, Sir John Fisher and the Politics of Naval Reform', *BIHR* (1987), pp.86–7, 98–9.
45 Insert in *The Navy* (January, 1910).

understand why the strength of imperialism as an organised political movement did not reside primarily in the political parties we must also examine the
trajectory of the party caucuses (or mass party organisations) in the years
following the Third Reform Act (1884). Imperial campaigning benefited from
a popular suspicion of organised party politics, a suspicion which stemmed
from the problems the National Liberal Federation and National Union of
Conservative and Constitutional Associations had in coming to terms with a
mass electorate.[46] At the turn of the century the NLF remained predominantly
a bourgeois organisation.[47] Few working-class voters joined its local associations or participated in the voluntary work upon which the caucus depended.
Low levels of popular participation were also a problem for the Conservative
National Union.[48] The impetus for the formation of the National Union came
from a handful of bourgeois luminaries craving recognition from the party's
leaders. Its core constituency was the propertied classes of suburban England
– the so-called 'Villa Tories'. Working-class membership of local Tory parties
was far less reliable, and was essentially negative in its nature, based upon
dislike of the moralising crusades of the Liberal caucus and religious hostilities
towards the Irish.

In 1902, a Russian refugee, Moisei Ostrogorski, published a damning critique of the recent development of political parties. His book, *Democracy and
the Organisation of Political Parties*, pilloried the caucus for having 'stereotyped
opinion', 'obliterated individuality' and ushered in an age of mere 'government by machine'. Not surprisingly, this exaggerated and highly polemical
account of the 'Americanisation' of party organisation in Britain was not well
received by fellow Liberals. Even its sponsor, the distinguished jurist and historian, James Bryce, made no effort to promote it.[49] But whatever its merits
as a work of political science, Ostrogorski's book tapped a powerful current
of opinion. Scepticism about the capacity of the caucuses to form and organise
mass political sentiment was widespread in Edwardian Britain.

The real problem with Ostrogorski's analysis was not that it was partisan, but
that it failed to explain *why* the caucus system had proved so disappointing.

---

46 For recent studies of this issue, see J. Vernon, *Politics and the People: A Study in English Political
Culture, c. 1815–1867* (Cambridge, 1993), esp. pp.7, 103–4, 182; and T.A. Jenkins, *Parliament,
Party and Politics in Victorian Britain* (Manchester, 1996), pp.111–26.
47 On the ascendancy of middle-class elites in the Liberal party organisation, see H.J. Hanham,
Elections and Party Management. Politics in the Time of Disraeli and Gladstone (1959), pp.127, 135–7;
T.R. Tholfsen, 'The Origins of the Birmingham Caucus', *HJ* (1959), pp.161–84; D. Fraser,
Urban Politics in Victorian England. The Structure of Politics in Victorian Cities (Leicester, 1976),
pp.194–5; M. Barker, *Gladstone and Radicalism. The Reconstruction of the Liberal Party in Britain*
(Brighton, 1975), pp.128–9; A. Briggs, *A History of Birmingham. Vol. II: Borough and City, 1865–
1938* (1952), pp.170–1.
48 J. Cornford, 'The Transformation of Conservatism in the Late Nineteenth Century', *Victorian Studies* (1963), p.66; J.A. Ramsden, *The Age of Balfour and Baldwin, 1902–40* (1978), p.48;
P.J. Waller, *Democracy and Sectarianism. A Political and Social History of Liverpool, 1868–1939*
(Liverpool, 1981), pp.48–52, and *Town, City and Nation. England, 1850–1914* (Oxford, 1983),
pp.110–11.
49 P. Pombeni, 'Starting in Reason, Ending in Passion: Bryce, Lowell, Ostrogorski and the
Problems of Democracy', *HJ* (1994).

Ostrogorski's treatment of party as a political institution was far too perfunctory. In particular, he failed to convey the seismic shift in the very meaning of party during the second half of the nineteenth century. As recently remarked, the 1870s, far from witnessing the full realisation of a two-party system first suggested in the 1830s, constituted a radical break with the past. Parties had previously been parliamentary institutions.[50] They were meant to be strong enough to prevent the executive from becoming dependent upon the monarchy, yet weak enough to prevent it from becoming too closely associated with popular sentiment. The effect of the franchise extensions of 1867 and 1884 was to transform parties into national institutions whose purpose was to secure an electoral mandate and to mobilise grass-roots support. However, at the same time as the meaning of party shifted to organisational structures outside parliament, a much more controlled and structured political environment was in the process of emerging. This transition is carefully charted in James Vernon's stimulating study of English political culture between 1815 and 1867. Examining the meaning of the constitution and the nature of citzenship in five parliamentary constituencies, Vernon offers a powerful critique of old 'triumphalist' accounts of the development of liberal Victorian democracy. Instead he argues for a 'trend towards closure' of democratic political forms, linking the growth of mass party organisation to the creation of a polity which was less open and less inclusive than the one which had preceded it.[51]

The deficiencies of the party caucuses, and the rigid control they often exerted over constituency politics, were a major spur to the development of imperialism and other political causes as extra-parliamentary movements. Not that imperialists could evade the problems of mass political mobilisation which the party caucuses were experiencing. They, too, had to think about how inclusively the political nation was to be defined; whether political authority could continue to be confined to the propertied classes; and what sort of constituency they were trying to appeal to.

IMPERIALISM AS A BROAD CHURCH

The professional middle classes were influential at all levels in the major extra-parliamentary movements inspired by the Empire, providing many of their local and national leaders. However, imperial politics was by no means an exclusively bourgeois affair. Each of the campaigns we have been discussing was grounded in class collaboration rather than in a sectional approach to politics. And each sought to incorporate working men, upper- and middle-class women and the aristocracy, in an effort to capture the middle ground.

50 A. Hawkins, ' "Parliamentary Government" and Victorian Political Parties, *c.* 1830–80', *EHR* (1989).
51 Vernon, *Politics and the People*, pp.6–7.

Working men

Imperial campaigns promoted popular involvement, even if they did not penetrate as deeply into the ranks of the working classes as they would have liked. There were two types of strategy for mobilising working-class support. The first was to 'domesticate' empire by linking it to the living standards of the mass of the British population. Tariff reformers were leading exponents of this technique. Upon the economic unity of empire, they argued, depended the strength of Britain's industrial base and the productive power of its economy. These, in turn, determined employment opportunities, wage levels, job security and the possibility of major instalments of social reform such as old-age pensions.

Like tariff reform, empire migration was understood by its advocates to be part of a long-term strategy of economic development. A steady stream of British migrants would help to make good the Dominions' shortages of labour, to improve the output of their economies and to enhance the purchasing power of their populations. It would also ensure a reliable and cheap supply of foodstuffs and raw materials for the mother country. The fact that the issue of empire migration re-emerged at a moment when Britain's governing classes were particularly sensitive to the plight of the country's urban poor no doubt gave it an even greater political purchase. Overcrowding and unemployment in towns and cities, and the fluctuating demands of the labour market, were very real problems in later-Victorian and Edwardian Britain.[52] In particular, the Labour-led 'right to work' agitation of 1907–10, and the threat to public order it presented,[53] suggested that existing social policy was in some sense deficient and in need of reform.

Relating the issue of naval supremacy to the everyday lives of British citizens was not so easy. It was possible to appeal to the material instincts of working-class voters by emphasising the commercial as well as strategic benefits of a strong navy. However, the introduction of state-funded old-age pensions in 1908–9 painfully exposed the potential for conflict between defence and social spending. Many Navy Leaguers responded to these events by attacking what they called 'social faddism', that is to say excessive government expenditure upon welfare programmes. When they did confront problems like unemployment, the preferred remedy lay in the realm of the voluntary sector, not the state. For example, in 1903 the Liverpool branch opened a 'Sea Training Home' at Clifton Hall. The home took poor boys (aged thirteen to fifteen) off the streets and prepared them for a life in the merchant navy. Five years later, in 1908, the executive committee of the Navy League organised a large conference in London, bringing together the officials of the home and the representatives of ten county councils to discuss the 'training of British seamen for British ships'.[54]

---

52 J.H. Treble, *Urban Poverty in Britain, 1830–1914* (1979), Chapters 2–3; J. Saville, *Rural Depopulation in England and Wales, 1851–1951* (1957), Chapters 1–2.
53 K.D. Brown, *Labour and Unemployment, 1900–1914* (Newton Abbot, 1971), Chapter 4.
54 Coetzee, *For Party or Country*, p.27.

Yet imperialists did not approach the problem of working-class political mobilisation purely in terms of policy – they also recognised the need to widen the social distribution of political power. Tariff reformers led the way here, supporting a series of initiatives which aimed to build a more constructive relationship with organised labour. The best known of these initiatives is the Trade Union Tariff Reform Association. Formed in April 1904, the TUTRA was intended to lure working-class voters away from pro-Labour Trade Unionism. Initially separate from the TRL, it claimed fifty-four branches and a membership of several thousand by 1907, though many of its branches lacked funds and were short-lived.[55] Demands for a more positive approach to the working classes also led to the formation of a Workers Defence Union in 1908. Significantly, its management was 'left largely in working-class hands as part of their political training'.[56] With a 'firm belief in England's imperial mission', the WDU supported tariffs and the exclusion of 'aliens' with a view to securing employment and fair wages. As well as the TUTRA and the WDU, the leading members of the TRL were actively involved in a wide range of other labour organisations, including the National Free Labour Association, the Unionist Labour Representation League, the Conservative Working Men's Association, and the British Workers' National League.[57]

What is important here is not the success of such projects but the enthusiasm of tariff reformers in directing and financing them. Tariff reformers were prepared to go to great lengths to present a more positive image for the party to Britain's working classes. In the run-up to the general elections of 1910, a fund was set up for working-class Conservative parliamentary candidates. Despite pressures from the grass roots of the party for the adoption of working men, the Conservative Central Office had remained highly ambivalent towards the idea. Politics, in its view, was essentially an occupation for the propertied classes – a 'stake' in society (i.e., wealth) was essential for nursing a constituency, meeting its electoral expenses, and for removing the temptation to turn politics into cash.[58] H.A. Gwynne at the *Standard* evidently disagreed. The newspaper's 'Working Men Candidates Fund', which raised £6,074 for the election in January and £7,866 for the election in December, supported a handful of working men to stand for parliament as Conservatives.[59] Significantly, Gwynne's efforts were applauded by Alfred Milner, Leo Maxse, Fabian Ware

---

55 On the TUTRA, see K.D. Brown, 'The Trade Union Tariff Reform Association, 1904–13', *JBS* (1970).
56 On the WDU, see A. Sykes, 'Radical Conservatism and the Working Classes in Edwardian England: The Case of the Workers Defence Union', *EHR* (1998), pp.1180–1209. The quotations are taken from this article.
57 R.J. Scally, *The Origins of the Lloyd George Coalition: The Politics of Social Imperialism* (Princeton, NJ), p.99.
58 S. Low, *The Governance of England* (1904), pp.174–82.
59 Blewett, *The Peers, the Parties and the People*, pp.271–2. Gwynne was later to support the payment of MPs for similar reasons. In the wake of the Osborne judgement in 1909 he argued that it was vital for the Conservative party to make it clear that it wished to retain a means of representation in parliament for trade unionists: Gwynne to A. Chamberlain, 30/9/1910, dep. 17, *Gwynne papers*.

and Leo Amery – all strong supporters of Chamberlain – but were ultimately frustrated by the wariness of the party managers who allocated constituencies which were mostly 'impregnable Liberal strongholds'.[60] Nor should we overlook working-class involvement in the TRL proper. Many of the League's local branches staged events in public houses to attract agricultural labourers and factory workers; a few even formed sub-committees composed entirely of working men, which organised their own meetings and lecture programmes.[61]

The political language of the Navy League also invested public opinion with a strong legitimacy. The Fleet was described as the 'property of the nation', and the nation was told in no uncertain terms that it would never have a better navy than it insisted upon having.[62] In this way, the League sought to reconcile the electorate to the heavy expenditure necessary to sustain an adequate margin of naval strength.[63] Yet up until 1909 its working-class membership was insubstantial. On the eve of the great naval scare, a special report regretfully concluded that the League had been 'too aristocratic' and 'too far above the level of the crowd'. Major organisational reforms were then implemented. The socialist agitator, Robert Blatchford, and the self-educated Lib-Lab MP, John Ward, were recruited to its executive; subscription fees were reduced; the social distinction between 'members' and 'associates' was abolished; and a new decision-making structure was devised. These changes appear to have had an effect. From 1909 to 1914, branch membership rose rapidly, many of the new recruits coming from the working classes. This broadening of the Navy League's social base owed a great deal to the efforts of a team of part-time lecturers who addressed large numbers of mass meetings up and down the country. The majority of these meetings were held outdoors in venues such as dockyards and engineering works, thus deliberately targeting working men.[64]

Middle- and upper-class women

Many historians speak of imperialism as if it was incurably masculine. Women are portrayed as the victims of empire, subject to sexual violence in Britain's colonies, and turned into scapegoats for the problems of 'social efficiency' and 'racial degeneration' at home.[65] More recently, however, feminist historians have begun to question this paradigm. New studies of the relationship between

---

60 A. Milner, *Constructive Imperialism: Five Speeches* (1908), pp.85–7; S. Koss, *The Rise and Fall of the Political Press. Vol. II: The Twentieth Century* (1984), pp.128–9.
61 These were Glasgow, Bristol, Portsmouth and Sunderland: *Monthly Notes* (March, 1905), p.246 and (March, 1906), p.161.
62 Speech of H.S. Trower at the 5th Annual General Meeting, *NLJ* (June, 1900), p.88.
63 Harold Wyatt speaking at the Navy League Dinner, 21/10/1904, *NLJ* (November, 1904), p.284.
64 Minutes of the Navy League executive, 15/2/1911, 25/9/1911, 12/6/1911, 9/4/1913, *Sea Cadet Association papers.*
65 On the masculine nature of Britain's imperial enterprise, and the sexual preoccupations of Britons overseas, see R. Hyam, *Empire and Sexuality. The British Experience* (Manchester, 1991). For a powerful critique of Hyam's work, see M.T. Berger, 'Imperialism and Sexual Exploitation: A Response to Ronald Hyam's 'Empire and Sexual Opportunity', *JICH* (1988), pp.83–9.

gender and imperialism have pointed to the need to be more open-minded about the way we incorporate women into the writing of imperial history.

Until 1918 women were excluded from the parliamentary franchise and had only a small say in municipal politics. Neither did party structures promote female participation.[66] Women were to provide hospitality at local meetings, recruit their husbands, organise educational lectures and stage fund-raising events, all of which were premised upon the ideology of separate spheres. However, many of the women who participated in the campaigns for tariff reform, naval supremacy and state-aided migration refused to be confined to a supportive and subordinate position. While they may not have adopted the more militant approach of suffragette organisations – heckling, marching and courting arrest – they did more than serve as hostesses and social workers. For a restricted circle of highly energetic and independently-minded women, imperial politics meant speaking on public platforms and asserting the right to make political decisions of their own.

Women in the Navy and Tariff Reform Leagues established their own separate organisations, which were affiliated to, but often in conflict with, the parent bodies. A Women's Organising Committee of the Navy League was set up in 1895, while women in the Tariff Reform League formed a Women's Association in December 1903.[67] One of the ways in which women in the Navy League asserted themselves was by trying to retain full control over the money which they raised. By 1904, female Navy Leaguers had gained a sub- stantial degree of autonomy in this respect, including the power to recruit their own members and to retain half of their subscriptions for a separate campaign fund. For five years the WOC operated free from the interference of men on the Navy League's executive. When it lost its semi-independent status in 1909 a hard bargain was struck – female Navy Leaguers negotiated a quota of seats on the central executive body, and female membership of the League's grand council was greatly expanded.[68]

Although the Women's Association of the Tariff Reform League was in- tended to be an essentially educative body, its role rapidly expanded to incor- porate canvassing, distributing literature and organising public meetings. Indeed this work was carried out with such efficiency that when Lord Ebury set up a fund for tariff reform constituency agents in 1907, it was to female tariff reformers that he turned for help. Ebury was the president of the Hertfordshire Federation of the TRL, and a major landowner in the county. The 'Ebury workers', as they became known, were assigned the task of organising sym- pathetic women, founding women's branches, and extending the work of the League into new constituencies. Three years on, Ebury noted how the fund

---

66 For an introduction to women's participation in party caucuses, see L. Walker, 'Party Polit- ical Women: A Comparative Study of Liberal Women and the Primrose League, 1890–1914', in J. Rendall (ed.), *Equal or Different. Women's Politics, 1800–1914* (Oxford, 1987).
67 A.S. Thompson, 'Thinking Imperially? Imperial Pressure Groups and the Idea of Empire in Late-Victorian and Edwardian Britain', University of Oxford D. Phil (1994), pp.93–9.
68 The grand council elected the executive: almost a third of its members were women by 1910.

had been administered with 'exemplary judgement' by the Women's Association, and offered an additional sum for its continuation and development.[69] A further measure of the WA's influence is apparent from its absorption of the Women's Committee of the Primrose League in 1904, and its amalgamation with the Women's Liberal Unionist Association two years later. Subsequently, all of the women's Unionist organisations were combined to form the Women's Amalgamated Unionist and Tariff Reform Association – the inclusion of fiscal reform in its title yet another indication of the political strength of female tariff reformers.

Women were also well represented in the empire migration movement. Women's emigration societies proliferated in the late-nineteenth and early-twentieth centuries, and six such organisations were affiliated to the Emigration Committee. Two of the representatives of the women's emigration societies which sat on the EC were active in the campaign for female suffrage. Mary Grimes belonged to the moderate National Union of Women's Suffrage Societies as well as the Conservative and Unionist Women's Franchise Association. And Lady Knightley of Fawsley, an experienced philanthropist, and author of the Committee's report on the emigration of women, was the first President of the CUWFA. It should, however, be noted that not all female emigration workers supported the idea of giving women the vote – a key anti-suffragist, Gladys Pott, later moved on to a career in imperial migration as the Secretary for the Society for the Overseas Settlement of British Women, formed in 1919.[70]

Possibly the most prominent female imperial activist was the writer, social worker and political activist, Violet Brooke-Hunt. At the end of the 1890s, Brooke-Hunt had set sail for South Africa to help care for British wounded soldiers. On returning to Britain in 1902, she immediately immersed herself in the work of various extra-parliamentary movements. Her role as the salaried Secretary of the Women's Unionist and Tariff Reform Association marks her out as one of the most outstanding – if now forgotten – female political activists of the Edwardian era. Displaying formidable energy and organisational zeal, Brooke-Hunt helped to form over forty women's branches of the Tariff Reform League. She was also a gifted public speaker, and regularly took to the platform to publicise her views on the fiscal question and the navy.[71] Despite this self-assertiveness, the issue of the vote for women does not appear to have been central to her political concerns. Her contribution to female emancipation was more subtle. It took the form of broadening and politicising the public role of women, and of acclimatising some men to women's political activism.

Imperial campaigning drew significant support from a female constituency. To be sure, the politicisation of women in these movements was gradual, and

69 Ebury to Bagley, 6/11/1910, *Ridley papers*, ZRI 25/99.
70 B. Harrison, *Separate Spheres. The Opposition to Women's Suffrage in Britain* (1978), pp.113, 228.
71 In her first year as organising secretary of the TRL, Brooke-Hunt addressed meetings in over twenty provincial towns and cities, see *Monthly Notes* (July, 1904), p.40.

possibly sometimes unconscious, among those involved. Only a handful of female imperialists were active in suffrage societies. For these individuals, participation in extra-parliamentary politics may well have been a means of validating their claim to full citizenship via the franchise. Many British feminists, for example, identified themselves with the cause of Indian women, supporting the abolition of child marriage, 'suttee' and prostitution as a way of asserting their right to political inclusion in the British state.[72] Nonetheless, many of the women who campaigned on imperial issues were not suffragists, and a few of them actually opposed giving women the vote. Women's emancipation cannot, therefore, be seen exclusively in terms of self-consciously feminist movements.[73] By organising their own groups at a local and national level, by instructing their members in the political issues of the day, by taking to the platform, and by demanding the right to participate in policy-making, female imperialists demonstrated a willingness to defy traditional expectations of what it was and was not possible for them to do in the public sphere. This is not to deny that long-established constructions of gender continued to influence men's attitudes towards women's politics – as late as 1912 a Navy League Ladies' honorary helpers' committee was being asked to help with clerical work at head office. Yet through these campaigns women became more visible in public life and challenged the notion that politics was primarily a male preserve.

The aristocracy

Several historians have speculated about why the aristocracy was attracted to the Empire. Some see the Empire as a form of aristocratic escapism; imperial service provided hard-up peers with an opportunity to re-create overseas an idealised world of aristocratic supremacy already in decline in Britain.[74] Others believe the Empire's purpose lay closer to home; imperial service advanced the political careers of ambitious peers, and reinforced the image of the aristocracy as a governing class.[75] It is possible that the variety of ways in which the aristocracy participated in extra-parliamentary imperial movements reflects the variety of attractions which the Empire held to Britain's peers. As already shown, the campaigns for tariff reform, naval supremacy and empire migration all benefited from aristocratic support. Many simply lent their names. Some stumped up money. And a few became more actively involved. Yet if the landed aristocracy often had its own particular reasons for enthusing about the Empire, it is important not to overlook the political beliefs which it shared with other parts of society. For a significant group of politically-motivated

72 A. Burton, *Burdens of History. British Feminists, Indian Women and Imperial Culture, 1865–1915* (Chapel Hill, NC, 1994), p.4.
73 See B. Harrison, 'A Different World for Women: Nineteenth Century Women Campaigners', *TCBH* (1992), pp.76–83.
74 D. Cannadine, *The Decline and Fall of the British Aristocracy* (New Haven, CT, 1990), pp.391–3, 420–9, 594–605.
75 A. Adonis, *Making Aristocracy Work. The Peerage and the Political System in Britain, 1884–1914* (Oxford, 1993), pp.210–39, 276–9.

peers, their commitment to imperial reorganisation was first and foremost ideological. That is to say that it was based on the same political premises as other participants in these campaigns.[76]

CONCLUSION

If the governors of Britain's colonies became accustomed to authoritarian stances, then the process of adjusting to home society must have been rather painful. Imbued with 'a bureaucratic mind-set', the Empire's great proconsuls are thought to have been leading proponents of the view that Britain's political structure was 'too free and open to be efficient'.[77] Milner's biographer, for instance, refers to his subject's central problem as a loathing of the political system in Britain.[78] Curzon, too, is understood to have been temperamentally unsuited towards the niceties of parliamentary politics. After returning to England from India in 1905, he was to spend four long years on the peripheries of public life, finding little to interest him in domestic politics until the crisis occasioned by Lloyd George's 'People's Budget' in 1909.[79] When he was eventually (and reluctantly) dragged into popular politics, it was to join hands with that other doyen of Edwardian imperialists, the Earl of Cromer, in resisting the vote for women.[80] It has been all too easy for historians to tar other enthusiasts for empire with the same brush.

Yet it would be wrong to assume that the authoritarian attitudes of the Empire's proconsuls were in any sense representative of wider public attitudes. On the contrary, by forging new, extra-parliamentary political structures, later-Victorian and Edwardian imperialists achieved a politicisation of empire which the two major parties had been anxious to avoid. This does not mean that there was not a recreational and populist side to their campaigning. However, the development of the social side of imperial politics was not incompatible with a more traditional emphasis on pamphlets, periodicals, and public meetings – types of activity which appealed to people's intelligence as much as their instincts. It has recently been suggested that 'the popular constituency for serious public discussion of politics in Edwardian Britain was larger in proportion to population than at any time before or since'.[81] In so far as this is true of public debate about the Empire, extra-parliamentary movements must take some of the credit.

Moreover, by invoking 'the people', imperialists were not simply laying claim to the popular will. They were challenging the representativeness of the party caucuses, and displaying a willingness to expand the notion of citizenship on behalf of some working men and upper- and middle-class women. That is

76 G.D. Phillips, *The Diehards. Aristocratic Society and Politics in Edwardian England* (1979).
77 B. Porter, *Britain, Europe and the World, 1850–1982: Delusions of Grandeur* (1983), pp.45–6, 62.
78 A.M. Gollin, *Proconsul in Politics. A Study of Lord Milner in Opposition and Power* (1964), pp.101–21.
79 D. Gilmour, *Curzon* (1994), pp.348, 358–64, 381–2, 400–2.
80 B. Harrison, *Separate Spheres*, pp.126–43, 147–71.
81 J. Harris, *Private Lives, Public Spirit: Britain, 1870–1914* (Penguin edn, 1994), ·p.196.

not to say that they, too, did not wish to balance the claims of democracy with a civilised polity, or to lay down the limits within which popular participation could be safely encouraged. It was certainly not the intention of imperialists to effect a sudden or radical redistribution of political power. Nevertheless, to hold them responsible for corrupting and brutalising British public life – as did many Radical Liberals like J.A. Hobson – is surely wide of the mark. For in challenging long-standing loyalties to party organisation and leadership, imperialists paved the way for a more open, lively and participatory political culture than is frequently imagined. Indeed the contribution of extra-parliamentary agitation to the formation of imperialism as an organised political movement might be likened to that of militant dissent, skilled labour and the provincial press in transforming the Liberal party from a parliamentary grouping into a truly national organisation. For just as mid-Victorian Liberalism drew its 'social strength' and 'social meaning' from outside parliament,[82] so imperialism derived its political muscle from the campaigns for tariff reform, naval supremacy and empire migration. Having said that, these extra-parliamentary campaigns could not have been so influential without the help of other factors, especially the publicity afforded by the press.

82 J. Vincent, *The Formation of the Liberal Party, 1857–68* (1966), pp.xxix–xxxiii.

CHAPTER 3

Propagating Imperialism

THE IMPERIALISING OF THE BRITISH PRESS

To understand how imperialism was propagated in Britain it is vital to look beyond parliament and party to consider the role of the press in circulating ideas and opinions among the general public. By the turn of the century, both the 'popular' and the 'political' press were printing more news of Britain's colonies. With respect to the 'political' press, imperialists were able to draw extensively on existing publications, but they also broke into the news by establishing papers and journals of their own. Nor was it simply a question of increased coverage. There was a change in attitudes too. Many of the most talented journalists, respected editors, and successful newspaper owners of this period were enthusiasts for empire, their inclination to 'think imperially' affecting the general management and editorial policy of some of the country's most widely read and politically significant papers. As the first section of the chapter sets out to show, empire helped to sell papers; newspapers, in turn, became powerful weapons for publicising empire and promoting the cause of imperial unity.

The second section of the chapter examines two of the most memorable orchestrated press campaigns of the late-Victorian and Edwardian era – tariff reform and naval supremacy. Journalists and editors became personally involved in these campaigns, delivering speeches under their auspices, helping to write their propaganda, and forging links with political groups in the colonies. In this way, they were to make a critical contribution to imperial political activity and to raise the profile of the Empire in national political debate. The final section of the chapter discusses a major, if much neglected, episode in the history of the Edwardian newspaper industry – the Imperial Press Conference of June 1909. Referred to by one journalist as 'a Parliament of the Empire', the conference brought together the Empire's leading newspapermen in order to give them an opportunity to exchange views on matters of common concern. The event is testimony to the complex associations which developed between the British press and its counterpart in the colonies after the turn of the century.

It took two years to plan, and enjoyed the backing of Fleet Street's most powerful personalities. On a practical level, it led directly to the formation of the Empire Press Union. The EPU described itself as a 'progressive movement towards the unity of the Empire'.[1] Among its more tangible achievements were a campaign for the reduction of cable rates, propaganda work during the First World War, and the summoning of two further conferences, one in Ottawa in 1920, and another in Melbourne in 1925.

THE NEW JOURNALISM AND THE OLD

During the last quarter of the nineteenth century the newspaper industry experienced rapid growth, propelled by the introduction of new technologies; by improvements in railway and telegraphic communication; and by the rise in literacy which followed the spread of elementary education. By the 1890s there was a greater quantity, quality and diversity of papers than ever before. Approximately 150 daily newspapers catered for the tastes of an expanding reading public; while the dailies were supplemented by a plethora of weekly papers, monthly periodicals, quarterly reviews and other miscellaneous publications.[2] In the absence of other methods of mass communication, the press continued to be the main medium for politicians to put their views to the electorate and for electors to keep themselves informed about public affairs.

The 'new journalism' targeted an increasingly prosperous and literate lower middle class by shifting the emphasis of news coverage away from education towards entertainment. Above all, the appearance and arrangement of papers was overhauled. Various typographical innovations were introduced (shorter paragraphs, more striking headlines, and an increased use of illustration), news commentary was cut down in favour of the 'human interest' story, novels were serialised, prize competitions were run, and sports coverage was extended.[3] Some of these developments affected long-established papers too, but not to the same extent, or with the same implications. I have therefore chosen to deal separately with the 'popular' press and the 'political' press.

The popular press

The two leading newspapers with a mass circulation – the *Daily Mail* and the *Daily Express* – were launched in 1896 and 1900 respectively. While coverage of foreign affairs was significant in both, it was the excitement and spectacle of empire which appealed most strongly to their readers. Expanded coverage of the Empire was made possible by the tremendous technological developments of the late-nineteenth century. Cheaper printing, and the spread of railways and telegraphs, gave readers access to the latest overseas news. Reporting

---

1 *Newspapers of Greater Britain associated with the Empire Press Union. With a Foreword by the Chairman, Robert Donald* (1918), p.10.
2 L. Brown, *Victorian News and Newspapers* (Oxford, 1985), p.4.
3 A.J. Lee, *The Origins of the Popular Press, 1855–1914* (1976), pp.117–20.

of colonial wars was particularly popular. Before the 1880s, few papers had special correspondents in the field: it was far too expensive, and news agencies such as Reuters were the main source of information.[4] However, by the late-1890s more and more editors were sending out their own staff, particularly to Africa,[5] and a large amount of capital was being sunk into the reporting of colonial wars.[6] This new-found popularity of war reporting received an especially strong stimulus from the South African War.

The paper which profited most from the war was Alfred Harmsworth's *Daily Mail*. Founded in May 1896, with an investment of £15,000, and sold at a halfpenny, the paper quickly became a success. It was the top-selling daily for virtually the whole of the period covered by this book. Harmsworth's stated intention was for the paper to be 'independent and Imperial' in its politics. This rather vague formulation typified his frame of mind.[7] His attraction to empire was of a sentimental kind – Cecil Rhodes and Joseph Chamberlain were admired as empire builders, but very little interest was displayed in imperial policy-making.[8] This was later to prove a problem at the height of the fiscal controversy. However, as an evangelist of empire in a more general sense, Harmsworth was a force to be reckoned with. A recent study of the popular press emphasises the importance of empire in the *Daily Mail*'s editorial policy – the paper even marketed itself as the 'voice of Empire in London journalism'.[9] Harmsworth's business partner, Kennedy Jones, went so far as to claim that the space allotted to imperial topics in the first years of publication was 'at least double the amount that any other London daily thought necessary for the same purpose'.[10] He also insisted that the Empire was central to the *Mail's* mission:

> It was the policy on which we worked throughout the whole of my journalistic career – One Flag, One Empire, One Home. We are a single family. ...I have always found the British public deeply interested in Imperial affairs. There is a personal bond, a domestic tie, but in Foreign affairs these were absent and, provided there did not happen to be a serious international crisis, it was well-nigh impossible to awaken a lively concern in Continental politics outside a limited circle.[11]

Harmsworth himself judged the public's thirst for imperial news to be one of the greatest untapped forces at the disposal of the press.[12] When criticised

4 For Reuters' domination of the supply of empire news, see D. Read, *The Power of News. The History of Reuters, 1849–1989* (Oxford, 1992), Chapters 3–4.
5 R.J. Wilkinson-Latham, *From Our Special Correspondent. Victorian War Correspondents and their Campaigns* (1979), pp.29–31.
6 R.T. Stearn, 'War Correspondents and Colonial War, *c.* 1870–1914', in J.M. Mackenzie (ed.), *Popular Imperialism and the Military, 1850–1950* (Manchester, 1992), pp.139–41.
7 R. Pound and G. Harmsworth, *Northcliffe* (1959), p.231.
8 H.J. Greenhall, *Northcliffe. Napoleon of Fleet Street* (1957), pp.48–9, 55–7.
9 M. Engel, *Tickle the Public. 100 Years of the Popular Press* (1996), p.75.
10 K. Jones, *Fleet Street and Downing Street* (1919), pp.147–9.
11 Ibid., p.150.
12 S.J. Taylor, *The Great Outsiders. Northcliffe, Rothermere and the Daily Mail* (1996), pp.36–7.

for warmongering in 1899, he is reported to have pointed triumphantly to the paper's circulation graph, recording the then unprecedented sale of over one million papers.[13] In the field of war reporting few papers could match the news-getting capabilities of the *Daily Mail*. By the end of the war, it had opened an editorial office in Cape Town and installed an expensive system of news cables. Famous among its correspondents were G.W. Steevens, Edgar Wallace, Lady Sarah Wilson, Ralph Hellawell, Julian Ralph and Charles Hands. Steevens was the paper's 'chief special', but his widely-acclaimed descriptive reporting was cut short by a bout of enteric fever from which he died in January 1900. Wallace, an ex-soldier, wrote with unusual sympathy for the lot of the ordinary private, and through an ingenious system of coded messages became the first to report the peace talks at Vereeniging. Sarah Wilson, the wife of an army officer at Mafeking, covered the siege of that town in a series of straightforward, matter-of-fact dispatches which proved enormously popular with the *Mail's* readers. Harmsworth even had the ingenuity to commission a war poem from Rudyard Kipling, entitled 'The Absent-Minded Beggar'. The profits from the poem were used to launch a fund for wounded soldiers, which had raised approximately £250,000 by the end of the war.[14]

The *Daily Mail* points to the symbiotic relationship between the 'new journalism' and 'new imperialism'. While the popular press fed off the passions and prejudices generated by imperial wars, the mass marketing of empire by popular dailies probably made it easier for imperial activists to awaken a response from the British public.

The political press

By the end of the nineteenth century, the 'serious' or 'quality' press – the equivalent of today's broadsheets – had established itself as an integral part of political society. There was at this time a 'press within a press' read by a 'nation within a nation' – papers and periodicals of real political consequence, with an influential if restricted readership, which expected to have an impact upon public affairs.[15] Standing outside the formal party caucuses, imperialists seized upon this type of paper as a way of drawing attention to themselves and their cause. In order to show how imperialists secured a voice in the 'political' press, this section will examine two daily papers, *The Times* and the *Morning Post*, and four periodicals, the *Outlook*, the *National Review*, *The Empire Review* and the *Round Table*.

Pre-eminently a political paper, *The Times* targeted the governing classes. Leo Amery was especially influential in shaping its colonial news coverage. Sent to South Africa in 1899, Amery was responsible for transmitting the reports of the paper's war correspondents, and for reporting on the political situation in

13 Engel, *Tickle the Public*, p.76.
14 R. Kipling, *Something of Myself* (1937), p.150.
15 S. Koss, *The Rise and Fall of the Political Press. Vol. I: The Nineteenth Century* (1981), pp.414–15 and *Vol. II: The Twentieth Century* (1984), pp.2–8.

South Africa more generally.[16] His own dispatches embraced Milner's vision of South Africa as a single, united, self-governing Dominion under the British Crown.[17] Returning to England in August 1900, Amery took over *The Times*'s colonial department, previously managed by Flora Shaw. Shaw was a remarkable woman; an uncompromising champion of the Uitlanders, she was questioned on her telegraphs to Rhodes at the government's official enquiry into the Jameson Raid.[18] She also contributed to the multi-volume *Times History of the South African War*, of which Amery was editor and principal author. For Amery, the *History* provided a platform from which to attack the War Office's handling of the conflict, and to preach the urgent need for reforms in the training and organisation of the army.

The *Morning Post* was London's oldest daily paper, with a reputation for lively and combative political commentary from a broadly Tory perspective. From 1876 to 1908, its proprietor was Algernon Borthwick (later Lord Glenesk); ownership passed to his daughter, Lady Bathurst, on his death. The paper's perspective on empire changed markedly during the nineteenth century. In the 1860s, it regarded the Empire as nothing more than a drain upon the exchequer. But during Disraeli's premiership, coverage of colonial affairs expanded, and a more positive attitude developed. In 1875, the *Morning Post* endorsed the purchase of shares in the Suez canal, and in 1876 it celebrated Queen Victoria's new title of Empress of India. In 1899, Glenesk intervened personally to make sure that proper recognition was given to the contribution made by colonial troops in Britain's fight against the Boers.[19] Hence the *Morning Post*'s support for tariff reform was but the final stage in its conversion to a fully-fledged imperial herald. Having suppressed its protectionist sympathies for much of the nineteenth century, the paper willingly became 'the mouthpiece of all those who put themselves under Mr Chamberlain's leadership and confidently reckoned on his ultimate triumph'.[20] Two of its long-serving editors, Fabian Ware and H.A. Gwynne, were uncompromising advocates of Chamberlain's programme. Before taking up the editorship in 1905, Ware had directed the education department of the Transvaal and Orange River Colony, and served as a member of the Transvaal's legislative council. He was succeeded as editor by Howell Gwynne. Gwynne had previously managed Reuters' correspondents in South Africa. At the helm of the *Morning Post* from 1911 to 1937, he used the paper to draw attention to the importance of economic co-operation in sustaining the sentimental and linguistic ties which united the Empire.[21]

In contrast to the daily papers, the periodical press was a more specialised medium; an amalgam of quarterly reviews, monthly journals, weekly papers,

16 L. Amery, *My Political Life. Vol. I: England before the Storm, 1896–1914* (1953), p.109.
17 W. Roger Louis, *In The Name of God, Go!: Leo Amery and the British Empire* (1992), p.45.
18 L. Heren, *Memories of* Times *Past* (1988), pp.120–1.
19 W. Hindle, *The Morning Post, 1772–1937. Portrait of a Newspaper* (1937), pp.221–6; R.J. Lucas, *Lord Glenesk and the Morning Post* (1910), p.387.
20 Ibid., p.408.
21 'The Policy of the *Morning Post* 1901–40' (undated), *Gwynne papers*, dep. 31.

and various other publications. The vast majority of periodicals were aimed at the university-educated, professional, middle-class reader. They were read in conjunction with newspapers as their function was to provide the in-depth commentary and opinion largely absent from the daily press. Many of the classic pieces of Victorian social and political thought first appeared in periodical form as long, reflective essays.[22] Periodicals were also more partisan than newspapers. Editorials were used to advise, cajole and criticise government. John Morley, editor of the *Fortnightly Review* and then the *Pall Mall Gazette*, liked to boast that an editor of an eminent review was equal in importance to twenty-five MPs. It was in the periodical press that imperialists were to find the most effective platform from which to develop in detail their views on the reorganisation of empire.

From 1904, J.L. Garvin edited the tariff reform weekly, the *Outlook*, recently purchased by C.S. Goldman, who had made his fortune in the Transvaal mining industry. Garvin later recalled Chamberlain having practically placed him in the editorial chair 'like a soldier at his post'.[23] If true, it was a shrewd choice. James Louis Garvin's was an outstanding journalistic talent. He was the son of poor Irish immigrants, born into a close-knit community in Liverpool in 1868. However, by the age of seventeen he had 'begun to feel the tug of a wider patriotism in which the Irish and English could share alike'.[24] This wider patriotism was fortified by his friendship with the Radical Liberal MP, Joseph Cowen, who edited the *Newcastle Daily Chronicle*. In his early twenties, Garvin worked for Cowen as a proof-reader, but with permission to write editorials. Cowen was a founder member of the Imperial Federation League, who saw the self-governing Dominions as shining examples of democratic polities from which even England might learn. Throughout his time in Fleet Street, Garvin's definition of empire was to be couched in very similar terms – an organic union of English-speaking states centred upon Britain.

Garvin's apprenticeship at the *Newcastle Daily Chronicle* served him well. True to its reputation as a training ground for London journalists, it led to a prestigious post as leader writer for *The Daily Telegraph*. It was at the *Telegraph* that Garvin got to grips with the main elements of the fiscal controversy, and his special articles on the subject gained him a reputation as a compelling propagandist. Garvin was thus ideally qualified to turn the *Outlook* into an effective rival of St Loe Strachey's free trade *Spectator*. Throughout the year 1905–6, he preached the value of imperial economic unity.[25] But frustrated by his lack of editorial freedom, Garvin was persuaded by Harmsworth (now

22 J. Mason, 'Monthly and Quarterly Reviews, 1865–1914', in G. Boyce, J. Curran and P. Wingate (eds), *Newspaper History from the Seventeenth Century to the Present Day* (1978), p.282.
23 J.L. Garvin to A. Steel-Maitland, 24/4/1912, *Garvin papers*, quoted in Koss, *The Rise and Fall of the Political Press*, Vol. II, p.28.
24 D. Ayerst, *Garvin of the Observer* (1985), p.11.
25 Quoted in J.D. Startt, *Journalists For Empire. The Imperial Debate in the Edwardian Stately Press, 1903–13* (Westport, CT, 1991), p.18.

Lord Northcliffe) to accept the editorship of *The Observer* in 1908 on the understanding that he was given a 20 per cent stake in the paper.

As editor of the *National Review*, Leopold Maxse was in the fortunate position of not having to answer to a proprietor. Maxse's father had bought the paper on his behalf in 1893, recognising his son's ill-health to be an obstacle to a parliamentary career. The *National Review* was the last major journal to appear in the nineteenth century. Its previous editor, the soon-to-be poet laureate, Alfred Austin, had intended to make it a 'glass hive of Conservative thought and Conservative opinion', and called for a return to a more aristocratic and paternalistic form of Toryism.[26] Maxse dispensed with his services, and made imperial and foreign policy the major topics of debate. Although invariably dogmatic and repetitive, Maxse's editorials could still be extremely entertaining. Within a decade, circulation figures for the *National Review* had increased from approximately 5,000 to between 7,000 and 8,000 copies per month. Subscribers included the Unionist party hierarchy and leaders of its constituency organisations, as well as journalists from other papers and periodicals. For Maxse, the publication of the *Review* was a labour of love. Under his watchful eye, it was transformed from a 'moribund, old-fashioned review into a lively journal of political opinion'.[27]

While Maxse liked to think of himself as the spokesman for the ordinary party supporter, many historians have fastened upon his more eccentric and wayward views. There is no denying that many of Maxse's opinions were couched in strong language. When attacking bureaucratic inefficiency, or the Conservative party hierarchy, his writing was uncompromising and full of scorn. This is partly to be explained by his long-standing distrust of those in authority, coupled with an irreverence towards any kind of establishment. Maxse's Germanophobia is widely commented upon too. It was fed by an unhealthy obsession with conspiracy theories – a close friend was once advised to dispense with the services of his children's German nanny, whose lengthy bicycle rides in the English countryside were sufficient to convince Maxse she was a spy! Yet for all his peculiarities and idiosyncrasies, Maxse's views upon empire were actually very similar to those of J.L. Garvin. Coached for Cambridge by an Australian tutor, Bernhard Wise, Maxse studied history at King's College from 1883 to 1886, precisely the time when John Seeley was delivering his famous lectures on 'The Expansion of England'. After leaving university, he embarked upon an extended tour of the Empire, gathering a large fund of knowledge about colonial life and politics, and establishing many contacts which were of great use to him as editor of the *National Review*.

Other periodicals focused exclusively upon imperial affairs. Founded in February 1901, *The Empire Review* was a monthly journal, priced at a shilling, and sold in Britain and the colonies. It strove to promote closer imperial

26 Mason, 'Monthly and Quarterly Reviews', p.291.
27 J.A. Hutcheson, *Leopold Maxse and the National Review, 1893–1914. Right-wing Politics and Journalism in the Edwardian Era* (1989), p.59.

union 'by placing before Britons, wherever they were domiciled, month by month the story of the Empire – its people, its policy and its trade'.[28] Just before the publication of the first issue, Milner wished its editor, Kinloch-Cooke, success in the enterprise, and favourable reviews soon appeared in the national dailies.[29] Like the *Outlook* and the *National Review*, *The Empire Review*'s conception of empire revolved around the self-governing colonies – pine rather than palm. It made no secret of its admiration of Chamberlain as a 'statesman of the highest order', and watched with 'special interest and sympathetic attitude' the progress of trade relations within the Empire.[30] Kinloch-Cooke's real passion, however, was empire migration. *The Empire Review* was one of the few journals to give continuous coverage of this topic. From as early as 1902, it argued the case for redirecting migrants away from foreign countries to the colonies, and for the necessity of state aid. It also examined schemes of colonisation for specific groups such as women, children and ex-soldiers, and ran features on what life was like in Australia and Canada in an attempt to get people to consider migrating there. Thus within a few years of publication, *The Empire Review* had established itself as a leading source of ideas on the issue of overseas migration.

The *Round Table* was the official organ of the Round Table movement – a non-party body, intent upon finding a form of imperial union which would be acceptable to the Dominions as well as to Britain.[31] The movement's magazine began publication in November 1910, with Philip Kerr (later Lord Lothian) as its editor. Kerr was Milner's private secretary, and later edited *The State*, a monthly review which advocated the federation of the South African colonies. As editor of the *Round Table*, he was assisted from 1913 by Edward Grigg.[32] The original plan for the *Round Table* was for a network of journals in each of the Dominions 'edited locally, but carrying a certain amount of material fed by an editorial clearing house in London'.[33] This plan was rapidly revised in favour of a quarterly review, edited in London, which aimed to prepare the ground for a reorganisation of the imperial system.[34] As was their habit, Round Tablers argued over the form and purpose of the magazine, as well as the nature of its intended readership. Nonetheless, under Kerr's guidance it gained a reputation as a well-informed journal of international affairs. Print-runs increased

28 The Earl of Hopetoun (Governor-General of Australia) to C. Kinloch-Cooke, 28/10/1900, reprinted in *ER* (February, 1901), pp.1–2; 'Learn to Think Imperially', The Editor, *ER* (February, 1904), p.2.
29 Milner to Kinloch-Cooke, 15/1/1901, *ER* (March, 1901), p.120; *ER* (April, 1903), pp.x–xi.
30 'Learn to Think Imperially', *ER*, pp.1–2.
31 Round Tablers used the word 'federation' in two senses, either to refer broadly to closer unity between Britain and the Dominions, or, more specifically, as a shorthand for some type of constitutional arrangement which would bind the empire of settlement together. See here J.E. Kendle, *The Round Table Movement and Imperial Union* (Toronto, 1975), pp.ix, xv, 64.
32 Grigg headed *The Times*'s colonial department from 1908.
33 A.C. May, *The Round Table, 1910–1966*, University of Oxford D.Phil thesis (1995), p.76. I am very grateful to Dr Alex May for allowing me to draw on his thesis for much of the information in this paragraph.
34 J.R.M. Butler, *Lord Lothian (Philip Kerr) 1882–1940* (1960), pp.43–4.

steadily from 3,500 for the first issue, to 13,000 for a special war issue in September 1914, settling down to around 10,000 for the rest of that decade. Two-thirds of the magazine's 3,000 subscribers lived in the Dominions, and free issues were distributed among leading politicians, national newspapers, hotels and London clubs.

THE PRESS AND IMPERIAL AGITATION

Orchestrated press campaigns were a feature of late-Victorian and Edwardian political life, and an important mechanism for reaching and guiding public opinion.[35] Throughout these years, the political press was highly partisan. Papers identified themselves not only with particular parties, but with particular causes, and the press played a crucial role in the politicisation of two of the most salient imperial issues of the day – tariff reform and naval defence.

Pressure groups like the Tariff Reform League were actively involved in publicity work. In an effort to keep the public's attention fastened on the subject of fiscal reform, and particularly the preferential tariff, the League's literature department supplied provincial papers with cartoons, news sheets and stereo blocks, formed a reference library, and oversaw the publication of its journal *Monthly Notes on Tariff Reform*.[36] Despite the considerable cost involved, the publication of a periodical was considered vital. Like the national airlines of 'third world' states, periodicals had a symbolic significance, and to be without one was to be incomplete. They were also crucial in fostering a sense of solidarity within movements which were constantly being criticised in the metropolitan press, and whose grass-roots activists often had little contact with each other or the group's executive.[37]

Chamberlain was equally successful in securing greater publicity for the tariff reform programme in the existing press. Seven months into the tariff reform campaign the former Liberal leader and Prime Minister, Lord Rosebery, lamented:

> At the beginning of last May I suppose there were hardly any newspapers in the country who realised that they were not as much attached to Free Trade as to the British Constitution and the Union Jack. All of a sudden there comes forward this magic musician, who plays a few notes on his pipe, and in a moment the whole mass of this highly respectable, and I thought, firm and convinced Free Trade Press begins to caper. . . . It matters very little what they are – large circulations or small – they all go hopping and bounding and skipping after the magic piper who has summoned them.[38]

35 Koss, *The Rise and Fall of the Political Press*, Vol. I, p.9; A. Jones, 'The Image Makers: Journalists in Victorian Popular Politics', in C.C. Eldridge (ed.), *Empire, Politics and Popular Culture: Essays in Eighteenth and Nineteenth Century British History* (1990), p.34.
36 V. Caillard, 'Suggestions as to the Organisation of the TRL', 1/10/1906, *Ridley papers*, ZRI 25/99.
37 B. Harrison, 'Press and Pressure Group Politics', in J. Shattock and M. Wolff (eds), *The Victorian Periodical Press: Samplings and Soundings* (Toronto, 1982), esp. pp.284–5.
38 Koss, *The Rise and Fall of the Political Press*, Vol. II, p.19.

Those who suffered most from Chamberlain's skill in marshalling the press were the Unionist Free Traders. As more and more papers fell under his sway, the UFTs became increasingly reliant upon the *Spectator* to put forward their point of view. Its editor, Strachey, led the way in attacking tariff reform as 'Tied-House' imperialism, and in elaborating a vision of empire firmly grounded in what he believed to be the interlocking principles of colonial autonomy and free trade.[39] But despite Strachey's best efforts, the UFTs were a faction in retreat after 1906.

When discussing press support for tariff reform, a distinction must be made between those papers which threw their weight wholeheartedly behind Chamberlain's campaign and those with tariff reformers on their staff which were sympathetic but by no means at Chamberlain's beck and call. Unequivocal support came from Maxse at the *National Review*, Garvin at *The Observer*, and Gwynne at the *Morning Post*. Chamberlain also benefited from the backing of an important figure in popular journalism – R.D. Blumfeld at the *Daily Express*. Garvin made a vital contribution to the tariff reform campaign. He was among the most skilful propagandists of the period,[40] who, during his brief time as a leader writer for *The Daily Telegraph*, helped to launch the cause of fiscal reform and to counterbalance the Balfourite leanings of E.B. Iwan-Muller.[41] Subsequently, as editor of the *Outlook* and then *The Observer*, Garvin elucidated the imperial aspects of Chamberlain's programme with great skill. Maxse, too, identified tariff reform as the major imperial issue of the epoch. He embraced the programme in its entirety, and even persuaded Garvin to write a special 100-page supplement on the 'Economics of empire' for the *National Review*.[42] Both men were close friends of the Tariff Reform League's organising chairman, Edward Goulding,[43] and both belonged to, and delivered papers at, the Compatriots Club.

The owner of the *Morning Post*, Lady Bathurst, was likewise a staunch Chamberlainite.[44] When the editorship of the paper fell vacant in July 1911, Kipling suggested his old friend Gwynne, who was offered the post at a salary of £2,000 a year.[45] Gwynne used the paper to attack the indecisiveness of Balfour on the fiscal question, and to argue that tariff reform was the only way to hold the Empire together.[46] Constantly being urged by his proprietor to take a harder line, he was at the forefront of that group of inveterate tariff reformers who opposed the dilution of the programme in 1912–13, and later exerted pressure upon Baldwin to revive the policy in the early 1920s.[47]

39 Startt, *Journalists for Empire*, pp.48–53.
40 Jones, *Fleet Street and Downing Street*, p.262.
41 The pro-Balfourite leader writer for the *Telegraph*.
42 Hutcheson, *Leopold Maxse*, p.194.
43 Maxse served for a time on the TRL's executive, but the demands of publishing the *National Review* prevented him from becoming deeply involved.
44 Lady Bathurst founded a local group of the Women's Tariff Reform Association.
45 G.D. Phillips, *The Diehards. Aristocratic Society and Politics in Edwardian England* (1979), pp.119, 134–5.
46 'Memorandum on the *Morning Post*' (October, 1936), *Gwynne papers*, dep. 31.
47 See p.180.

Ralph Blumfeld – or RDB as he was called – was another important ally. He was part of a small group of journalists who in 1903 engineered an interview between Chamberlain and Harmsworth's rival, Arthur Pearson. RDB wrote in his diary for 23rd of that month: 'Mr. Chamberlain has not until now been able to secure the support of a single London daily, and we, who are ardent Tariff Reformers, felt that it was time to see to the support of his plans. . . . We knew that if Joe once succeeded in talking to Pearson we would win.'[48] What Chamberlain said at the meeting we do not know, but soon afterwards Pearson was to put his own formidable organisational skills at Joe's disposal. Pearson's mornings were spent at the Tariff Reform League's headquarters, overseeing the production and distribution of literature, and thinking up new forms of propaganda.[49] He also spent freely to promote tariff reform in the press, and over the next two years established control of provincial papers in Birmingham, Leicester and Newcastle. More importantly, by placing the *Daily Express* at their disposal, Pearson gave tariff reformers a golden opportunity to reconcile the working classes to the prospect of duties on food.[50] RDB, whom Pearson recruited to the paper in 1902, and who became its editor in 1904, was instrumental in this task. His memoirs recall how the Liberal press 'hypnotised a large section of the public into the belief that if tariffs of any kind were imposed on any kind of foreign goods, the British working man would starve'.[51] RDB's analysis of the fiscal question therefore focused upon the question of employment. It was he who conjured up the slogan 'Tariff Reform Means Work For All', and who 'flaunted it day after day, week after week on the front page of the *Daily Express*'.[52]

The other national daily paper controlled by Pearson proved somewhat less dependable. The *Standard* was purchased in November 1904 with the help of Sir Alexander Henderson, the TRL's treasurer. It had previously sided with the UFTs and was therefore a welcome addition to the tariff reform press. Winston Churchill, who defected to the Liberals over the fiscal question, was scathing about the deal:

£700,000 was found – I wonder where – *The Standard* passed into the hands of the champion hustler (Chamberlain) of the Tariff Reform League. The group of able writers who expected so much influence is scattered. Their places are filled by the obedient scribes of a mammoth trust and the protest of the last remaining free trade newspaper is silenced.[53]

Potentially the paper was a great asset. Under the editorship of the brilliant W.H. Mudford (1877–99), its daily sale rose from about 180,000 to 250,000

48 R.D. Blumfeld, *R.D.B.'s Diary, 1887–1914* (1930), pp.194–5.
49 R.D. Blumfeld, *All in a Lifetime* (1931), p.184; D. Porter, 'A Newspaper Owner in Politics: Arthur Pearson and the Tariff Reform League, 1903–05', *Moirae* (Trinity, 1980).
50 Koss, *The Rise and Fall of the Political Press*, Vol. II, p.23.
51 R.D. Blumfeld, *The Press in My Time* (1933), p.48.
52 Ibid., p.49.
53 Speech of Winston Churchill at Glasgow, quoted in D. Griffiths, *Plant Here* The Standard (Basingstoke, 1996), pp.161–2.

copies, and it came to be regarded as the oracle of the landed and commercial classes. But whatever satisfaction Chamberlain derived from the acquisition was short lived. In February 1905, Gwynne ran a series of articles on imperial preference. These articles diverged from Chamberlain's scheme of a 10 per cent duty on foreign manufactures, and proposed a 5 per cent tax on all imports. They were printed with the full approval of Pearson, and greatly annoyed Chamberlain. The following month Pearson resigned as chairman of the Tariff Reform League.

If the *Standard* was a disappointment to Chamberlain, the Northcliffe press proved to be a thorn in his side. The fitful, transitory and partial allegiance of *The Times* and the *Daily Mail* had the effect of impeding the progress of tariff reform, while at the same time damaging the influence of those papers and exposing them to charges of instability and opportunism. Northcliffe was the supreme waverer on the fiscal issue. The chance to put himself at the forefront of a great press campaign, with a strong imperial appeal, was clearly a strong temptation. Northcliffe's instincts, however, told him that a food tax must be unpopular and might well damage the circulation of his papers.[54] He probably also resented following the lead of Pearson, his chief rival. Thus although pledging a vague general support for the programme, a vigorous campaign against 'stomach taxes' was conducted in the Northcliffe press in 1903.

In view of its vast circulation, and its separate northern edition, reconciling the *Daily Mail* to the idea of a preferential tariff was a priority for Chamberlain. An opportunity presented itself when H.W. Wilson, a leader writer on the paper and a loyal Chamberlainite, was offered a position at the *Express*. Chamberlain advised Wilson to accept unless Northcliffe gave him greater freedom of action at the *Mail*; and Wilson succeeded in securing the promise of a column in the paper to fight his case.[55] He then persuaded Chamberlain to consider some sort of concession to make it possible for the *Mail* to speak up for the full tariff reform programme without losing face. Chamberlain obliged by guaranteeing that more taxes on food would be removed than imposed. This seemed to do the trick, and for a while criticism of tariff reform was tempered. However, Northcliffe and Kennedy Jones continued to cling tenaciously to their view of the *Mail* as a paper catering 'to the popular taste' which had a duty to 'treat its customers honestly' and to 'reflect the public mind'.[56] It came as no surprise, therefore, when, at the end of 1912, the *Mail* defected on the issue of food duties, and renewed its pressure on the Unionist leadership to drop them once and for all.

The attitude of *The Times* to tariff reform was most confusing of all. W.F. Monypenny (assistant editor), Valentine Chirol (head of its foreign department), and Leo Amery all came out strongly in favour. But its editor, G.E. Buckle,

---

54 In August 1904, the paper polled some 2,000 people on the issue of tariff reform, and the response appeared to confirm Northcliffe's fears of a mass hostility to Chamberlain's scheme, *Daily Mail*, 29/08/1904, p.4.
55 J. Amery, *Joseph Chamberlain and the Tariff Reform Campaign*, Vol. 5 (1969), pp.296–7.
56 Jones, *Fleet Street and Downing Street*, pp.308–10.

'a thorough and lifelong Balfour man', was only really interested in the retaliatory and revenue-raising functions of tariffs, while C.F. Moberley Bell, the manager, lacked confidence that the programme could carry.[57] Without Amery's input it is likely that the overall tone of *The Times* would have been fairly hostile. For example, it was Amery who engaged W.A.S. Hewins to produce a series of sixteen articles extolling the virtues of fiscal reform and imperial preference. And it was Amery who, under the pseudonym 'Tariff Reformer', responded to the famous letter from the 'fourteen leading economists' condemning Chamberlain's proposals. However, at the end of 1912, following the appointment of Geoffrey Robinson as its new editor, *The Times*, like the *Mail*, declared against food duties. It appears that Robinson was urged by Grigg to drop preference.[58] Certainly, Amery blamed the attitude of the paper as much on Robinson and Grigg as on Northcliffe. He later recalled how Robinson's and Grigg's 'very strong Round Table views' had inclined them to 'minimise the economic side' of imperial unity.[59]

British naval supremacy was the greatest imperial subject other than tariff reform to be debated by the Edwardian press.[60] The state of the navy hit the front pages of the nation's newspapers in 1909 with the acceleration of the German battleship programme. Throughout February, the Liberal cabinet had debated whether the naval estimates should provide for four or six dreadnoughts. Reginald McKenna, First Lord of the Admiralty, held out for a minimum of four capital ships to be laid down immediately, and two more at the beginning of 1910. Lloyd George and Churchill insisted that four ships were sufficient, and hotly disputed the Admiralty's projections of German battleship construction. After angry debates, in which McKenna came close to resigning, a compromise was reached whereby the Admiralty agreed to the construction of four dreadnoughts with the building of a further four if required.

The compromise was like a red rag to the navalist press. It immediately sparked off a campaign for the government to lay down all eight ships without delay – 'we want eight and we won't wait' was the slogan of the hour. The *National Review*, *The Observer*, *The Times*, *The Daily Telegraph*, and the *Pall Mall Gazette* were all swept up in this storm of naval hysteria. In the case they constructed for a 'big navy', the Empire figured very prominently. There was much discussion of the withdrawal of ships from the Atlantic and the Pacific to the North Sea – a key aspect of the debate on the defensibility of Britain's imperial frontiers, which we shall return to in Chapter 5. Yet notwithstanding the apparent unanimity of the press agitation of 1909, there was in fact a great diversity of opinion in the nation's newspapers regarding imperial defence. Above all, there was a rift between the 'Admiralty press', which expressed

57 Startt, *Journalists for the Empire*, pp.42, 164; N. Blewett, *The Peers, the Parties and the People. The General Elections of 1910* (1972), p.305.
58 Startt, *Journalists for Empire*, pp.197–9.
59 Amery to Gwynne, 3/1/1913, *Gwynne papers*, dep. 14.
60 Startt, *Journalists for Empire*, p.175.

Fisher's views on the condition of the navy, and the 'Patriotic press', the mouthpiece for Fisher's critics. Among the charges levelled at the Admiralty press by its critics was that of neglecting the defence of the Empire; a charge which was, of course, vigorously denied.

Fisher had a shrewd sense of the influence wielded by the press. He was particularly reliant upon the backing of Spender at the *Westminster Gazette* and Garvin at *The Observer*. Both men were supplied with privileged information and expected to support Admiralty policy in return.[61] The *Westminster Gazette*'s support was significant because the paper was recognised as the most author-itative expression of moderate Liberalism.[62] But Fisher was even more indebted to Garvin. Under Garvin's editorship, *The Observer* was turned into a weekly organ of Admiralty policy.[63] From the beginning of 1905, Garvin was shown a range of confidential documents and became privy to secret cabinet discus-sions. This not only helped him in fighting the Radicals in the Liberal party, it put him in a far stronger position when defending Fisher's policy of reducing and redistributing ships against its critics on the political right. In particular, Garvin ridiculed Beresford's demand for an enquiry into Admiralty policy. He warned that such an enquiry would sour relations between the government and the Admiralty, undermine discipline in the navy, and provide material for Radical backbenchers wishing to cut defence expenditure.[64]

Fisher's critics in the press – the 'Syndicate of Discontent' as he labelled them – included Blumfeld at the *Daily Express*, Maxse at the *National Review*, and Gwynne at the *Standard* and subsequently the *Morning Post*. From the summer of 1907, when it became known that Fisher had co-operated with the Liberal ministry in reducing the naval estimates, they contrived to put the First Lord under pressure to resign. The following *Daily Express* leader of March 1909 is a good example of their coruscating criticism:

> The sole responsibility for the fact that in a few months Great Britain will be in a more vulnerable position than she has been since the battle of Trafalgar belongs to the First Sea Lord. . . . Above all, he is responsible for the starving of the Navy during the last three years. . . . If he had threatened resignation when an unsatisfactory programme was being prepared he would have forced the hands of the economaniacs. . . . We arraign Sir John Fisher at the bar of public opinion, and with the imminent possibility of national disaster before the country we say to him, 'Thou art the man!'[65]

Beresford was the source of many of the accusations levelled against Fisher. Although admired by many for his frank personality, sincere patriotism, and profound attachment to the Royal Navy, he was an impulsive character who

---

61 A.J. Marder, *From Dreadnought to Scapa Flow: The Royal Navy in the Fisher Era, 1904–19* (Oxford, 1978), p.82.
62 J.A. Spender, *Life, Journalism and Politics*, Vol. I (1927), pp.110–11, 188, 228.
63 A. Gollin, *The Observer and J.L. Garvin, 1908–1914. A Study in a Great Editorship* (1960), pp.28, 49.
64 Ibid., p.37.
65 *Daily Express*, 20/3/1909, quoted in Marder, *From Dreadnought to Scapa Flow*, p.186.

craved publicity. When in May 1907 ships were withdrawn from the Channel fleet – which Beresford commanded – to form a new Home fleet, his response was to turn to the press for support. Having already twice championed Beresford for First Sea Lord in October 1900 and August 1901, Maxse was an obvious ally.[66] Maxse's intense hostility to Germany, and deep distrust of the Kaiser, made him hyper-sensitive about the operational efficiency of the Home and Channel fleets. Gwynne, too, sympathised with the objectives of the anti-Fisherites, and exploited his position as editor of the *Standard* to publicise Beresford's demand for an enquiry into Admiralty policy.[67] The two men corresponded regularly throughout the years 1907–12. Beresford supplied information relating to the shortcomings of the navy, which enabled Gwynne to mount an assault on the Fisher regime.

It was Beresford's contention that under Fisher the Royal Navy had become a fraud and danger to the Empire. Gwynne marshalled his specific criticisms into a public manifesto, and arranged for a special commissioner to tour around naval posts 'to corroborate certain points and pick up fresh information'.[68] The manifesto aimed to expose the inadequacies of the Home fleet, to draw attention to the withdrawal of cruisers from colonial stations and the injury which their absence inflicted upon 'Imperial prestige', and to stress the urgent need for increases in the number of small craft and naval personnel.[69] Gwynne then pressed the leadership of the Conservative party to look into these issues, albeit to no avail. The 'Syndicate of Discontent' did, however, get its enquiry. In April 1909 the Asquith government announced a review of Admiralty policy, only to reject criticisms of the organisation and distribution of the Fleet, and broadly endorse the Fisher reforms. Not a man to give up easily, Beresford continued to campaign through the press. In 1912, he supplied Gwynne with a lengthy indictment of official policy, intended for 'private circulation' among MPs. The document called for increased spending on naval construction and the 'building of a new fleet in the Mediterranean'.[70] The controversy surrounding the policy of redistribution will be explored in greater detail in Chapter 5.

THE IMPERIAL PRESS CONFERENCE (1909)

The idea for an Imperial Press Conference originated with Harry Brittain, part of the *Standard*'s management staff, and a Conservative MP from 1918 to 1929. While visiting Canada in 1907 as a representative of the Board of Trade, Brittain was struck by the ignorance of many people in the United Kingdom

66 Hutcheson, *Leopold Maxse*, pp.142, 158.
67 Griffiths, *Plant Here* The Standard, p.178; Gwynne to Beresford, 23/5/1907, *Gwynne papers* dep. 16.
68 Gwynne to Beresford, 28/5/1907, *Gwynne papers*, dep. 16.
69 Copy of a typed memorandum explaining Beresford's reasons for resignation (undated and unsigned), *Gwynne papers*, dep. 16.
70 'Great Britain and Germany. The Naval Danger', printed memorandum by Beresford (1912), *Glenesk–Bathurst papers*, 1990/1/2075.

regarding the Dominions and vice versa. Working on the assumption that the press itself could be a powerful factor in promoting co-operation within the Empire, he devised a plan to bring together its newspaper editors at a conference in Britain.[71] The next two years of his life were devoted to turning the idea into a reality. The first step was to secure the support of leading newspaper magnates. A committee was formed with Lord Burnham as President, Northcliffe as Treasurer, Pearson as Chairman, and Brittain as Secretary. Other well-known press personalities actively involved in making arrangements for the conference included Spender, Gwynne, Robert Donald (editor of the *Daily Chronicle*), and Harry Lawson MP (who managed *The Daily Telegraph* from 1903, when his father, Edward Lawson, was raised to the peerage as Lord Burnham). Letters were sent to the owners of the Empire's major daily papers to inform them of the conference, and to ask those from larger cities to elect a delegate. There were fifty-four delegates in total. They came from Australia, New Zealand, Canada (including a representative of the French-Canadian press), South Africa (including two representatives of the Afrikaans' press, both of which had fought for Transvaal independence in 1899), India (there were five representatives of the Anglo-Indian press, but only a single spokesman for the 'native' press[72]), Burma, Ceylon, the Straits Settlements of Malaya, and the West Indies. It was, as W.T. Stead remarked, the first time in the history of the Empire that 'the keepers of the eyes and ears of King Demos had been gathered together from Britain and from Britain's dominions overseas'.[73]

The visitors were welcomed on 5 June at the Imperial International Exhibition halls in Shepherd's Bush. Six hundred newspapermen from the United Kingdom were present. A moving opening address was delivered by the seasoned platform orator, Lord Rosebery. Begging the forgiveness of the Indian press delegates, Rosebery directed his remarks mainly to the self-governing parts of the Empire. His closing words bade the guests: 'Welcome home! Welcome home to the home of your language, your liberties and your race. Welcome home to the source of your parliaments, your free institutions and of this immeasurable Empire.'[74] Spender, who had been responsible for stage-managing the speech, but had failed to silence the appalling noises from a display of fireworks outside, later judged it to have been the 'most extraordinary performance by a public man' he had ever witnessed.[75] A week later on 11 June, the overseas delegates were welcomed by the government at another banquet at which the Prime Minister, Asquith, acknowledged the significance of their visit, and recognised the special function of the press in promoting imperial unity.[76]

71 H. Brittain, *Pilgrims and Pioneers* (1946), pp.5, 181–98.
72 Surendranath Banerjee of *The Bengalee*.
73 W.T. Stead, 'The Editors of the Empire at Home', *The Contemporary Review* (July, 1909), p.48.
74 T.H. Hardman, *A Parliament of the Press. The First Imperial Press Conference, 1909* (1909), pp.12, 15.
75 Spender, *Life, Journalism and Politics*, p.227.
76 *The Times*, 12/6/1909, p.6.

In between the more serious business of the conference debates, a busy social itinerary was organised for the overseas delegates. There was a military display at Aldershot, and a great demonstration of sea power at Spithead; a garden party was hosted by the Prince of Wales at Marlborough House; a banquet was held by the Corporation of the City of Glasgow; and there were guided tours of the Edinburgh offices of the *Scotsman*, and of the General Post Office by the Postmaster-General. There were also visits to the Daimler works in Coventry, steel works in Sheffield, and cotton mills in Manchester; and outings to Warwick Castle, All Souls and Worcester colleges in Oxford, and Chatsworth House.[77] It was a demanding schedule, but not without a purpose, for it was meant to give Dominion journalists a more rounded view of British society, and an opportunity of forging relationships with their British counterparts.

The centrepiece of the event was a series of debates, modelled upon the colonial conference system. Spender chaired a small sub-committee which decided upon the subjects to be discussed. It was resolved to hold daily meetings at which ministers, ex-ministers and British journalits would discuss key aspects of imperial affairs with the overseas guests.[78] These meetings deliberately excluded the fiscal question as newspapers of every shade of political opinion were represented. The programme was as follows:

Day 1: *Imperial cable communications:* The Colonial Secretary, Crewe, presiding, with Austen Chamberlain and Sydney Buxton in support.
Day 2: *The navy and imperial defence:* McKenna presiding, with Grey, Cromer, Lyttelton, and Amery present.
Day 3: *Imperial defence:* Balfour presiding, with Haldane and Roberts present. (Emigration was also discussed.)
Day 4: *Literature and journalism:* Lord Morley presiding.

A further debate on naval defence was held on the penultimate day of 26 June, under the chairmanship of Lord Esher, with Beresford and General Sir John French present. The conference's political debates were judged to be of such importance by *The Times* that each one was reported in detail and made the subject of a leading article.

As well as developing a dialogue between British and Dominion journalists, the conference also lobbied for a reduction of cable rates. It was in the years between 1850 and 1870 that submarine cables grew from infancy to maturity.[79] In 1852, they totalled a mere 46 kilometres; by 1895, they stretched over some 300,000 kilometres. Cables reached North America in 1866, India in 1870, Australia in 1871, South Africa in 1879, and West Africa in 1886. They had a remarkable effect. For instance, when the cable from London to Australia was opened, news that had taken fifty-four days to travel by the fastest ship now took only fifteen to twenty-four hours. Yet since international

77 *The Newspaper Press Directory* (1910), pp.6–9.
78 Spender, *Life, Journalism and Politics*, p.224.
79 For a fuller discussion of this subject, see D.R. Headrick, *The Invisible Weapon. Telecommunications and International Politics, 1851–1945* (Oxford, 1991), Chapters 2–3.

telegraphy was left to private enterprise for many years, cable rates tended to be very high. Indeed, until 1895 telegrams between Australia and Britain were so expensive that all the Australian newspapers together could only afford to cable a few hundred words a day. In order to reduce the rate, the Australian colonies had to subsidise the relevant company, the Eastern Telegraph, to the tune of £32,400 a year. But it was not until the Pacific Ocean cable was opened to the public in December 1902 that the situation really began to improve. Built by a consortium consisting of Australia, New Zealand and Canada, and subsidised heavily by the British government, the new cable forced the Eastern Telegraph to lower its rate to 3s per word. The Pacific's telegrams were also faster, taking an hour instead of a day.

The conference's committee on cable rates and press inter-communication organised a deputation to Asquith. Its case for cheaper cables was premised upon the benefits of closer contact between the distant parts of the Empire.[80] High cable rates, it was argued, had curtailed the discussion of imperial affairs in the press, and frequently led to misunderstandings between Britain and its colonies. Lower cable rates would permit the colonial press to provide wider and more accurate coverage of events in Britain, as well as facilitating a free exchange of ideas on imperial subjects. They were therefore a necessary foundation of imperial unity.[81] While sympathising with what the deputation had to say, Asquith emphasised that the Canadian and North American cable companies were 'commercial bodies acting on commercial principles'; government could do little more than encourage them to reduce their rates. Needless to say, the suggestion of another state cable, either from Britain to Canada, or across Canada linking the Atlantic and Pacific, was not well received.[82] Yet the committee had more joy with the cable companies. In response to its representations, the cost of a telegram from Britain to Australia was reduced substantially by the Pacific Cable Board from 1s to 9d a word. Two years later, a much desired cheapening of the trans-Atlantic message rate was secured when it was agreed to transmit messages of non-urgent character at half-rates.[83]

Immediately after the delegates departed, the Empire Press Union was formed. It was a permanent body charged with the task of carrying on the work of the conference and improving communication between the newspapers of the Empire. Its headquarters were in Fleet Street, and branches were organised throughout the Dominions. The EPU dealt with questions concerning cables, and was responsible for making arrangements for further conferences. During

80 Letter from Hudson Berkeley (New South Wales) to the Editor, *The Times*, 6/6/1909, p.17.
81 *Newspapers of Greater Britain* (1918), pp.1–3.
82 The idea of a state-owned Atlantic cable originated with the Canadian delegates, who were authorised by the Canadian Postmaster-General (Lemieux) to say to Asquith that Canada would pay one half of the cost of such a cable if Great Britain financed the other half. See Hardman, *A Parliament of the Press*, p.121; P.D. Ross, *Retrospects of a Newspaper Person* (Toronto, 1931), pp.148–9.
83 The latter was a delayed message rate, the cable companies reserving the right to hold back a cablegram for up to 19 hours. The EPU continued to agitate for a flat rate of 2.5d per word, without deferment, and this was eventually conceded by the Western Union Cable Co. in 1912. *Newspapers of Greater Britain*, pp.36–42.

the First World War it also participated in propaganda work, arranging for the correspondents of colonial papers to be admitted to the lobby of the House of Commons, to visit important industrial and military centres in Britain, and to travel to the Western Front.[84]

CONCLUSION

Towards the end of the South African War, Milner had urged the need for journalists at home to launch a campaign for the better organisation of the British Empire.[85] How far were his hopes fulfilled? The late-Victorian and Edwardian era saw the arrival of the modern newspaper magnate, buying up and marshalling the press on a grand scale. Northcliffe and Pearson acquired huge stakes in national and provincial newspapers. They were men of abounding energy, with a great zest for life, and a hands-on approach to the management of their papers. In founding the *Daily Mail*, Northcliffe chose to put particular emphasis on the Empire, convinced that it would increase the paper's circulation. Yet despite his abiding interest in politics, and his admiration of Chamberlain, Northcliffe was unable to offer consistent support for tariff reform. His stable of papers pursued an 'erratic middle course' on the fiscal question.[86] In contrast, Pearson, who had previously shown very little interest in politics, rallied to Chamberlain's banner. In its first two years, the TRL benefited from his ingenuity, imagination and organisational flair, and although the *Daily Express* was by no means a political organ, it devoted a large number of column inches to explaining the case for tariff reform.[87] Turning to the 'political' press, it is impossible not to be struck by the large number of journalists who identified their careers with the cause of imperial unity, and who wrote extensively on the reconstruction of the Empire. Men like Amery, Garvin, Grigg, Gwynne, Kerr, Kinloch-Cooke, Maxse and Ware shared a profound belief in the importance of the press in forming and directing public opinion. In putting forward their views on empire they displayed great strength of character, often ignoring their proprietors or the party managers in order to criticise existing policy. They were not so much spectators as participators in the drama of imperial politics, and they regarded their papers as instruments of agitation which had a function beyond that of disseminating 'hard' news.

Throughout these years, the overriding concern of imperial journalists was Britain's relations with the self-governing Dominions. They all agreed that the Empire was evolving into some form of partnership based upon the shared political ideals and institutions of its English-speaking peoples.[88] So much was apparent from the Imperial Press Conference. For if the event had acted as a

84 *Newspapers of Greater Britain*, pp.8–31.
85 Koss, *The Rise and Fall of the Political Press*, Vol. II, p.8.
86 Blewett, *The Peers, the Parties and the People*, p.305.
87 S. Dark, *The Life of Sir Arthur Pearson* (1922), pp.13–14, 94–100; R. Allen and J. Frost, *Voice of Britain. The Inside Story of the Daily Express* (Cambridge, 1983), pp.18–21.
88 Startt, *Journalists for Empire*, pp.207–9.

great demonstration of imperial kinship and solidarity, it had also fought shy of the problems associated with governing different races and cultures. W.T. Stead, a pioneer of the 'new journalism', was quick to take up this point. Acknowledging how the presence of the Dominion delegates in Britain had helped to 'quicken the sense of the unity of the Empire, so far at least as the white-skinned races are concerned', he complained bitterly of the conference's failure to confront 'the greater and deeper trouble involved in the collision of the white and coloured races of the Empire'.[89] Similarly, the Secretary of State for India, John Morley, was struck by the 'extraordinarily small attention, almost amounting to nothing' that was given to India by the delegates; an impression confirmed by Lord Esher, who on the final day observed how the term 'Empire' now referred primarily to Great Britain and the white Dominions.[90] In the next three chapters we shall be examining how this particular concept of empire influenced national political debate about trade, defence and migration.

89 Stead, 'The Editors of the Empire', p.55.
90 'Lord Morley at Oxford', *The Times*, 14/6/1909, p.6; *The Annual Register* (1909), pp.131, 149.

CHAPTER 4

Imperial Trade: Tariff Reform

JOSEPH CHAMBERLAIN AND THE ORIGINS OF TARIFF REFORM

Public expenditure ballooned during the South African War. Already facing severe fiscal problems, the Treasury was forced to impose a registration duty upon imported corn. The origins of the tariff reform campaign lie in Chamberlain's decision to stake his political future upon preserving this new corn tax and securing a permanent exemption for grain grown inside the Empire.[1] This was the policy of imperial preference, designed to 'establish preferential commercial arrangements with the colonies, and secure for British producers and workmen a further advantage over foreign competitors in Colonial markets'.[2] Although tariff reformers also hoped to protect the home market against 'unfair' competition, and to open up foreign markets to British goods, it was the preferential part of the policy to which they attached the greatest importance. For example, in response to the argument that foreign trade was more valuable than colonial trade, Chamberlain declared:

> My conclusion is exactly the opposite. I say it is the business of British statesmen to do everything they can, even at some present sacrifice, to keep the trade of the colonies with Great Britain; to increase that trade, to promote it, even if in doing so we lessen somewhat the trade with our foreign competitors.[3]

Preferential tariffs were intended to transfer trade from international to imperial channels and to pave the way towards a more self-contained, self-sustaining Empire akin to the German *Zollverein* (customs union). Underpinning this vision lay the assumption that there was no article of food or raw material or

---

1 After Ritchie repealed the registration duty in his 1903 budget, Chamberlain's proposal became even more radical as it was no longer that of amending existing duties but of implementing new ones.
2 'The Inaugural Meeting of the TRL', *The Times*, 22/7/1903, p.7.
3 Speech of Joseph Chamberlain at Birmingham on 'Imperial Union and Tariff Reform', 15/5/1903, quoted in C.W. Boyd (ed.), *Mr. Chamberlain's Speeches* Vol. I (1914), pp.131–2.

manufactured good which could not be produced somewhere in the British Empire.

This emphasis upon the imperial dimension of tariff reform goes against the grain of much of the existing scholarship. Despite the variety of interpretations of tariff reform, historians have tended to conceive it as more of a domestic political strategy than an imperial one.[4] Some follow the path trodden by free traders by drawing attention to a protectionist impulse behind tariff reform. In the face of general anxieties about British economic decline, and the clamour of specific manufacturing interests, Chamberlain was supposedly drawn to tariffs as a way of protecting the home market or of prising open markets overseas.[5] Others have set tariff reform in the broader context of a resurgent 'new' Liberalism. Tariff reform, it is argued, was an anti-socialist strategy, designed to generate funding for social legislation without alienating core Conservative constituencies by resorting to progressive taxation.[6] Another and more cynical view of tariff reform is that it was simply a party political programme, either an attempt by Chamberlain to breathe new life into a fast-decaying Liberal Unionism,[7] or a bid by Chamberlain for the leadership of the Tory party.[8] The latest addition to this burgeoning historiography portrays tariff reform as an electoral strategy designed to adapt the Unionist party to an age of democratic politics by consolidating its support among the working classes.[9]

To understand why it has been possible for historians to offer such a range of competing and conflicting interpretations, it is vital to grasp that tariff reform was a multi-dimensional policy, sheltering many different types of tariff: protective, retaliatory, revenue-raising, and preferential too. Tariffs, then, were supposed to serve different functions. Nonetheless, the *preferential* tariff had a privileged status as it promised to do most to unite the Empire. The primacy of imperial motivation among tariff reformers was widely recognised at the time. As the Fabian, Sidney Webb, remarked, it was Chamberlain's enthusiasm for empire which was infectious and which made him so dangerous a political force.[10] Hence what fired the imaginations of committed tariff reformers (or 'wholehoggers' as they were known) was the opportunity of using fiscal policy

4 For an imperial emphasis, see P.J. Cain, 'The Economic Philosophy of Constructive Imperialism', in C. Navari (ed.), *British Politics and the Spirit of the Age* (Keele, 1996); A. Marrison, *Business and Protection 1903–1932* (Oxford, 1996), p.19; and my own, 'Tariff Reform: An Imperial Strategy, c. 1903–13', *HJ* (1997).

5 For the view that protectionism steadily assumed more importance in the campaign, see B. Semmel, *Imperialism and Social Reform. English Social Imperial Thought, 1895–1914* (1960), p.124; P.J. Cain and A.G. Hopkins, *British Imperialism. Vol. I: Innovation and Expansion, 1688–1914* (1993), pp.212, 218.

6 D. Judd, *Radical Joe. A Life of Joseph Chamberlain* (1977), pp.241–2.

7 A.J.P. Taylor, ' "Joe" at his Zenith', *Essays in English History* (Harmondsworth, 1976), p.189.

8 P. Fraser, 'Unionism and Tariff Reform: The Crisis of 1906', *HJ* (1962), p.150, and *Joseph Chamberlain. Radicalism and Empire, 1868–1914* (1966), p.246.

9 E.H.H. Green, 'Radical Conservatism: The Electoral Genesis of Tariff Reform', *HJ* (1985), pp.674–87.

10 S. Webb, *Fabianism and the Fiscal Question. An Alternative Policy*, Fabian Society Tract, no. 116 (1904).

to draw together the different parts of 'Greater Britain'. It was never their intention simply to line the pockets of British businessmen, or for that matter to prop up the farming community. Throughout the campaign, protectionist sentiment was strictly subordinated to the goal of preference.[11] Thus when the 'domestic' attractions of tariff reform threatened to overshadow its wider imperial implications, vigorous efforts were made through the offices of the Tariff Reform League, and its sister organisations, to publicise the goal of economic unity within the Empire and to show that a preferential tariff was a necessary first step towards it.

Among the more eloquent exponents of this new fiscal policy was Leo Amery. In 1907, Amery published a series of papers which presented preference not as an abstract economic theory but as a fundamental political principle. Supporters of preference, it was explained, took as their starting point the unity of the Empire, and then analysed economic policy from that viewpoint. They regarded free trade as indifferent to empire, and inconsistent with the higher political objective of reconstructing relationships within the British world.[12] Indeed, without imperial reconstruction the whole future of the British state was thought to be at risk – its long-term industrial competitiveness, its employment and wage levels, and its funding of social reforms. Like so many of the other major texts on tariff reform, Amery's pamphlets treated imperial preference as the principal plank of Chamberlain's programme.

THE BACKGROUND TO THE CAMPAIGN

In the early 1880s the National Fair Trade League was established to campaign for protection for industry and agriculture.[13] The NFTL's strongest support came from urban regions suffering from the impact of tariff barriers and foreign exports, especially Sheffield, Birmingham and Bradford.[14] It was in the face of its agitation that Salisbury decided to appoint a Royal Commission to enquire into the 'Depression of Trade and Industry'. Reporting in 1886, the Commission acknowledged the problem of foreign competition in 'home' and 'neutral' markets, but its majority report rejected a return to protectionism, urging instead improvements in technical education, and the gathering of commercial information by overseas consuls.[15] Even the proposals of the Commission's minority report did not favour a system of imperial preference,

11 For a fuller exploration of this issue, see Thompson, 'Tariff Reform: An Imperial Strategy', pp.1033–54.
12 L. Amery, 'Preference as a Principle', *The Times*, 30/4/1907, reprinted in *Union and Strength. A Series of Papers on Imperial Questions* (1912), pp.246–7.
13 For the fair trade movement of the 1880s and 1890s, see S.H. Zebel, 'Fair Trade. An English Reaction to the Breakdown of the Cobden Treaty System', *JMH* (1940).
14 The best account of the NFTL remains that by B.H. Brown, *The Tariff Reform Movement in Great Britain* (New York, 1943), pp.17–28, 88–95, 129–37.
15 A.L. Friedberg, *Britain and the Weary Titan. Britain and the Experience of Relative Decline, 1895–1914* (Princeton, NJ, 1988), pp.39–40.

arguing instead for a 10–15 per cent duty upon manufactured goods imported from foreign countries. The Trade and Industry Commission did, however, indicate a new-found willingness to question the benefits of free trade.

In parallel to this fair trade agitation of the 1880s and 1890s there emerged a new school of economic thought; the first major challenge to existing fiscal policy since the Anti-Corn Law Movement had protested against protection in the 1840s. The leading lights of the so-called 'historical economy' school were W.J. Ashley, William Cunningham, W.A.S. Hewins, H.S. Foxwell and L.L. Price – all except Foxwell lent their active support to the campaign for tariff reform. In their attack on the foundations of economic liberalism, individualist philosophy and the doctrine of *laissez-faire*, historical economists helped to reopen a debate upon the state's economic responsibilities.[16] They also challenged liberal cosmopolitanism's refusal to distinguish between the value of foreign and colonial markets. The basis for future economic policy, they argued, lay in a recognition that the Empire was Britain's most prized market and best resource base with a huge potential for further development.

Neither should we ignore Chamberlain's own experience as President of the Board of Trade from 1880 to 1885. At the Board of Trade, Chamberlain had become acutely aware of the problems of overproduction, declining prices, and falling profit margins facing the British economy. Despite a resurgence of protectionist feeling among manufacturers in the West Midlands, he had continued to defend Britain's fiscal orthodoxy in the election campaign of 1885. Privately, however, he began to doubt the wisdom of clinging to the policy of free trade.[17] These doubts were amplified in 1894–95 when serving on Lord Aberdare's Royal Commission on the Aged Poor. Sir Herbert Maxwell – later to join the TRL – was a member of this Commission. His memoirs recall how Chamberlain was ardently in favour of establishing a scheme of old-age pensions. Upon being asked how the necessary revenue for such a scheme was to be raised, Chamberlain suggested a tax on corn. He then went on to explain how his faith in *laissez-faire* economics had first been shaken in 1882 when asked to prepare arguments against a motion in favour of fair trade.[18]

The 1890s were a very difficult decade for a politician like Chamberlain whose reputation rested upon his achievements as a social reformer. In local politics, Chamberlain had pioneered urban planning and municipal reform, mindful of the need to improve the condition of the working class. But when Chamberlain later championed a more active role for the Colonial Office in developing Britain's tropical colonies, he was vigorously opposed by the Treasury,[19] which

16 For a skilful elucidation of their beliefs, see E.H.H. Green, *The Crisis of Conservatism. The Politics, Economics and Ideology of the Conservative Party, 1880–1914* (1995), pp.162–3, 176–83.
17 R.V. Kubicek, *The Administration of Imperialism: Joseph Chamberlain at the Colonial Office* (Durham, 1969), pp.6–8.
18 Sir Herbert Maxwell, *Evening Memories* (1932), pp.245–6.
19 S.B. Saul, 'The Economic Significance of Constructive Imperialism', *JEH* (1957), pp.187–90; P. Marsh, *Joseph Chamberlain. Entrepreneur in Politics* (1994), pp.408–13; M. Havinden and D. Meredith, *Colonialism and Development. Britain and its Tropical Colonies* (1993), p.88.

was facing a budgetary crisis.[20] No wonder, then, that Chamberlain's mind turned to tariffs. As customs revenue fell, and income outstripped expenditure, the existing fiscal regime became an increasing source of irritation to a minister intent upon expanding the sphere of the state.

A further and final element in the background to tariff reform is to be found in the discussions of imperial preference at the Colonial and Imperial Conferences of 1887, 1897 and 1902, and at a special meeting at Ottawa in 1894. At the Colonial Conference of 1887, Jan Hofmeyr, from the Cape, suggested levying an imperial customs tariff on foreign goods entering the Empire. Though the idea received strong backing from the majority of colonial delegates,[21] the caution of the British government prevented a resolution from being proposed. Yet fair traders took heart from the discussion, especially from the way it broadened the debate about tariffs from an industrial into an imperial problem.[22] In 1894, delegates from the colonies met again in Ottawa, where they resolved to give a preference to each other's produce. The Foreign Office and Board of Trade took fright at this proposal, fearing it would harm commercial and manufacturing interests in the United Kingdom. But the Colonial Office intervened to defend the right of the colonies to adjust their tariffs with a view to obtaining trade concessions from other powers.[23] At the Colonial Conference of 1902, Wilfrid Laurier, the Canadian premier, then stepped up the pressure upon the British government to adopt a policy of reciprocal preference. Laurier had indicated beforehand that Canada was in a position to make offers to Britain which it could not have made at the previous gathering in 1897. This was the so-called 'colonial offer' which tariff reformers seized upon as evidence of a mutual desire for closer economic relations within the Empire to be realised through a system of preferential tariff arrangements.[24]

IMPERIAL PREFERENCE AND THE ECONOMIC UNITY OF EMPIRE

In the words of W.A.S. Hewins, the tariff reform movement came into being as 'the expression of a necessary change in the economic relations of the Empire and the manner in which we regarded them'.[25] Tariff reformers wished to channel trade in those directions which enhanced imperial unity. They criticised the policy of free trade for undermining the sense of a 'Britannic' community and for turning the United Kingdom into a cosmopolitan clearing house for money and goods. The likely consummation of such a policy,

20 Green, *The Crisis of Conservatism*, pp.48–53; R. Shannon, *The Age of Salisbury, 1881–1902: Unionism and Empire* (Harlow, 1996), pp.475–6.
21 Brown, *The Tariff Reform Movement*, p.101.
22 J.E. Kendle, *The Colonial and Imperial Conferences, 1887–1911. A Study in Imperial Organisation* (1967), p.11.
23 L. Trainor, 'The British Government and Imperial Economic Unity 1890–5', *HJ* (1970), pp.74–6; Brown, *The Tariff Reform Movement*, pp.123–6.
24 J. Chamberlain, 'Retaliation', speech delivered at the Town Hall, Greenock, 7/10/1903, quoted in *Imperial Union and Tariff Reform. Speeches delivered from 15 May to 4 November, 1903* (1903), p.63; C. Kinloch-Cooke, 'Mr. Chamberlain's New Chapter', *ER* (June, 1903), p.448.
25 W.A.S. Hewins, *The Apologia of an Imperialist: Forty Years of Empire Policy*, Vol. I (1929), p.5.

they argued, was the disintegration of the Empire into a number of separate states.

Underlying this belief that fiscal unity constituted the best strategy for reconstructing the Empire was the historical experience of the German *Zollverein*. Not that Germany was thought to provide an exact model for the development of British imperial trade. Rather, the *Zollverein* was important because it demonstrated the long-term significance of commercial and economic association in consolidating links between states.[26] This argument was repeated again and again in tariff reform propaganda. In his book *The Britannic Question*, Jebb expressed the view that common economic interests were the *only* firm foundation upon which imperial unity could be built.[27] 'Real Imperial Union', he declared, could not rely on the racial bond since many of the king's subjects in the Dominions, although white, were not Anglo-Saxon. Trade matters were of first concern, reciprocity being integral to the idea of a united Empire. Hewins agreed and predicted that unless Britain secured the trade of the colonies it would lose them altogether, sentiment having little to do with the destiny of nations.[28] Amery too felt that political co-operation could only develop within a coherent economic system: 'In our case, the development of mutual interests is required both to hold the Empire together as it exists and to pave the way to the Empire as it ought to be.'[29] Milner, as ever, was more circumspect, claiming to be 'the last man to contend that preferential trade alone is a sufficient bond of Empire'. But even he accepted that the maintenance or creation of other bonds became very difficult in circumstances where Britain refused to distinguish between trade with 'foreigners' and trade with its 'fellow-citizens across the seas'.[30] Austen Chamberlain was more hopeful. Speaking of preference as a 'problem of Empire', he expressed confidence in the capacity of mutual trade to 'spin a web, ever increasing in strength, between every portion of the Empire' and to 'make our interests so inseparable that when the days of stress and trial come no man can dream of breaking bonds so intimate and so advantageous to all of those whom it concerns'.[31]

Hence the overriding objective of tariff reformers was a policy of planned empire development. At the centre of their ideology lay a new conception of the role of the state in reorganising the Empire. Formed in 1904, the Compatriots Club provided the forum for elaborating and publicising this 'constructive' approach to imperial policy.[32] According to the Compatriots, the issue

26 J. Parker Smith, 'Tariffs and Federation', *Monthly Notes on Tariff Reform* [hereafter *Monthly Notes*] (November, 1904), p.205.
27 R. Jebb, *The Britannic Question* (1913); 'The Clue to the Great Alternative', address on Tariff Reform to the East Marylebone Conservative and Liberal Unionist Association, 22/11/1909, *Jebb papers*, d/7.
28 Speech by W.A.S. Hewins to Lewes branch of the TRL, 22/11/1907, reported in *Monthly Notes* (January, 1908), p.72.
29 Amery, *Union and Strength*, pp.233–4.
30 A. Milner, *Constructive Imperialism: Five Speeches* (1908), p.21.
31 Speech by A. Chamberlain in Newcastle, 9/3/1911, reported in *Monthly Notes* (April, 1911), p.297.
32 Milner, *Constructive Imperialism*, p.43.

of the epoch was imperial consolidation. As with the Round Table movement, Milner provided the main political focus for the group. Other prominent personalities included Amery, Garvin, and Mackinder from journalism and politics, and Ashley, Cunningham and Hewins from academe. Partly financed by the Rhodes Trust, Compatriots met privately to read and discuss papers; and public lectures were also held under the Club's auspices.

The Compatriots looked back on the last sixty years as a period when political economy had been dominated by a 'futile' and essentially 'negative' conception of the state. They saw their encounter with free traders more as a moral crusade than a normal political confrontation. Amery, for instance, described it as a 'fight for freedom of thought' in the sphere of economic theory, and a 'fight for freedom of action' in the sphere of fiscal policy. In future, government was to be guided not by *laissez-faire*, but by *vouloir-faire* (the will to act) and *savoir-faire* (the knowledge to act).[33] Compatriots also considered the policy of free trade to be fundamentally antagonistic to the consolidation of the Empire. It was a 'policy of drift' which had left the colonies short of people, neglected their natural resources, and risked losing a position of 'permanent and assured advantage' in some of the 'greatest and growing markets in the world'.[34] Thus the fact that the colonies could not afford to contribute their share in defending the Empire was not their fault but the mother country's. Britain had left them weak when they might have been made strong; Britain had left them languishing when, like the United States, they could have supported a growing and prosperous population.[35] The Compatriots' conception of the state was neatly summarised by J.L. Garvin's phrase, 'the doctrine of development'. According to Garvin, government was a creative and dynamic agency which had a positive and vital function to play in mobilising the Empire's manpower and resources, and in consolidating Anglo-Dominion relations.[36]

The Compatriots, then, were of one mind that trade and empire were interdependent. The power and wealth of Britain depended upon the maintenance of empire. Britain, in turn, had a duty to pursue a fiscal policy which would increase the economic, and especially the industrial strength, of the Empire as a whole, without retarding the development of its component parts or consigning the colonies to agricultural production.[37] Free trade within the Empire, while in the long-run desirable, was recognised to be impracticable in the short or even medium term. Amery was quite forthcoming on this problem: 'I have no hesitation in saying that, Imperial preference with moderate internal tariffs . . . is vastly preferable to the immediate introduction of an Imperial *Zollverein* with complete internal Free Trade.'[38]

---

33 L. Amery, *The Fundamental Fallacies of Free Trade. Four Addresses on the Logical Groundwork of the Free Trade Theory* (1908, popular edition), p.40.
34 Milner, *Constructive Imperialism*, pp.17–8.
35 Amery, *The Fundamental Fallacies*, p.39; Amery, *Union and Strength*, pp.5–7.
36 J.L. Garvin (ed.), *Compatriots Club Lectures. First Series* (1905), p.9.
37 Lecture by W.A.S. Hewins at a meeting of the canvassing committee of the Primrose League, 17/6/1907, *Milner papers*, dep. 129, fo. 78.
38 Amery, *The Fundamental Fallacies*, p.55.

In examining economic relations within the Empire, the Compatriots focused their analysis on markets rather than finance. Under free trade, they maintained, the needs of metropolitan industry were being sacrificed to those of metropolitan finance. Fiscal policy had to be refashioned in such a way as to secure Britain's manufacturing base, to increase the competitiveness of British industry, and to promote Britain's export trade. This argument was advanced very forcefully in Amery's collection of speeches, *Union and Strength*. Considering the connection between preferential trade and imperial unity, he remarked:

> It is not only a policy of stimulating the Colonies, but also a policy of stimulating and maintaining the industrial strength of the Mother Country. That industrial strength has declined enormously of recent years . . . and is declining more rapidly every year. Yet it is upon that industrial strength that the main burden of the defence of the Empire . . . must fall for the next generation. To develop the industrial strength of England in every way is one of the most essential measures for the preservation of the Empire.[39]

Yet it was Joseph Chamberlain, erstwhile screw manufacturer, who offered the most striking reassessment of Britain's comparative advantage. Addressing a group of City bankers in 1904, Chamberlain asked if they were entirely beyond anxiety as to the permanence of their great position. He continued:

> Banking is not the creator of our prosperity, but is the creation of it. . . . If the industrial energy and development which has been going on for so many years in this country were to be hindered or relaxed, then finance, and all that finance means, will follow trade to the countries which are more successful than ourselves.[40]

Was there any substance to Chamberlain's assertion? In their study of British overseas expansion, Cain and Hopkins observe how, under free trade, the needs of metropolitan industry were to some degree sacrificed to those of metropolitan finance.[41] But tariff reformers made much bolder claims. They argued that the British economy was undergoing a structural shift from manufacturing to services which was dangerous and damaging, and jeopardising Britain's success as an economic power by compelling the country to live on 'parasitic' rather than 'productive' wealth.[42]

The late-nineteenth century was, of course, a period of rapid economic change. International competition intensified as a number of recently industrialised powers began to experience more rapid rates of growth than Britain. Furthermore, as science and technology developed, so new industries emerged, utilising the latest techniques in mass production. In most of these areas of innovation Britain lagged behind her major rivals.[43] It was not that the British

39 Amery, *Union and Strength*, p.244.
40 Speech of J. Chamberlain, 1/19/1904, quoted in Friedberg, *The Weary Titan*, p.76.
41 Cain and Hopkins, *British Imperialism*, Vol. I, p.275.
42 Green, *The Crisis of Conservatism*, pp.169, 174.
43 Marrison, *British Business and Protection*, p.9.

economy stopped growing: industrial decline was relative, reflecting the fact that Britain's lead on her major competitors was being eroded during these years. Nevertheless, tariff reform propaganda exploited this news to the full, stressing how Britain's rate of manufacturing progress fell far behind that of its chief rivals, and predicting the future loss of Britain's industrial supremacy.[44] For example, one expert claimed that in the period 1895–1907 British exports to foreign protected markets had increased by only 37 per cent, compared with a rise in Germany of 112 per cent, and 330 per cent in the United States. More recent comparative analysis of relative growth rates in foreign countries has tended to corroborate these figures. In the period 1870–1913 Germany's economy expanded 1.6 times more rapidly than Britain's, while America's economy grew at twice the rate.[45]

Economic historians disagree on whether it was within the British government's capacity to slow down or reverse the country's relative industrial decline. Some believe the government might have gone further to frame the sort of economic policies under which industry could have thrived. Others refuse to accept that economic policy impeded manufacturing progress or that high levels of overseas investment obstructed the introduction of new technologies in the British economy.[46] As far as the merit of a preferential tariff is concerned, the critical factor is the potential for Anglo-Dominion trade. It is often said that Chamberlain's proposals represented a bad bargain for Britain, or for the colonies, or both. Either tariff reform is criticised for having 'stereotyped' the colonies as suppliers of foodstuffs and raw materials to the mother country at the expense of their growing industrial sectors,[47] or the colonies are said to have been unprepared to lower their tariff barriers sufficiently to benefit British industry. With regard to the former, we have already seen how tariff reformers were careful to avoid the charge of exposing colonial industries to the full blast of British competition. Their aim was not so much free trade within the Empire as *freer* trade within the Empire – the colonies were not expected to abandon plans for industrialisation or to sacrifice young industries. In fact, throughout the campaign, a great effort was made to show that imperial preference was perfectly consistent with colonial economic aspirations.[48] Nevertheless, the accusation that the colonies were at best lukewarm towards preferential tariffs, or only willing to enter into such agreements for their own benefit, struck a raw nerve for tariff reformers. It is necessary, therefore, to consider how far the tariff reform debate was influenced by colonial reactions to Chamberlain's proposals.

44 H.D. Gregory, 'Tariff Reform and Colonial Preference', *ER* (May, 1911), pp.240–2.
45 A. Maddison, *The Phases of Capitalist Development* (Oxford, 1982), pp.37–8.
46 For a useful summary of these debates, see the review article by N. Woodward, 'Britain's Relative Decline, 1870–1914', in C.C. Eldridge (ed.), *Empire, Politics and Popular Culture: Essays in Eighteenth and Nineteenth Century British History* (1990).
47 Friedberg, *The Weary Titan*, pp.83–4; W. Ross Johnston, *Great Britain. Great Empire. An Evaluation of the British Imperial Experience* (1981), Chapter 7; Saul, 'Constructive Imperialism', p.183.
48 Chamberlain, *Imperial Union and Tariff Reform*, pp.9–10, 29–31, 63.

THE COLONIAL PERSPECTIVE

Ever since the mid-nineteenth century, a rising sense of economic nationalism in the English-speaking empire had led to calls for fiscal policy to be redirected towards colonial rather than British needs. By introducing protective tariffs, the 'white' Dominions were able to safeguard their indigenous industries and to raise vital revenue. By the end of the century, Canada even began to assert its freedom to make separate trading arrangements with foreign countries.[49] These developments posed problems for tariff reformers who were anxious to persuade opinion in Britain that the Empire was willing to favour its trade. In the winter of 1903–4, *The Empire Review* ran a series of articles on the trend of colonial opinion towards the fiscal question. Its editor, Kinloch-Cooke, produced detailed analyses of the so-called 'colonial offer', tracing it back to the Colonial Conference of 1887 and the gathering of Dominion statesmen at Ottawa in 1894. He directly challenged the free traders' assertion that the colonies did not desire preference, arguing that criticism of preferential tariffs expressed in the Dominions did not represent official thinking:

> In a great controversy it is well to keep up to date with colonial criticism, but keeping up to date does not necessarily involve, as the free importers would have us believe, the avoidance of official records. Moreover, it is surely wrong to attach more value to a statement made by an unauthorized individual than to the statements delivered after mature consideration by the official representatives appointed for the express purpose by colonial governments of the time. Yet these are the tactics practised by opponents of fiscal reform.[50]

But though it was essential for the tariff reform press to portray the colonies' reaction to Chamberlain's proposals in a positive light, men like Kinloch-Cooke faced formidable obstacles in turning tariff reform from a home-grown into a truly imperial campaign. Part of the problem lay in the constitutional structure of the Empire, which kept the colonial viewpoint out of the mainstream of British parliamentary politics.[51] If Dominion statesmen were implacably opposed to the home government interfering with their domestic policies, they could hardly enter the fray of British political debate.[52] As a result, official support from the colonies for imperial preference tended to be muted.

Nevertheless, for all of the 'white' Dominions, there were obvious economic advantages in retaining an imperial link.[53] Britain was a major outlet for their exports, and the demands of debt repayment gave them an added interest in

---

49 R.A. Shields, 'Imperial Policy and Canadian-American Relations, 1880–1911', *BIHR* (1986), pp.108–21.

50 C. Kinloch-Cooke, 'Imperial Fiscal Union: Trend of Colonial Opinion', *ER* (January, 1904), p.596.

51 J. Darwin, 'The Fear of Falling. British Politics and Imperial Decline since 1900', *TRHS*, 5th series (1986), p.40.

52 M. Beloff, *Imperial Sunset. Vol. I: Britain's Liberal Empire, 1897–1921* (1969), p.16.

53 Ross Johnston, *Great Britain. Great Empire*, p.58.

proposals which promised improved access to its market.[54] Admittedly, few colonies were completely dependent upon the mother country to take their exports. But the British market was valuable, and it was only Canada which did not look first to Britain as an outlet for its products. In the years 1910–12, 83 per cent of New Zealand's exports went to Britain. Even the figure for Canada was substantial at 43 per cent.[55] It is no surprise therefore that strong support for tariff reform came from South Africa – it was almost completely dependent upon the British market. In 1896, Cecil Rhodes inserted a clause in the charter of the British South Africa Company which stated the tariff on British goods entering Rhodesia should not in future exceed the level of the Cape Colony tariff prevailing at the time of the Charter. The clause is significant because it made it possible for Rhodesia to discriminate between British and foreign goods if the Cape Colony tariff was ever raised.[56] This latent Rhodesian preference finally came into effect in 1906 when the level of South Africa's general tariff was increased. The general tariff, which treated British imports preferentially, had been adopted at a Customs Union Conference in Bloemfontein in 1903. Afrikaner Bond leaders like Hofmeyr opposed the idea of giving Britain a unilateral preference, arguing instead for full reciprocity. But the measure was passed by the Cape legislature, if only by the very narrowest of margins.[57] As it transpired, neither the preference offered by the four South African colonies nor that by Rhodesia had a material impact upon trade. Competition in the South African market remained fierce, while the exchange of goods with Rhodesia was too small in volume to matter.

Opinion in New Zealand was likewise favourable to Chamberlain's policy. Both the Liberal Prime Minister, Richard Seddon, and the Leader of the Opposition, Sir John Ward, reacted positively. Furthermore, in June 1903, the Chambers of Commerce passed a series of resolutions approving preferential trade.[58] Fortified by these resolutions, the New Zealand parliament carried a Preferential Trade Bill, which granted preferences to Britain and provided for similar reciprocal arrangements with Canada and Australia. The principle of preference incorporated in the 1903 New Zealand tariff was subsequently extended in a new tariff in 1906. Tariff reform propaganda in Britain trumpeted the benefits of the New Zealand tariffs in a special memorandum.[59] While it was recognised that the United Kingdom had always occupied a predominant position in the New Zealand market, it was argued that the measures had helped to arrest a steady decline in British exports to the Dominion dating from the 1890s. For example, under the revised tariff of 1906, the duty upon some British exports had dropped by nearly one per cent to 12 per cent;

---

54 Cain and Hopkins, *British Imperialism*, Vol. I, p.275.
55 L.E. Davis and R.A. Huttenback, *Mammon and the Pursuit of Empire: The Political Economy of British Imperialism, 1860–1912* (Cambridge, 1986), p.189.
56 Saul, 'Constructive Imperialism', p.183.
57 J. Amery, *Joseph Chamberlain and the Tariff Reform Campaign*, Vol. 5 (1969), pp.329–31.
58 Ibid., p.331.
59 For a summary of the report, see 'The New Zealand Tariff. Tariff Commission Memorandum', *Monthly Notes* (1908), pp.97–106.

foreign goods, on the other hand, had their duties increased from 15.9 per cent to 16.2 per cent. Moreover, the 1906 tariff had extended preference to a larger proportion of British trade, particularly via the 'Empire Free List' (i.e., goods admitted free from within the Empire but subject to duties when imported from foreign countries). The memorandum went on to speculate upon the possibility of the New Zealand government extending preference to other categories of British manufactures, especially categories where a significant percentage of trade was presently in the hands of foreign countries (principally the United States, Germany, Belgium and Japan). By adopting a system of reciprocal preference, it claimed that more of New Zealand's imports could profitably be diverted to the United Kingdom from these foreign producers.

In Australia, tariff autonomy was achieved in 1870. By the time the Commonwealth was founded in 1901, the requirements of the exchequer, the jobs created by industry, and the interests of the business community meant that both the Liberal and Labour parties were strongly protectionist.[60] Thus there was little chance of reducing tariffs in Britain's favour. Rather, preference was to take the form of maintaining present tariffs against Britain and increasing duties upon the foreign producer. The first Prime Minister of the Commonwealth, Edmund Barton (1901–3), welcomed Chamberlain's proposals on this basis, though resistance came from the deputy leader (Sir William MacMillan) and Leader of the Opposition (G.H. Reid), who believed such a tariff would hamper Australia's trading relations with foreign countries.[61] Many Australian newspapers were also hostile to tariff reform. However, the effect of negative press reporting was to some extent counteracted by the declaration of the Australian Chambers of Commerce in favour of reciprocal preferences in August 1903.

Chamberlain's most dependable ally in Australia was Barton's deputy, Alfred Deakin. At the Colonial Conference of 1887, Deakin, then Chief Secretary of Victoria, had been strongly in favour of establishing a preference policy, declaring that the Australian colonies would gladly take their part in any movement for an imperial tariff. A month after the launch of the tariff reform campaign, Deakin sent a telegram to the editor of *The British Australasian* stating that the Commonwealth government and all the governments of the separate states approved of Chamberlain's proposals. In his second term of office as Prime Minister of Australia (1905–8), Deakin continued to treat preferential tariffs as 'an indispensable foundation of the Empire', and piloted a new Australian tariff bill through the Commonwealth parliament in 1907. The 1907 tariff was introduced at a time when Anglo-Australian trade was increasing more slowly than trade between Australia and other countries. In 1895, Australian trade with the United Kingdom (total imports and exports) was 72 per cent of overseas trade, the balance being divided between other British possessions (10 per cent) and foreign countries (18 per cent). Ten years later, the United Kingdom

60 Cain and Hopkins, *British Imperialism*, Vol. I, p.253.
61 Amery, *The Life of Joseph Chamberlain*, Vol. 5, pp.334–6.

had 52 per cent of the share, other British possessions 19 per cent, and foreign countries 29 per cent.[62] Thus within a decade Anglo-Australian trade had grown by a quarter, while the foreign trade of the Commonwealth had more than doubled. As the Agent-General for Western Australia observed, Britain was currently Australia's best market, but the chief avenues for the expansion of trade were to be found in countries other than the United Kingdom.[63] Deakin shared the Agent-General's concern. In a speech to the Imperial Conference in 1907, he graphically depicted how British exports to Australia had fallen by £4 million in the period from 1881–85 to 1901–5, while foreign exports had increased by £7 million. Preference was presented as a way of reversing this trend.

Of course, Deakin had also to address a domestic audience. Yet in responding to criticisms of the 1907 tariff, he emphatically denied that protection and preference were incompatible policies, other than in a very limited number of trades.[64] While recognising that tariffs would still be essential to raise revenue, he maintained that there was ample room to give preference to British imports. The preference proposed was to exclude foreign goods and favour British goods by increasing duties upon the former. In addition, it was suggested that the 1907 preferences might be expanded, especially in relation to the 'Empire Free List'. Adamant that the framing of a new tariff would ultimately be determined by Australia's needs, Deakin was not afraid to draw out its wider imperial context. As he explained to the Commonwealth parliament:

> It is scarcely possible to use a single word which shall cover all that is associated with the greatest of great movements within the Empire for the co-operation of all its parts. What we aim at is, as a British minister put it, 'the free union of free Commonwealths'. . . . From the very first I pointed out that 'the policy is large, and the principle of that policy applies not only to trade and commerce, but is capable, as already suggested, of indefinite expansion'.[65]

Later that year, Chamberlain's Tariff Commission extolled the benefits of the new Australian Tariff.[66] Refuting the free trade criticism that the Australian preference was illusory, it reminded people in Britain that the old Australian tariff had been surprisingly low – 6 per cent, compared to 18 per cent under the old Canadian tariff. Moreover, it argued that the use of tariffs by the colonies to raise extra revenue and to foster industry was perfectly compatible with the policy of preferential trade. Britain merely sought to export the goods Australia could not make for herself, and to exclude foreigners from this trade.

62 Figures from: C.H. Rawson, the Agent-General for Western Australia, 'Trade Development in Australia 1902–06', published in *ER* (December, 1907), p.344.
63 Ibid., p.352.
64 A reprint of Deakin's speech was published under the heading 'British Preference' in the *ER* (January, 1908), pp.415–37.
65 The speech was given in October 1907: ibid., pp.419–20.
66 For a report of the Tariff Commission's memorandum (no. 31), see *Monthly Notes* (November, 1907), pp.303–9.

By adopting a preferential tariff, the Australian government had ensured that British goods would always receive an advantage over non-British goods. The Commission claimed that the new tariff would help to transfer a substantial amount of non-British trade to British firms.

Fiscal policy was an equally important topic of debate in Canadian politics. By the late 1870s, a strong coalition of Canadian interests clamoured for protection. Conservatives exploited this atmosphere to the full. They campaigned vigorously for a 'National Policy', the main elements of which were higher tariffs, the promotion of a western railway, increased immigration to the western prairie, and a positive attitude to investors. Fighting on this platform, the Conservative party was returned to power in 1878 with a substantial majority. It immediately raised the Canadian tariff to an average of 25 per cent, arguing that the tariff was not just for raising revenue, but also for safeguarding industries facing stiff competition from abroad and suffering from the practice of 'dumping' by American producers.[67] So strong were the interests succoured by this 'National Policy' that by the time the Liberals regained office in 1896 a return to free trade was out of the question. Hence when Laurier's finance minister, W.S. Fielding, introduced a revised tariff in 1897, a high level of protection was maintained. The 1897 tariff also provided for reduced import rates for nations who reduced their charges on Canadian exports. In particular, the rates on British imports were reduced by nearly a third, it being hoped that Britain would then grant similar concessions to Canadian exports.

From Chamberlain's point of view, the Canadian reaction to his proposals was most critical of all. Canada was the oldest and richest of the Dominions with the greatest development potential; Canada had raised the question of reciprocal preferences at the Colonial Conference of 1902; and Canada was at risk of being pulled into the economic orbit of another power, namely the United States. The initial responses were quite encouraging. A positive reaction to Chamberlain's Birmingham speech came from the Canadian press, from Hodgeson (the President of the Board of Trade) and from Borden (the leader of the opposition). There was an enthusiastic welcome from the British Empire League, and Laurier and Fielding were satisfied by the move, although they did not make any public statements to this effect since the Liberal party was dependent for support upon French-speaking Quebec and the free trade provinces of the west. So far so good. Yet British opinion had still to be convinced that Canada was prepared to make a genuine gap in its protective walls in return for favoured access to the 'home' market. Attention focused upon the impact of the 1897 tariff. Just how valuable had it been to Britain? The fluctuating trend of Anglo-Canadian trade meant that there was no easy answer to this question.

Britain's share of Canada's imports decreased during the depression of the 1890s. It then remained steady at around one-quarter of the total, declining

---

67 'Dumping' meant selling abroad at or below cost price.

again from 1910 to 1914. British manufacturers suffered from a shift in Canadian imports towards capital goods, a sector in which American exporters enjoyed the greatest technical and geographical advantages. The value of American exports of iron and steel goods to Canada rose from $6.1 million (Can.) in 1893–97 to $80.4 million in 1910–14, whereas the value of British exports increased from only $4.1 million to $13.9 million over the same period. Sales of British consumer goods tell a similar story. They fell sharply until 1899, remained steady for some years, before recovering slightly in the years up to 1908. This meant that tariff reformers could make only very modest claims for the effect of the 1897 preference in opening up the Canadian market to British manufacturers. To convince people that preference might be of greater benefit to British manufacturers, it became necessary to find out more about the state of Canadian opinion. At first Chamberlain relied chiefly on Lord Minto (the Governor-General) for his information on Canadian affairs. In the summer of 1903, Minto forwarded a series of reports indicating a desire in Canada for closer commercial relations with the mother country. But he made it clear that Laurier was not prepared to go beyond his resolution at the 1902 Colonial Conference expressing support for inter-imperial trade.

Chamberlain's next step was to instruct Hewins to travel to Canada to discuss preference with government officials.[68] Hewins's task was to find out what Britain might expect in return for granting a preference on Canadian corn. During his stay he met Laurier and Fielding. Laurier stressed the importance of the two shilling duty on wheat and asked for an extension of preference to other items (including dairy products and bacon). Hewins pressed Laurier on his suggestion that certain classes of British manufactures not produced in Canada might enter upon a more moderate duty than imports from foreign countries. This was a significant step forward for tariff reformers in Britain, for it made it possible for them to contest two of the more damaging criticisms of free traders. The first was that the colonies were being asked to sacrifice their industries in return for an assured market for their agricultural produce in Britain. The second stated that the colonies were unprepared to give worthwhile concessions to British manufacturers. As a result of Hewins's negotiations with Laurier and Fielding it was clearer to both sides which goods were essential to a workable scheme of preference, and what the margin of preference on those goods might be. Armed with this information, the Tariff Reform League was able to engage with the propaganda of the Free Trade Union far more effectively. The League's leaflets and pamphlets were revised to show that there were at least three areas in which British business might receive an advantage in colonial markets: the Empire Free List; goods entering on a very low rate compared with foreign imports; and goods designed to assist colonial development. In each case, it was asserted that preferential tariffs could be decisive in diverting trade from foreign into British channels.

---

68 For an account of Hewins's trip to Canada in 1905, see *The Apologia of an Imperialist*, pp.132–42.

Up until 1910, therefore, opinion in Canada, even within Laurier's Liberal party, did not appear to have ruled out the possibility of closer trading relations with Britain. Then came the 1911 Trade Reciprocity agreement between Canada and America. After touring western Canada in 1910, Laurier saw the potential for tapping a new political constituency and decided to take action to appease western prairie interests, which were denouncing protection and eastern industrial domination.[69] In contemplating a revised tariff, the Liberal government was heavily influenced by US fiscal policy. As a result of the adjustments made by Fielding to the Canadian tariff in 1906, the United States introduced the Payne–Aldrich tariff. This allowed America to impose a maximum scale of duties on imports from countries which discriminated against its goods.[70] In order to avert a trade war between Canada and America, President Taft had to intervene personally to negotiate with the Laurier administration. These negotiations led to an agreement with Washington for the free importation of most natural products and selected manufactured goods, lower duties on a range of processed food products and a second group of manufactures, and special rates on other products.

When the Canadian-American Trade Reciprocity agreement was signed in January 1911 tariff reformers exploded in a fit of indignation. They prophesied that this act of American expansionism would damage British trade, increase the cost of British food, and eventually lead to the incorporation of Canada into the United States. They also feared that the agreement would set a precedent for other Dominions to negotiate similar treaties. Indeed, so distressed was the TRL by this turn of events that it decided to launch an 'Imperial Preference campaign' to re-establish tariff reform as imperial policy and to demonstrate the grave dangers involved in the refusal of the British government to reciprocate colonial preferences. Amery acted as chairman of the committee organising the campaign, and a total of forty public meetings was staged, culminating in large demonstrations in Manchester and London.

To the TRL's delight, the Liberal government in Canada was defeated by the Conservatives in an election later that year. Laurier's sudden reversion to free trade had shattered his support in the business world, which feared that the reciprocity proposals would open the door to a wider free trade agreement with America. Moreover, throughout the election campaign the Conservatives had played mercilessly upon Canadian fears of US annexationist designs. Behind Borden's favourite slogan 'No truck nor trade with the Yankees', lay a reminder of the substantial numbers of Americans migrating to Canada, and the big rise in US investment in Canadian industry. Anti-American sentiment was likewise exploited by elements of the press. In particular, a war was waged on the reciprocity treaty by *The Ottawa Journal* and its editor, P.D. Ross. Ross did not deny that the trade agreement had good points in 'purely

69 K. McNaught, *The Penguin History of Canada* (1988), pp.200–3.
70 Shields, 'Imperial Policy and Canadian-American Reciprocity', p.161.

commercial terms'. His objection was based upon American intentions.[71] A great many people in America, he argued, saw the treaty as a stepping stone to the political incorporation of Canada. This argument was echoed in the tariff reform press in Britain. Garvin celebrated the fact that Canada had saved itself, and had saved the Empire by its example, while Maxse portrayed the result as victory for Canadian independence as well as for imperial unity.[72]

Too many studies of the tariff reform campaign have overlooked how the fiscal debate in Britain was shaped by attitudes and events elsewhere in the Empire. Mobilising support in the Dominions was essential if tariff reformers were to rebut the charge of ignoring the interests of colonial industries. Much was made of the endorsement of Chamberlain's proposals by New Zealand, and of the enthusiasm expressed by other groups of colonials. In fact, pro-Chamberlainite journalists went to great lengths to show that the Dominions were on their side. The outstanding example here is the editor of the *National Review*, Leo Maxse, who not only pressed a number of willing Canadians into his service, but reproduced in his journal the views of papers such as the *Toronto News*, the *Montreal Star*, the *Mail and Empire* and the *Toronto Globe*. Maxse also commissioned articles from the leading Canadian imperialist and chief writer of the *Montreal Star*, A.R. Carman, an implacable opponent of the US Trade Reciprocity agreement. Likewise, it was vital for tariff reformers to show that preference would be of benefit to producers and consumers in Britain. To this end, the advantages of New Zealand's and Australia's revised tariffs were loudly trumpeted by tariff reformers, while following Hewins's negotiations in Canada, the movement's literature was revised to show how Britain's access to colonial markets would be improved under a preferential trading system. Thus, although tariff reform was pre-eminently a British political campaign, fiscal policy and argument in the colonies impinged directly upon it. Had tariff reformers not consulted with colonial opinion, their imperial credentials would have been weaker, their propaganda less convincing, and their ideas about fiscal reform much more inchoate. We now need to consider why this exchange of opinion between the Dominions and Britain was largely lacking in the case of India.

INDIA AND IMPERIAL PREFERENCE

Historians of tariff reform have been almost as guilty as Chamberlain and company in ignoring India. Their oversight is all the more surprising given India's importance to the British economy. India accounted for a substantial share of British overseas trade, taking on average about 12 per cent of its

71 See here Ross's own account of the controversy in his memoir *Retrospects of a Newspaper Person* (Toronto, 1931), pp.179–80.
72 S. Potter, ' "A Great Imperial Disaster"? Canadian-American Reciprocity and British Party Politics', University of Oxford, Masters Dissertation (1997), pp.32, 34.

exports.[73] It was also among the leading recipients of British capital.[74] Furthermore, in helping to resolve Britain's balance of payments problems, India was a lynchpin of its position in the world economy. India ran a growing trade deficit with Britain from the 1870s, supplying less than 10 per cent of total British imports. Crucially, however, she developed sizeable export markets in a number of countries from which Britain imported large quantities of goods but exported little in return. Profits earned by exporting rice and opium to the Far East, and other goods to continental Europe and North America, enabled India to settle trade deficits with Britain which, in turn, provided Britain with the flexibility essential to a great capital exporting nation.[75] As B.R. Tomlinson concludes, 'from 1870 to 1914 India formed the vital third leg in a triangular pattern of settlements between Britain and the rest of the world'.[76]

The ambiguous place of India in Chamberlain's vision of empire did not escape criticism.[77] For a small circle of free traders, a resounding objection to the doctrine of constructive imperialism was that it overlooked the largest part of the very Empire which it was designed to preserve. Lord George Hamilton, Secretary of State for India from 1895 to 1903, claimed that if other parts of the Empire enjoyed the benefits of protection and preference, then these could not be denied India.[78] Another attack upon the imperial aspect of tariff reform came from the journalist Sidney Low. After travelling in India as special correspondent of the *Standard* in 1905, Low produced a remarkably subtle and perceptive analysis of the *swadeshi* movement in Bengal, remarking wryly that it was a movement 'which should command the sympathy of many Englishmen of these Tariff Reform days'.[79] Behind this apparently flippant remark lay a serious point. The aim of *swadeshi* was to encourage the growth of home industries by abstaining from the purchase of imported foreign manufactures and relying instead upon local production. It seemed inconsistent for tariff reformers to be championing the protection of British producers against foreign competition and then refusing to extend this logic to India.

Perhaps the most serious attack upon the imperial implications of tariff reform came from Lord Curzon. Curzon thought it absurd that Chamberlain had 'forgot all about India' in launching his new imperial policy:

> I often wonder what would have become of him and us, if he had ever visited India. He would have become the greatest Indian imperialist of the

73 Although Britain's share of total Indian imports did gradually fall after 1870. For the geographical distribution of India's foreign trade, see B.R. Tomlinson, *The New Cambridge History of India: III.3. The Economy of Modern India, 1860–1970* (Cambridge, 1993), p.54.
74 In 1870, 20.3 per cent of British foreign investment went to India; by 1913 the figure had dropped to 9.5 per cent. See Cain and Hopkins, *British Imperialism*, Vol. I, pp.173–6.
75 See here S.B. Saul, *Studies in Overseas Trade 1870–1914* (Liverpool, 1960), Chapters 3–4.
76 B.R. Tomlinson, 'India and the British Empire, 1880–1935', *The Indian Economic and Social History Review* (1975), p.342, see also p.344.
77 See pp.32–4.
78 A.S. Thompson, 'Thinking Imperially? Imperial Pressure Groups and the Idea of Empire in Late-Victorian and Edwardian Britain', University of Oxford D.Phil (1994), p.142.
79 S. Low, *A Vision of India* (1906), p.345.

time. The Colonies would have been dwarfed and forgotten; and the pivot of the Empire would have been Calcutta. Not having enjoyed this good fortune, we are now forgotten, and the Empire is to be bound together without reference to the requirements of its largest and most powerful unit.[80]

Even if India were to be included in a scheme of preferential tariffs, Curzon was highly sceptical about whether it would be fairly treated. His reservations were reiterated in a preliminary note on the likely effect of tariff reform on India, produced in September 1903, which provided the basis for the subsequent official report, *Views of the Government of India on the Question of Preferential Tariffs*.[81] This report noted that India already had very low duties. If they were to be cut for British goods, the Government of India would be denied much-needed revenue; if they were raised for foreign imports and kept low for Britain, there was a danger of the subcontinent's substantial European trade being damaged by foreign retaliation. Drawing attention to the importance of India's export surplus in upholding the multilateral settlements system which enabled Britain to run trading deficits with Europe and North America, the Government of India counselled against any change in fiscal policy likely to close markets to Indian exports. It also pointed out that the likely consequence of British manufactures receiving preferential treatment in India would be heightened agitation in favour of India's own import-substituting industries.

Yet not all old India hands supported the position adopted in the blue book. Sir Charles Elliott was a long-serving Indian civil servant with considerable expertise in revenue questions and famine relief. After entering the Indian Civil Service in the 1850s, he rose through its ranks to become Lieutenant-Governor of Bengal from 1890 to 1895. On returning to England, Elliott was recruited by Hewins to the Tariff Commission. He accused the Government of India of 'constitutional timidity' in dealing with the tariff reform question.[82] In India's case, he argued, a preferential tariff would not involve protective duties on British imports. Rather it would allow India to maintain its import duties at the present, or at a slightly lower rate, while lowering duties on British and colonial goods by about 25 per cent. Under this policy, the Government of India might lose a small amount of revenue – estimated by Elliott at £420,000 – but the loss would be amply repaid by the advantages accruing to India from favoured treatment from Britain for Indian industries.

Elliott rejected both the Government of India's view that a preference of 25 per cent calculated on a low rate of duty would be of little advantage to British manufacturers, and its argument that India had very little to gain from preference. In relation to the former, he was able to point to the slow

80 Curzon to Northbrook, 12/8/1903, *Curzon papers*, MSS Eur fo. 111/182.
81 Many of the opinions in this document were reiterated in a 'Memorandum on Preferential Tariffs in their application to India', presented by the India Office to the Colonial Conference in 1907. See Papers Laid Before the Colonial Conference, 1907, Cd 3524, XXIII.
82 Sir Charles Elliott, 'The Indian Government on Preferential Tariffs and Retaliation', *ER* (May, 1904), p.290.

but steady growth of foreign manufactures competing with British exports, and the low profit margins on goods such as cotton, flax, woollens and hardware.[83] As regards the latter, he listed tea, tobacco, coffee, indigo and wheat as trades which all stood to benefit from a discriminating tariff. Moreover, it was suggested that an extension of the area under wheat cultivation would afford India immense security against famine. In the light of Elliott's widely acclaimed work in organising famine relief in Mysore in 1878, and his secretaryship of the Royal Commission on Indian famines, this particular line of argument had added force.[84] Elliott went on to contest the Government of India's prediction of reprisals from foreign nations. He maintained that most foreign countries had already raised their tariffs as high as they safely could without detriment to themselves. Hence India was in a strong position to enter into fair trade negotiations with any state which set up a hostile tariff. Finally, Elliott concluded that a preferential tariff in India would be a very valuable relief to an import trade worth £24 million, and that a similar tariff in England would do equal or even greater good to a trade worth about £7 million of Indian goods, besides reinforcing the measures taken to secure the country against famine. Since these proposals involved no increase of duty against foreign goods, it was argued that there was no danger of reprisals being organised in the shape of hostile tariffs.

Another acknowledged authority on Indian affairs who supported the inclusion of India in a system of imperial preference was Sir Roper Lethbridge. Lethbridge, a Vice-President of the Tariff Reform League, had studied the external trade of India, edited the *Calcutta Quarterly Review* (1871–78), and worked as a professor and examiner in the subject of political economy for the University of Calcutta. Hence he was well qualified to comment upon India's fiscal policy. Like Elliott, Lethbridge argued that free traders were badly mistaken to think that Britain was holding its own in Indian trade. Citing the blue book, *Statement of the Moral and Material Progress of the Government of India* (1903), he produced detailed statistics for the period 1881–82 to 1901–2, which charted the rapid growth of the protected trade of foreign countries and the stagnation of British trade in all but a few favoured lines.[85] As we have seen, although total British exports to India were rising in the period from 1870 to 1914, Britain's share of India's imports was falling. It stood at 83 per cent in 1880–81, but had dropped to 66 per cent by 1913, mainly due to a rise in exports from the European continent.[86] There was therefore genuine cause for concern.

Looking to the future, Lethbridge identified three possible fiscal frameworks for economic development in India. These were: 'Bengal *swadeshi*'

83 See the figures for exports from continental Europe, Japan and the United States in the period 1870–1911, tabulated in Tomlinson, *The Economy of Modern India*, pp.54, 291.
84 Elliott, 'The Indian Government on Preferential Tariffs', pp.292–3.
85 Sir Roper Lethbridge, *India and Fiscal Policy* (1903), p.1.
86 For example, Belgian metal trades and the German wool trade increased their market share in India: A.J. Latham, 'Merchandise Trade Imbalances and Uneven Economic Development in India and China', *Journal of European Economic History* (1978), p.40.

(regional protection), 'Indian *swadeshi*' (national protection), and 'Imperial *swadeshi*' (imperial preference). He thought it inconceivable that the House of Commons would assent to either of the first two options, but believed that imperial preference could benefit India and Britain.[87] In the proposals put forward by Lethbridge, exports from India to Britain were to be granted an advantage equivalent to that enjoyed by British manufactures entering the Indian market. It was envisaged that a range of Indian imports would be given more or less free entry to Britain, with the exception of tea, which would be subject to a small duty for revenue purposes.[88] This left open the vital question of how indigenous industry would fare under a preferential system. Having ruled out 'absolute protection', Lethbridge enumerated the benefits he expected to accrue to Indian manufacturers under preference. First, they were to be protected against foreign if not British producers, so that those raw materials now manufactured in Hamburg or Bremen or Antwerp or Marseilles might in the future be 'better done on the spot'.[89] Second, it was argued that preference would lead to a large and rapid increase in total Indian exports, thus helping to divert labour from 'the congested industry of agriculture' into various branches of manufacturing. Finally, in constructing a case for tariff reform, Lethbridge refused to measure the outcomes of present fiscal policy in purely economic terms. Unlike the Dominions, he observed, the strength of the 'Imperial connection' in India depended to an unusual degree upon the ties of 'mutual interest' and 'mutual respect'. After years of 'dragooning' the dependency under the pretence of free trade, it was now time to make amends by placing her on the 'honourable footing of a sister State of the Empire'.[90]

Speaking in a private capacity, the imperialist Richard Jebb went even further in condemning the way in which the doctrine of free trade was being upheld in India for the benefit of the Lancashire cotton textile industry. Indeed, Jebb's analysis anticipated arguments advanced in Peter Harnetty's study of the Lancashire cotton industry, in particular its emphasis upon the mercantilism inherent in the Manchester school's attitudes to empire, attitudes which ensured India's 'effective subordination to British imperial power'.[91] The book which brought Jebb to public notice was *Studies in Colonial Nationalism*. In it he launched a ferocious attack upon 'exploitative imperialism', describing how the Indian tariff had been manipulated in the interests of Lancashire manufacturers to the detriment of India's public finances and its native industry.[92] Accusing Britain of imposing a 'fiscal strait-waistcoat' upon its greatest dependency, and labelling the cotton excise duty as 'the new slavery',[93] Jebb

---

87 Lethbridge, *India and Fiscal Policy*, p.11.
88 R. Lethbridge, *India and Imperial Preference* (1907), p.15.
89 Ibid., pp.61–2.
90 Lethbridge, *India and Fiscal Policy*, p.3.
91 P. Harnetty, *Imperialism and Free Trade: Lancashire and India in the Mid-nineteenth Century* (1972), pp.6, 125.
92 R. Jebb, *Studies in Colonial Nationalism* (1905), p.312.
93 The countervailing excise duty was imposed upon Indian manufacturers in order to compensate the Lancashire cotton industry for the reintroduction of import duties in 1894.

pulled no punches in asserting that the Lancashire textile industry had attained its present size only by the forcible restriction of competition in the Indian market.[94]

Admittedly, Jebb's analysis of the state of India's cotton textile industry was not without its problems – such was the industry's growth that by 1914 India stood second only to Britain as an exporter of cotton yarns.[95] However, in view of the vast market in India for cotton textiles, the pace of development seemed sluggish, while India's fiscal policy contrasted sharply with the rise of tariff barriers across Europe. Indeed, a leading study of the Lancashire cotton industry shows considerable sympathy with the criticism that the countervailing excise duty was arbitrary and exploitative.[96] We cannot, therefore, write off Jebb's critique of Indian fiscal policy simply as an act of revenge upon Lancashire for its hostility to tariff reform. On the contrary, for a person whose interest in imperial relations was essentially confined to the Empire's self-governing territories, Jebb displayed a striking sensitivity to Indian opinion, presenting the abolition of cotton duties as a step well worth taking if the loyalty and affection of the Indian people could thereby be retained.

It is worth remembering that at the time *Studies in Colonial Nationalism* was published India was by far Lancashire's single most important market, taking around 40 per cent of its cotton piece-good exports.[97] Moreover, the depreciation of silver against sterling had given the Bombay textile industry an enormous competitive advantage over Lancashire in Asian markets until India was put on the gold-exchange standard in 1898.[98] Aware of the danger of alienating an important political constituency, the leadership of the Tariff Reform League was noticeably more conciliatory towards the Lancashire cotton industry than Jebb. In a speech at the Manchester Free Trade Hall in 1913, Austen Chamberlain confronted head-on the problem of the cotton excise duty.[99] The legitimate purpose of the duty, he accepted, had been to ensure fair play between manufacturers in Lancashire and their competitors in India. Yet it was a system which was 'hateful' to the people of India. The alternative, he ventured, was to do away with the customs and excise duties on cotton goods, and to allow India to recoup the lost revenue by increasing duties on foreign produce. The effect would be to strengthen simultaneously Indian industries and those of the motherland.[100]

94 Jebb, *Studies in Colonial Nationalism*, pp.314, 320–1, 324–5.
95 N. Charlesworth, *British Rule and the Indian Economy, 1800–1914* (Basingstoke, 1982), pp.36–7.
96 D.A. Farnie, *The English Cotton Industry and the World Market 1815–1896* (Oxford, 1979), pp.114–15.
97 Ibid., p.91.
98 Green, *The Crisis of Conservatism*, p.42; Tomlinson, 'India and the British Empire', p.344.
99 'Speeches of the Month', A. Chamberlain at Manchester, 15/12/1913, *Monthly Notes* (January, 1914), pp.49–50; *The Times*, 16/12/1913, p.10.
100 The previous year, Austen Chamberlain had exercised more caution. In an introduction to Roper Lethbridge's book, *The Indian Offer of Imperial Preference*, he had suggested that the exact position of India in a system of imperial preference 'could only be finally determined after conference and consultation between Indian and British Governments'.

Austen Chamberlain's proposals were intended to square the circle of conciliating native opinion in India while keeping the Indian market open to Lancashire and protecting India's public finances. Yet it is often claimed that preferential tariffs offered nothing to the Lancashire cotton industry because there was no import penetration of the Indian market by foreign producers. Strictly-speaking this is not true, since by the turn of the century textiles from a number of European countries were beginning to penetrate the Indian market, though not to any significant extent.[101] It was not until the 1920s that a serious rival emerged to the United Kingdom, and then it came from Japan not Europe. However, it was the protective rather than preferential part of the tariff programme which was of greatest interest to Lancashire. Following the revival of Indian cotton production in the 1870s, Lancashire's main competition came from the spinning and weaving industry located in Ahmedabad and Bombay.[102] The tariff reform campaign thus raised the possibility of a modification of the Indian tariff in favour of indigenous industry. Even if Lancashire's trade with India had reached a record height in 1907 (and improved thereafter), the Manchester Chamber of Commerce was still conscious of the stagnation of cotton exports during the last two decades of the nineteenth century, and was still troubled by the prospect of a falling off of Indian demand.[103]

Nevertheless, the rather half-hearted attempts by tariff reformers to adapt imperial preference to the needs of Britain's greatest dependency betrayed their overriding objective of forging closer links with the self-governing Dominions. When India was mentioned in tariff reform propaganda it was largely as an afterthought. Significantly, the TRL made no detailed statements regarding India's future fiscal system; and the pronouncements of ex-civil servants like Lethbridge were *obiter dicta* rather than official policy. How far can the neglect of India be attributed to a hardening of racial attitudes in later Victorian and Edwardian Britain? It is tempting to conclude this was so, but on closer inspection such an argument is difficult to sustain. As we have seen, the handful of tariff reformers who did pay attention to the likely impact of preference and protection upon the Indian economy were surprisingly sympathetic towards native opinion, even to the point of supporting some of the Indian National Congress's demands. Another explanation is that the marginalisation of India in fiscal debate in Britain resulted from the widely remarked upon ignorance of many backbench MPs regarding the jewel in Britain's imperial Crown. Yet tariff reformers did not forget India; rather they decided it was not central to their strategy for promoting economic competitiveness and growth. The whole

101 One estimate put the total value of cotton manufactures entering the Indian market at £817,000 in 1901–2: Elliott, 'The Indian Government on Preferential Tariffs', p.291.
102 Farnie, *The English Cotton Industry*, pp.111–12; Tomlinson, *The Economy of Modern India*, p.106, p.109.
103 A. Redford, *Manchester Merchants and Foreign Trade. Vol. II: 1850–1939* (Manchester, 1956), pp.43–6.

emphasis of Chamberlain's proposals was upon the 'white Dominions'. It was these colonies which were the chief destination of empire investments, and which accounted for an increasing share of Britain's imports. Moreover, if the proportion of British exports to the Dominions had not changed markedly after 1850,[104] it was thought to be Britain's fault for failing to develop them properly.

Of course, the importance tariff reformers attached to the Dominions rankled with other imperialists, especially with those involved with India. Having said that, neglect of India was not the only criticism levelled at tariff reform by free trade imperialists. Much of the opposition to Chamberlain's proposals was based on the belief that his whole conceptualisation of Anglo-Dominion relations was fatally flawed.

CRITICS OF PREFERENCE: PAST AND PRESENT

Free trade remained a very potent idea in the early-twentieth century. Across the political spectrum, there was a strong commitment to 'His holiness free trade', as Marx called it; a commitment held by many with all the passion and emotion of a religious belief. Support for free trade represented not only opposition to tariffs but to government interference more generally. Indeed the most popular and powerful line of attack upon tariff reform probably stemmed from the continuing purchase of the 'minimal' conception of the British state. Whereas many constructive imperialists looked to Germany for ideas and inspiration, embracing a neo-Hegelian view of the state as a dynamic agency which had a key role to play in the Empire's consolidation, the dominant attitude in Britain was quite different. It was reflected more faithfully in the writings of free trade imperialists who feared that further state intervention in imperial policy would prove costly and counterproductive, perhaps placing Britain's relations with the colonies under intolerable strain.[105] In contrast to tariff reformers, 'liberal' imperialists, like St Loe Strachey and Alfred Spender, espoused a gradual, organic and evolutionary approach to imperial reconstruction. Strachey's *Spectator* proclaimed that protection and preference had ill-served Britain in the past, and represented a false hope for its imperial future:

> Imperial federation, when the time is ripe, is an ideal well worth working for. What we will not consent to do is to rush, in a panic or a flurry, or because it will help politicians at home out of a temporary or local difficulty, into some wild, ill-considered, and altogether premature scheme of Federation which is bound to prove unworkable, and instead of uniting, must carry in it the seeds of disintegration.[106]

104 W. Schlote, *British Overseas Trade. From 1700 to the 1930s* (Oxford, 1952), pp.92–3.
105 A.S. Thompson, 'Imperial Ideology in Edwardian Britain', A. Bosco and A. May (eds), *The Round Table, the Empire/Commonwealth and British Foreign Policy* (1997), pp.9–14.
106 'The Federalist Fallacy', *Spectator*, 15/1/1910.

For Strachey, imperial preference was precisely such a scheme. It threatened to destroy the freedom of action which was the defining feature of modern imperial relations by forcing the colonies into a commercial union which they did not really want and which would produce friction and jealousies between them. Likewise for Spender, the uniqueness of the British Empire lay in the fact that it existed independently of material ties, deriving its unity from the long-term action of race, sentiment, and tradition rather than from 'mere material bonds'. It was simply not possible to produce an economic policy suited to the geographically diverse elements of the Empire.[107]

Another, related criticism of tariff reform was that a self-contained Empire was not in any sense a rational economic proposition. This was the focal point of Asquith's attacks upon Chamberlain. In a series of cool, dispassionate speeches, Asquith defended free trade as a 'concrete and living policy' essential to the long-term success of the British economy. The United Kingdom, he argued, was the Empire's greatest asset, and anyone who struck a blow at the root of its prosperity was endangering the very fabric of Britain's imperial system. Disputing the claim that Britain's trade with the colonies was growing faster than its trade with the rest of the world,[108] Asquith warned that tariff reform was likely to inflict severe damage upon Britain's trading relations with the United States and Russia.

Historical analysis of the overall feasibility of the tariff reform programme has tended to plough the Asquithian furrow. Tariff reformers, we are told, greatly overestimated the economic potential of the English-speaking empire.[109] The trade statistics for the period from 1890 to 1914 go some way to corroborate this claim. As Table 1a shows, the Empire as a whole received about one-third of Britain's exports and accounted for no more than a quarter of Britain's imports. Imperial trade was significant, then, but it was only a component of Britain's international trade.

Table 1a   The Empire's share of Britain's overseas trade

	Imports (%)	*Exports (%)*
1885–89	23	35
1895–99	22	34
1905–9	23	33
1915–19	30	31
1925–29	28	42

107 J.D. Startt, *Journalists for Empire. The Imperial Debate in the Edwardian Stately Press, 1903–13* (Westport, CT, 1991), pp.53–7, 157, 160–1.
108 H.H. Asquith, *Trade and the Empire. Mr. Chamberlain's Proposals Examined in Four Speeches and a Prefatory Note* (1903), pp.16–17, 21, 86.
109 Saul, *Studies in Overseas Trade*, p.165.

Table 1b   The Dominions' share of Britain's trade with the Empire

	Imports (%)	Exports (%)
1885–89	46	46
1895–99	56	48
1905–9	58	47
1915–19	55	45
1925–29	57	49

Source: Tables 1a and 1b are adapted from W. Schlote, *British Overseas Trade from 1700 to the 1930s* (Oxford, 1952), pp.162–3, Table 20b.

It is very difficult to guage how far was there the potential for an expansion of inter-imperial trade.[110] The Dominions' share of Britain's exports increased markedly in the first half of the nineteenth century, but then stabilised, to rise slightly in the years from 1895 to 1913 (Table 1b and Figure 2). Fierce competition from foreign manufacturers meant that Britain was struggling to hold its own in Dominion markets by the turn of the century. It still supplied 60 per cent of New Zealand's imports in 1913, but Britain's share of Canadian imports fell from 54 per cent in 1872–74 to 21 per cent in 1913, while its share of Australian imports decreased from 73 per cent to 52 per cent over the same period. Similarly, Britain supplied 83 per cent of South Africa's imports in 1881 but only 56 per cent in 1913.[111] It is possible that a bigger margin of preference for British exporters could have helped to reverse this trend. However, the technological superiority of American and German firms in capital goods would have made it difficult for Britain to compete in this sector under all but the most favourable of tariff regimes. In terms of imports from the Empire, the pattern of trade changed considerably from the 1870s – the result of the building of railways, a reduction in maritime freight rates, and the use of refrigeration in transport. The opening up of new sources of supply of temperate foodstuffs – wheat, meat, butter and cheese – meant that there was a big increase in the proportion of imports from the settlement colonies, and especially from Australasia (Table 1b and Figure 3). The share of Britain's imports from the Dominions rose from about one-third to over a half between the mid-1850s and 1914. The increase was most marked in the case of Australia and New Zealand – the value of their exports to Britain multiplied ten-fold over this period.

Thus tariff reformers could justifiably argue that Britain was being edged out of Dominion markets by foreign competition,[112] and that certain avenues of Anglo-Dominion trade were becoming more important. However, it was

110 Marrison, *British Business and Protection*, p.20.
111 Figures from F. Crouzet, 'Trade and Empire: The British Experience from the Establishment of Free Trade until the First World War', in B.M. Ratcliffe (ed.), *Great Britain and Her World, 1750–1914* (Manchester, 1975), p.224.
112 Ibid., p.223.

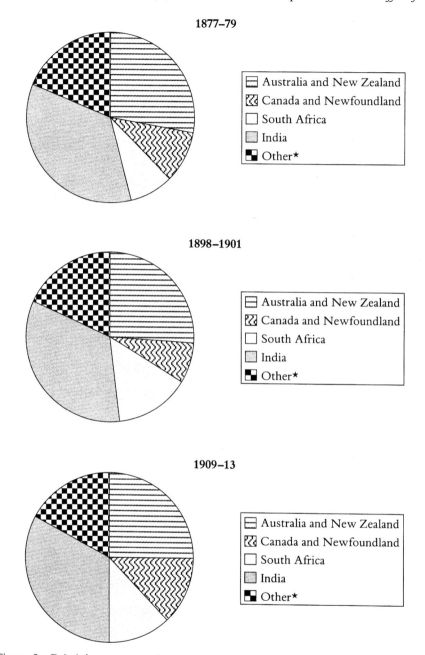

1877–79

Australia and New Zealand
Canada and Newfoundland
South Africa
India
Other★

1898–1901

Australia and New Zealand
Canada and Newfoundland
South Africa
India
Other★

1909–13

Australia and New Zealand
Canada and Newfoundland
South Africa
India
Other★

Figure 2   Britain's exports to the Empire by region
★ mainly British Asia (excluding India), British Africa (excluding South Africa) and the West Indies

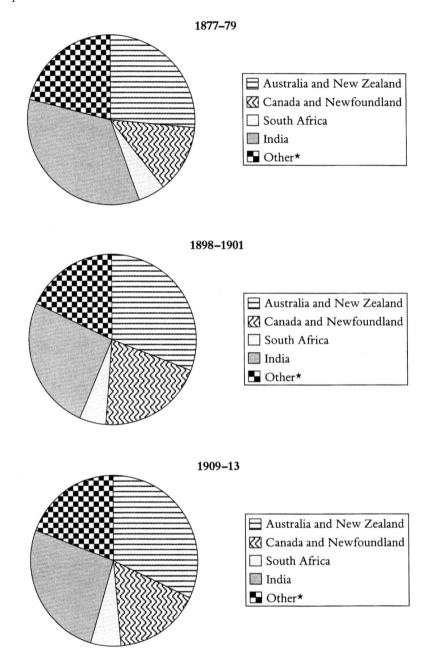

Figure 3   Britain's imports from the Empire by region
* mainly British Asia (excluding India), British Africa (excluding South Africa) and the West Indies
Source: Piecharts in Figures 2 and 3 are adapted from W. Schlote, *British Overseas Trade from 1700 to the 1930s* (Oxford, 1952), pp.162–3, Table 20b.

clearly wishful thinking to imagine the Dominions would some day replace America and Europe as Britain's trading partners. Such overly optimistic assumptions ignored the very real climatic and geographical restraints on their population growth.[113] Similarly, in the light of recent reinterpretations of the growth of the British economy in the nineteenth century,[114] it has become fashionable to accuse tariff reformers of failing to come to terms with the central role of the service sector in generating wealth and employment. If it is accepted that Britain was as much a service-based economy as an industrial or manufacturing economy, then the prescriptions of tariff reformers begin to look misguided – a system of preferential tariffs manifestly had little to offer so-called 'gentlemanly capitalists'. The problem with this critique of tariff reform is that it misses the point. Chamberlain and his principal supporters did not dispute the fact that there had been a shift from manufacturing to services, but they did deny that this shift was likely to be beneficial. According to Amery, for example, the concentration of free traders on 'exchange' rather than 'production' was destroying the 'national capital' of the country by eliminating skilled trades, bankrupting manufacturers, driving skilled labourers into the ranks of the unskilled and unemployed, and leaving valuable natural resources undeveloped.[115]

Finally, it needs to be emphasised that tariff reformers refused to conduct a debate on Britain's fiscal policy in purely economic terms. As this chapter has shown, tariff reform was not simply a debate about living standards. There was a visionary aspect to Chamberlain's proposals: the ideal of a united Empire was intended to infuse British society with a new sense of mission. Viewed in this way, tariff reform was as much a question of national character as of national wealth, which aimed at raising the moral, intellectual and spiritual welfare of the population, and not just its material well-being.[116] Equally, it must be recognised that, notwithstanding the imperial idealism of tariff reformers, there remained a substantial body of opinion in British politics wedded to free trade, and opposed to the argument that fiscal bonds were the only or even the optimal way of uniting the Empire. For many of these free trade imperialists, naval defence offered the safest and securest route to imperial reconstruction, and it is to their ideas that we must now turn.

---

113 Cain, 'The Economic Philosophy of Constructive Imperialism', p.58.
114 W.D. Rubinstein, *Capitalism, Culture and Decline in Britain, 1750–1990* (1993); C. Lee, *The British Economy since 1700* (Cambridge, 1986); Cain and Hopkins, *British Imperialism*, Vol. I, Chapter 1.
115 Amery, *The Fundamental Fallacies*, pp.31, 43, 55.
116 Cain, 'The Economic Philosophy of Constructive Imperialism', pp.42–4.

CHAPTER 5

Imperial Security: Naval Supremacy and Defence Planning

DEFENDING THE EMPIRE: THE DEBATE

Today British defence policy arouses little public interest, despite the considerable expenditure involved. This was not the case in later-Victorian and Edwardian Britain. Far from being conducted behind closed doors in Whitehall, debates on naval policy rippled throughout political society during these years. Of course, informed political interest in the navy did wax and wane. The atmosphere of general public quiescence regarding the adequacy of the navy evident in the 1870s and early 1880s was not seriously challenged until 1884, when W.T. Stead's agitation was launched through the pages of the *Pall Mall Gazette*. After Stead's agitation, there was growing public concern for the navy, although it was not continuous, at least not until after the turn of the century when the race to build battleships injected a new (and popular) dimension to the development of the Fleet.

The late-nineteenth and early-twentieth centuries were also a time when many of the long-established orthodoxies relating to the Royal Navy were being challenged.[1] The rapid pace of technological change, intensifying foreign naval rivalry and escalating defence costs all required a rethinking of existing conceptions of defence. For some strategic thinkers this re-evaluation of Britain's naval capabilities led to the conclusion that a 'national' fleet and an 'imperial' fleet were not one and the same thing, and that a navy which served (and was seen to serve) the defence requirements of the whole empire could

---

1 The historiography on the navy is huge, but we lack a satisfactory study of contemporary debates about its imperial role. Even A.J. Marder's *magnum opus* contains relatively few passages upon the specifically imperial aspects of naval strategy. See *From Dreadnought to Scapa Flow: The Royal Navy in the Fisher Era, 1904–19* (Oxford, 1978) and *The Anatomy of British Sea Power: A History of British Naval Policy in the Pre-Dreadnought Era, 1880–1895* (1964). Paul Kennedy's, *The Rise of Anglo-German Naval Antagonism, 1860–1914* (1980), draws attention to the importance of colonial disputes in European naval rivalries, and charts the 'surrender of local naval mastery' in the Atlantic and Pacific from the 1890s. However, Kennedy gives short shrift to measures of Anglo-Dominion co-operation in the naval sphere, and is generally dismissive of the idea of 'imperial federation' as applied to defence. See *The Rise and Fall of British Naval Mastery* (1976), Chapters 7–8.

not continue to be organised along existing lines. Through the concept of a *kriegsverein* (defensive union), a school of imperial navalists sought not only to forge a system of collective imperial security, but to link Britain's naval dispositions to the wider question of imperial unity. It is their ideas which provide the focus for this chapter.

THE DOCTRINE OF SEA POWER AND THE DEFENCE OF EMPIRE

A major landmark in the emergence of an imperial–naval conception of defence came in 1867 with the publication of a pamphlet by J.C.R. Colomb entitled *The Protection of Our Commerce and the Distribution of Our War Forces Considered.*[2] Colomb, a prominent member of the Imperial Federation League, argued that the essence of imperial security was naval and not military. Beyond Canada and India, he insisted, no part of the Empire was susceptible to landward attack, unless enemy troops were first transported by sea. A supreme navy was therefore the only way of defending the Empire.[3] Though initially slow to catch on, Colomb's ideas gained ground in the 1880, partly thanks to the IFL and the first Colonial Conference (1887). By 1889, the Naval Defence Act, and the extra expenditure it provided for shipbuilding, had marked out the navy as the senior service, while relegating the army to the 'second division' of imperial defence.[4] The Act led to the adoption of the so-called 'Two-Power Standard' – Britain's Fleet was to be equal in numbers of major warships to the combined strength of the next two largest navies.

Although the issue of inter-service rivalry cannot be investigated in any depth here,[5] we must consider briefly the 'Blue Water' school's strikingly successful propagation of theories of sea power. During the 1890s and early 1900s, naval enthusiasts showed great skill in mobilising public opinion in favour of a maritime concept of empire defence. Britain was depicted as an oceanic power with an empire created and maintained by supremacy at sea. In their study, *Imperial Defence*, Charles Dilke and Spenser Wilkinson spoke of the Empire as the 'possession of the sea', and spelt out how, without naval supremacy, the colonies would be left isolated, without an assured British future.[6] Other writers made much of the link between naval supremacy and imperial communications, or focused upon the navy's responsibility for defending the Empire in wartime. The Navy League's envoy to the colonies, Harold

2 D.M. Schurman, *The Education of a Navy. The Development of British Naval Strategic Thought, 1867–1914* (1965), Chapter 1; J. Beeler, 'Steam, Strategy and Schurman: Imperial Defence in the Post-Crimean Era, 1856–1905', in K. Neilson and G. Kennedy (eds), *Far Flung Lines. Studies in Imperial Defence in Honour of Donald Mackenzie Schurman* (1977), pp.32–4.
3 See Colomb's speeches to the RCI on 18/6/1886 and 10/4/1900: Captain J.C.R. Colomb, *Imperial Defence* (1886), pp.1–11 and *British Defence* (1900), p.10.
4 J. Gooch, *The Plans of War. The General Staff and British Military Strategy c. 1900–1916* (1974), pp.11–18.
5 For a fuller discussion of the obstacles standing in the way of the army defining its role in national and imperial defence, see W.S. Hamer, *The British Army. Civil–Military Relations, 1885–1905* (Oxford, 1970), Chapter 2.
6 C.W. Dilke and H. Spenser Wilkinson, *Imperial Defence* (1892), pp.39–48.

Wyatt, went so far as to predict that without a supreme navy the fabric of the Empire would dissolve like the fragments of a dream.[7]

The doctrine of naval supremacy was likewise trumpeted by the press. The eminent naval columnist, Archibald Hurd, likened the navy to an 'insurance department' of the Empire – the only effective protection for its overseas commerce – while his fellow journalist, J.R. Thursfield, proclaimed the British Empire to be 'the gift of sea power', recalling how during the recent war in South Africa the Royal Navy had guaranteed the security of transit necessary to the success of British troops.[8] It seems likely that figures like Hurd and Thursfield had a significant impact. Certainly, the level of public support for a strong navy was commented upon by defence experts. For Viscount Esher the notion that the navy was the first line of imperial defence was accepted almost as an 'act of faith', while the Committee of Imperial Defence's first Secretary, Sir George Sydenham Clarke, believed it to be universally acknowledged that the 'command of the sea' was essential to the existence of empire.[9] As one commentator remarks, in the 'naval revival' of the late-nineteenth century, 'the British Empire and the Royal Navy dwelt together in close juxtaposition in the popular mind'.[10] The general perception was that owing to its imperial commitments, Britain depended upon the strength and efficiency of its Fleet to a far greater extent than other foreign powers. This, in turn, provided the principal justification for Britain maintaining a higher level of naval armaments.

THE SIZE, DISTRIBUTION AND COMPOSITION OF THE FLEET

If the security of empire was to be measured by naval strength, then that strength was conceived primarily in terms of the number of battleships in service and commission.[11] It was also judged in relation to the fleets of rival colonial empires. In the 1880s and 1890s the threat came from a possible combination of Russian and French fleets in the Mediterranean; by the early 1900s it came from Germany in the North Sea. Moreover, any assessment of British naval strength had to be revised in the light of new technologies, which rendered older ships obsolescent. The main development at the turn of the century was the new model battleship, *HMS Dreadnought*, launched in 1905. The *Dreadnought*'s firing power and turbine propulsion made Britain's preponderance in pre-dreadnought type battleships of far less significance. Indeed, by the early 1900s Germany was thought to have enjoyed almost a level start in challenging for naval supremacy.

7 H. Wyatt, 'Navy League Envoy', *NLJ* (October, 1904), p.285.

8 A. Hurd, *The British Fleet. Is It Sufficient and Efficient?* (1901), p.ix; J.R. Thursfield, *Nelson and Other Naval Studies* (1909), p.342.

9 T.H. Hardman, *A Parliament of the Press. The First Imperial Press Conference, 1909* (1909), p.230; G.S. Clarke and J.R. Thursfield, *The Navy and the Nation or Naval Warfare and Imperial Defence* (1897), p.8.

10 Schurman, *The Education of a Navy*, p.10.

11 M. Howard, *The Lessons of History* (Oxford, 1993), pp.86–7.

Although the literature upon Anglo-German naval rivalry in the Edwardian era is daunting, an insight into the official mentality which sustained it can be gained from the diaries of Edward Goschen, the British Ambassador to Berlin from 1908 to 1914.[12] Goschen's diaries are especially interesting upon the question of German perceptions. They record the sense of British triumphalism which the German press associated with the construction of *HMS Dreadnought*. According to the Kaiser – the self-proclaimed 'Admiral of the Atlantic' – it was this triumphalism which had increased Germany's determination to show that it could build battleships as well as it could build huge passenger liners.[13] Two months later, Goschen's diary noted the equally determined resolve of the British people to build sufficient ships to maintain supremacy at sea. Yet responding to the German Naval Laws of 1908 and 1912 entailed a huge commitment from the British taxpayer, as shown by Table 2. Even with naval expenditure on this scale, it was clear that Britain could not be strong everywhere. As early as 1890, Dilke expressed anxiety about the tendency to concentrate the Fleet in the waters closest to the British Isles, which he thought tantamount to abandoning 'Greater Britain'.[14] He warned that the colonies would remain reluctant to pay into a scheme of naval defence which was not truly imperial in its scope. After the turn of the century, his fears and forebodings were amplified by the Navy League, whose agitation for an 'adequate margin of naval strength' was based squarely upon a concept of imperial (not merely national) defence.

Table 2   Gross public expenditure on the Navy, 1904–14 (£000,000)

1904	35.5	1910	35.8
1905	36.8	1911	40.4
1906	33.3	1912	42.9
1907	31.4	1913	44.4
1908	31.1	1914	48.8
1909	32.2		

Source: B.R. Mitchell, *Abstract of British Historical Statistics* (Cambridge, 1962), p.398.

The received wisdom on the distribution of the late-Victorian and Edwardian Fleet largely ignores these critiques of official policy, presenting the principle of concentration as a widely, in fact almost universally, accepted tenet

12 C.H.D. Howard (ed.), *The Diary of Edward Goschen, 1900–1914*, Camden 4th series, Vol. 25 (1980), pp.203, 214.
13 For the way in which the anglophobia of Germany's Kaiser and press fed off the naval rivalry between the two countries, see H.H. Herwig, *Luxury Fleet: The Imperial German Navy, 1888–1918* (1980), pp.38–9.
14 C.W. Dilke, *Problems of Greater Britain* (1890), p.653.

of naval thinking. The policy of concentration, we are told, was doubly justified. First, in strategic terms, the Admiralty saw the command of the sea as one and indivisible, it being imperative to amass naval strength where it was most needed. Certainly, this refrain was sung from the topmasts by many contemporary naval writers. Mahan's work, *The Influence of Sea Power upon History, 1660–1783*, insisted upon concentration as the predominant principle of naval warfare,[15] and popularisers of Mahan like Thursfield packaged this principle for public consumption. In *Nelson and Other Naval Studies*, Thursfield defended the stationing of the greater part of the Fleet in the 'home waters' on the ground that the Fleet's distribution simply reflected the 'momentous change in the strategic situation' brought about by the rise of German naval power. As long as the enemy's ships were in waters adjacent to the British Isles, the nation's main fleets would have to be stationed there too. If the enemy's fleets moved to distant waters, the British Fleet would follow. Looking to the future, Thursfield predicted that the continued growth of a German fleet, with its bases in the North Sea, would have the effect of further shifting 'the centre of strategic moment' away from the Mediterranean and placing it closer to the home waters, where the newest and most powerful vessels would be stationed. The earlier concentration of battleships in the Far Eastern waters, he reflected, had been due to 'exceptional and transient circumstances'.[16] Much of the historiography recycles this view.

Second, redistribution is explained in financial terms. When Fisher became First Sea Lord the need for naval economies was firmly established on the political agenda. In fact, Fisher's popularity with the politicians rested in no small part on his skill in ushering in a new period of naval economy under the cloak of 'modernising' the training, equipment and administration of the Fleet. In an effort to cut costs, the naval reserve was reconstituted; many older, slower and poorly armed vessels were recalled from the 'outer margins' of empire and scrapped; and the entire system of fleets and squadrons was reorganised. As a result, the cost of the navy was reduced from £41 million to £37.2 million in less than two years, and substantial savings continued to be achieved for a further two years, much to the relief of the new Liberal government.[17]

The implications of the policy of concentration pursued by Fisher after 1904 were far-reaching. British sea power in the Atlantic and Pacific was dealt a terrible blow. Thursfield had argued, somewhat complacently, that the 'strategy of position' had little application to the Atlantic waters because of the remote contingency of a war between Britain and the United States. Considering the rise of the American navy as a neutral or even positive event, he felt the disestablishment of the North American station presented no real problems for

---

15 P.A. Crowl, 'Alfred Thayar Mahan: The Naval Historian', in P. Paret (ed.), *Makers of Modern Strategy from Machiavelli to the Nuclear Age* (Oxford, 1986), p.457.
16 Thursfield, *Nelson and Other Naval Studies*, pp.xxi–xxiv, 286, 289–90.
17 A.L. Friedberg, *Britain and the Weary Titan. Britain and the Experience of Relative Decline, 1895–1914* (Princeton, NJ, 1988), pp.128–31.

imperial defence.[18] Yet by 1907, when the Pacific squadron at Esquimalt had been disbanded, and the North American squadron relocated to Britain, the United States was third in the world's league table of battleships built and being built.[19] In the event of a war with America, even the CID had to admit that it was at a loss as to how to respond. A joint meeting with Canadian ministers in 1910 proved an awkward occasion for the British defence establishment. Maurice Hankey, then secretary of the CID, explained the difficulty:

> The peculiar delicacy of this question is that in 1905 the Committee of Imperial Defence came to the conclusion that the Admiralty could not either themselves undertake the Defence of the Canadian Lakes, nor recommend any measures by which Canada could herself undertake their defence . . . *and this conclusion was not discussed with Canada, nor communicated to her Government.*[20]

The foundations of British sea power in the Pacific were weaker still. Britain's alliance with Japan in 1902, its renewal in 1905, and its revision and extension in 1911, demonstrated that Britain was no longer capable of defending its interests in this region without the assistance of another power.[21] In its first phase, the alliance was a response to the growth of the Russian navy in the Far East. After Russia's defeat at the hands of Japan in 1905, it was deemed necessary to meet the German naval threat in the North Sea. Within ten years of the Japanese alliance being signed, the number of British battleships and cruisers stationed in the Far Eastern waters was halved. When Churchill became First Lord of the Admiralty in November 1911, additional ships were withdrawn from the Far East, thereby placing even greater reliance upon Japan to defend British interests in the region. By this time the British China squadron was not much stronger than the German Pacific squadron.

British diplomacy did little to allay the anxieties which Fisher's policy of redistribution caused Australasia and western Canada. When, in May 1911, the British government consulted Dominion leaders upon the Japanese alliance, only reluctantly did they agree to its renewal. Moreover, public opinion in Australasia and Canada continued to express itself against the measure in strong terms. It was, therefore, very fortunate for the British government that the full extent of its dependence upon Japan did not become apparent until after the outbreak of the Great War. In 1914, Australian expeditions captured the islands of New Guinea and Samoa, but Japan occupied the German Pacific islands north of the equator. British naval weakness in the Pacific prevented

18 Thursfield, *Nelson and Other Naval Studies*, pp.295–300.
19 By this date, the strength of the US fleet would have required Britain to send the greater part of its navy across the Atlantic in order to guard against an invasion of Canada. See Kennedy, *The Rise and Fall*, p.211.
20 Quoted in J. Gooch, 'Great Britain and the Defence of Canada, 1896–1914', *JICH* (1975), p.383. Original italics.
21 For a study of the Alliance and the debates it provoked, see P. Lowe, *Great Britain and Japan, 1911–15. A Study of British Far Eastern Policy* (1969).

the transfer of these possessions to Australia, emphasising how far the balance of power had tipped in Japan's favour.

The assumption that opinion in Britain welcomed the policy of redistributing naval forces, and the informal and formal alliances it spawned, needs subjecting to more rigorous examination. Objections were certainly raised by the Colonial Office and to a limited extent by the Foreign Office.[22] Even opinion within the Admiralty was not clear cut. A memorandum presented to the Colonial Conference in 1902 appeared to endorse a broad range of 'Mahanian' positions: destroying the enemy's fleet was the primary duty of the navy; battleships were to be concentrated; and local defence was not to divert attention from the Fleet from which an attack was to be expected.[23] Significantly, however, the memorandum added the rider that it would be necessary for Britain to have 'sufficient power available to carry on a vigorous offensive against [the] hostile outlying squadrons without unduly weakening the forces concentrated for decisive battle'.

Reactions to redistribution outside the Service were not nearly so restrained. Although initially supportive of Fisher's reforms, the Navy League understood Australasia's sense of isolation from areas of imperial strength, and refused to accept the Anglo-Japanese alliance as sufficient security for British interests in the Pacific. While the Foreign Office reluctantly acquiesced to the alliance as a disagreeable necessity, and Colonial Office officials rued the way it was straining the loyalty of the Australasian colonies, Navy Leaguers carried their criticism much further. They argued that Britain was renouncing its overseas commitments by concentrating the Royal Navy in the North Sea. The 'hurrah party' visit of the American fleet to Australasia in 1908 was the occasion for a particularly strong attack upon existing policy. To abdicate the defence of the Pacific to the Americans, it was claimed, was to put an end to the 'Imperial dream'.[24] Furthermore, following Fisher's resignation, each successive stage in the withdrawal from the Far East was vocally opposed. The decision to station the New Zealand dreadnought in the home waters met with angry protest, as did the drastic reduction in the number of ships on the Australian station. And the renewal of the Japanese alliance in 1911 was said to be 'weakening the imperial bond'.[25] To be sure, few Navy Leaguers believed Britain's resources would stretch to a 'sufficient force' in the Far East – a cheaper alternative was thought to be the re-establishment of a 'flying squadron' of battle cruisers to visit the outlying ports of the Empire with a view to showing 'Britons overseas' the latest developments in warship construction.[26]

22 N. d'Ombrain, *War Machinery and High Policy: Defence Administration in Peacetime Britain, 1902–14* (1973), p.225.
23 'The Admiralty Memorandum on Imperial Defence (1902)', quoted in full in A.B. Keith (ed.), *Selected Speeches and Documents on British Colonial Policy, 1763–1917* (Oxford, 1948), pp.230–7.
24 Unsigned, 'The Problem of the Pacific', *NLJ* (September, 1908), p.259.
25 Editorial, *The Navy* (July, 1912), pp.173–4; A.H. Burgoyne, *The Navy League Annual* (1909–10), p.8.
26 H.T.C. Knox, 'Why Not a Flying Squadron?', *The Navy* (November, 1911), p.304.

But a minority held out for a Pacific fleet. Jebb doubted that a concentrated fleet could be moved easily from one arena of conflict to another, when in practice it took several weeks for battleships to get from the North Sea to the Pacific. He pleaded for two fleets; one British, the other 'Britannic'. The Britannic fleet was to be stationed permanently in the Pacific, and to be strong enough to prevent a rival fleet from securing command of the sea until reinforcements arrived.[27]

If the withdrawal of ships from the Pacific was a matter of some controversy among navalists, their withdrawal from the Mediterranean was the cause of complete consternation. The Mediterranean held a unique place in British maritime history. It controlled access to the Suez canal and provided the fastest route to India.[28] Ever since the Napoleonic Wars, it had been the station for the main fleet, and an important highway for British overseas trade.[29] Yet by the end of 1904 the number of battleships stationed in the Mediterranean had been cut to eight, and in 1906 an additional two ships were recalled. Although the Admiralty defended these reductions by designating the Atlantic fleet as a mobile reserve to be moved to the Mediterranean in the event of a crisis, the Foreign Office took fright, complaining of the likely impact upon British prestige of the absence of permanently stationed warships in the region. After the passing of the new German Naval Law of 1912, the situation again deteriorated. Unable to find trained men for the additional 'home water' battleships, the Admiralty decided to recall the Mediterranean squadron. So strong was the opposition to this decision that Churchill was compelled to offer its critics an olive branch. The First Lord committed himself to the restoration of a one-power standard in the Mediterranean (eight dreadnought-class ships by 1915), promising four battle cruisers based on Gibraltar as an interim measure.[30]

Churchill's policy of treating the Mediterranean as a subsidiary naval theatre antagonised large sections of the navalist community in parliament, the press and the country at large. The vital importance of retaining a fleet in the Mediterranean was a long-established principle of British defence.[31] In the summer of 1912 the Navy League launched a full-scale public campaign to restore British naval supremacy in these waters.[32] It told its audiences that the Mediterranean was a region in which British naval might had predominated for centuries, and which was central to the defence of empire since it was the 'avenue of approach' to Egypt, India, and Australasia.[33] It declared the policy of withdrawal

27 R. Jebb, 'The Admiralty and the Dominions – A Retrospect, 1914', *Jebb papers*, G1.
28 D.G. Halpern, *The Mediterranean Naval Situation, 1908–1914* (Cambridge, MA, 1971); G.S. Graham, *The Politics of Naval Supremacy. Studies in British Maritime Ascendancy* (Cambridge, 1965), Chapter 3.
29 A. Lambert, 'The Shield of Empire, 1815–1895' in J.R. Hill (ed.), *The Oxford Illustrated History of the Royal Navy* (Oxford, 1995), p.166.
30 Halpern, *The Mediterranean Naval Situation*, pp.17–18.
31 Clarke and Thursfield, *The Navy and the Nation*, p.241; H.S. Wilkinson, *Thirty-Five Years 1874–1909* (1933), p.189.
32 Minutes of the Navy League executive committee, 5/7/1912 and 9/10/1912.
33 'The Mediterranean Situation', unsigned, *The Navy* (September, 1912), p.245.

to be the negation of 'all our history', condemned by 'national honour', 'practical interest', and the 'eternal principles of strategy'.[34] In organising this campaign, the League's resolve was stiffened by support from the political and service worlds. In October 1913, Selborne spoke at its Trafalgar Day dinner, warning of the dangers which would befall the Empire if the Mediterranean continued to be neglected.[35] The same month, Beresford, who had previously commanded the Mediterranean fleet (1905–7), contributed a pessimistic article to *The Empire Review* on the naval outlook. The article berated Churchill for failing to send the promised battle cruisers, anticipating a combined strength of fifteen 'first class heavy armoured ships' for the Triple Alliance by the beginning of 1916.[36] In order to meet this emergency, it called for a conference between Britain and the Dominions as a necessary preliminary to restoring naval supremacy beyond the 'home waters'.

Most accounts of British naval policy before 1914 make little mention of the anger provoked by the principle of concentration and the redistribution of ships it required. Yet the reactions evoked by this part of Fisher's reform programme were very strong indeed. Typically, Leo Amery did not mince his words. Writing in 1914, he argued that the removal of the bulk of the Fleet to the 'home waters' had involved the 'practical abandonment of the rest of the world's ocean highways'. In the Pacific sea power had passed into the hands of the Japanese. In the Atlantic it was in the hands of the Americans. The French and Italians now controlled the Mediterranean:

> We exist as an Empire today, to some extent at least, by the grace of the Americans and Japanese. No empire can live long by foreign favour or foreign alliances. If its strength is not within itself it must in the end come to grief.[37]

The policy of redistribution also caused widespread alarm in English Canada (after the 1909 naval scare) and across Australia (particularly after the Russo-Japanese War of 1905). In the minds of many, redistribution called into question Britain's position as the 'cradle of sea power for the whole Empire' and exposed the Dominions to unnecessary danger.[38] It thereby strengthened the hand of those in favour of organised schemes of localised naval defence.[39]

The controversy surrounding the redistribution ships was compounded by British politicians' fixation with battleships. Here it is essential to distinguish between the battleship and the battle cruiser. Whereas the main principle governing the disposition of the former was convergence, that governing the latter was dispersion.[40] Thus despite looking very similar to the general public,

34 'A Navy Imperial', unsigned, *The Navy* (June, 1912), p.154.
35 Speech by Selborne to the NL, *The Navy* (November, 1913), pp.320–2.
36 Admiral Lord Charles Beresford, 'The Naval Outlook', *ER* (November, 1913), pp.219–24.
37 L. Amery, *Union and Strength. A Series of Papers on Imperial Questions* (1912), p.3.
38 Frank Hodgins, 'Shall Canada Have a Navy of its Own?', *NLJ* (February, 1908), p.53.
39 R. Muirhead Collins, 'Australian Naval Defence', *The Navy League Annual* (1908–9), p.159.
40 Thursfield, *Nelson and Other Naval Studies*, p.292.

these vessels were assigned quite different roles. It is only recently that historians have begun to probe Fisher's feelings on this important issue of strategy. We now know that the fleet Fisher built was not the fleet he wanted. Despite the fact that most accounts of the 'dreadnought revolution' focus upon the battleship and overlook the battle cruiser, Fisher was actually much more impressed by the latter than the former.[41] He felt battleships to be vulnerable to torpedoes launched from submarines or fast surface craft. He also believed them to be ill-suited to defending Britain's imperial interests. More lightly armoured and faster than the dreadnought, the advantage of the battle cruiser lay in part with its greater speed and transportability – 'speed is armour' was one of Fisher's favourite refrains. A fleet of battle cruisers, he believed, was far easier to move to other arenas of naval action, and could therefore operate far more effectively upon Britain's far-flung lines of maritime supply and communication.

Nevertheless, Fisher's preference for the battle cruiser over the battleship was not popular with the politicians for whom the battleship remained a symbol of national prestige as well as a readily comprehensible numerical measure of naval strength.[42] Constrained by political necessity into channelling resources into the battleship programme, Fisher was forced to build a fleet which was dangerously one-sided. Not only were there too few battle cruisers, but large capital ships were constructed at the expense of flotilla craft, further impairing the navy's fighting capabilities.[43] Hence the transition from colonial naval subsidies to separate colonial fleets described below should not be understood simply as a reflection of a growing national sentiment and self-confidence in the Dominions. The construction of Dominion navies was a perfectly rational response to the type of navy Britain decided to build in the years after 1904.

COLONIAL PARTICIPATION IN IMPERIAL DEFENCE

The issue of colonial contributions to the Royal Navy dominated imperial defence thinking from the 1870s. Both fiscal and strategic considerations called for fuller Dominion participation in the task of defending the Empire. A tide of opinion in Britain – how strong it is difficult to say – felt that the taxpayer should not have to defray the entire cost of the navy. This was not merely a parliamentary preoccupation, though there were many calls from this quarter for the colonies to make a bigger contribution to defence expenditure. Public opinion, too, demanded an equalisation of the burden – even music hall entertainers were known to make reference to the colonies' duty to contribute to Britain's armed forces. The same sermon was preached by British politicians

41 J.T. Sumida, *In Defence of Naval Supremacy: Finance, Technology and British Naval Policy, 1889–1914* (1989).
42 N. Lambert, 'British Naval Policy, 1913–1914: Financial Limitation and Strategic Revolution', *JMH* (1995), p.324.
43 Ibid., p.325.

at the Imperial Press Conference of 1909. Rosebery's opening speech reminded overseas delegates of the Dominions' responsibility for defending the Empire, as did the great naval display staged at Spithead on 12 June. The Empire's outlying parts occasionally saw vessels drawn from less powerful classes of ships, but at Spithead the main fleet was assembled in all its glory. The spectacle included twenty-four battleships, sixteen armoured cruisers, eight other cruisers, four scouts, forty-eight destroyers, thirty-five submarines, and nine auxiliaries, occupying about 18 miles of water. As the Conference's official history explained, the aim was to convey what the mother country had done in the way of 'sacrifice, expenditure and invention' in order to maintain mastery of the oceans. In this way, it was hoped to persuade the colonial press delegates of the need for the Dominions to share more of the defence burden.[44] But the devil lay in the detail. While the South African War may have shown that the Dominions were under certain circumstances willing to rally to the Empire's cause, it had also reinforced the local pride and distinctive identity of the colonial troops which had fought alongside Britain. No colony was likely to continue writing cheques for the Royal Navy unless it was clear that the Fleet was capable of meeting their defensive needs. This, in turn, required the Admiralty to consult the colonies on important matters of defence policy.

It is necessary to recall how the maritime defences of the self-governing colonies developed from the mid-nineteenth century. Under the provisions of the Colonial Naval Defence Act (1865), the Australian colonies organised schemes of coastal and port defence, beginning with Victoria, which established a small naval brigade. Subsequently, Victoria, Queensland and South Australia placed orders for gunboats and torpedo boats.[45] The next step came in 1887 at the Colonial Conference, when it was agreed to base a Royal Navy auxiliary squadron permanently in the waters of the Australian station in return for an annual subsidy of £126,000 towards its maintenance. From the outset, the Admiralty expressed reservations about tying warships to a particular coastline as it was felt the enemy would 'either evade them completely or defeat them in detail'.[46] At the following conference in 1897 considerable pressure was exerted by the Colonial Office to persuade the Australian colonies to waive their right to stop ships being moved out of local waters, but to no avail. The veto remained a condition of the subsidy from Australia and New Zealand, which was eventually raised to £240,000 a year, the actual cost of the squadron to the Admiralty being about £670,000.

After intensive Admiralty lobbying, the veto was finally removed at the Colonial Conference of 1902. Britain agreed to increase the number and size of ships on the Australian station, and to man two of the vessels with Australian personnel. In return, the new Commonwealth government consented to

44 Hardman, *A Parliament of the Press*, p.71.
45 Canada did nothing to acquire vessels under the legislation.
46 M.L. Hadley and R. Sarty, *Tin-Pots and Pirate Ships: Canadian Naval Forces and German Sea Raiders, 1880–1918* (Montreal, 1991), p.8.

the free movement of the squadron in the Australasian, Indian and China seas. In the hope of extracting bigger defence subsidies from the Dominions, British officials then produced tables comparing the naval contributions per capita of different parts of the Empire.[47] The response was disappointing. Australia and New Zealand agreed to slightly larger subsidies; the Cape undertook to contribute £50,000 annually to the navy (an increase of £20,000 on its former contribution), and Natal £35,000 (an increase of £23,000); and Newfoundland offered to pay £3,000 annually towards the cost of a branch of the Royal Naval Reserve. Meanwhile Canada offered to take more responsibility for local defence, suggesting that it might build a coastal naval militia on its existing Fisheries Protection Service.[48] Although this new agreement came in for fierce criticism from the Australian parliament and press, it survived until the next conference in 1907, by which time even the Admiralty was preparing to make a concession to the demand for local squadrons.

By 1907 it was apparent that Britain was reluctant to share control of the Royal Navy for relatively insignificant cash contributions from the colonies. Time and time again the Admiralty had shown itself unwilling to surrender control over vessels which the colonies had provided (in full or part). For their part, British politicians gradually began to accept that colonial statesmen were unlikely to go on handing over money or ships without having any say in what they paid for. As Arthur Balfour reflected, Britain was asking the parliaments of the Dominions to vote monies for a navy over which they had next to no control.[49] Neither did the difficulty of the situation escape Harold Wyatt, the Navy League's envoy to the colonies in 1904–5.[50] While in Canada, Wyatt experienced first-hand the sense of colonial vexation with Britain's arguments for increased participation in imperial defence. Parts of the Canadian press even labelled him (unfairly) as an agent of imperial centralisation. Upon returning to Britain, therefore, Wyatt was well placed to explain how the theory of 'no taxation without representation' was a major factor in colonial opposition to naval subsidies.

Some historians have taken a different view, however. Exploring the distribution of defence costs between Britain and its colonies, it is argued that the contribution from the Dominions to the defence of the Empire was artificially low. Britain, we are told, shouldered the burden of imperial defence by maintaining two military establishments – one for home defence, the second for imperial protection – while failing to recover anything other than a most

---

47 Friedberg, *The Weary Titan*, p.117.
48 Some Canadian historians now locate the origins of the Royal Canadian Navy in this decision. The proposed Naval Militia Act never materialised, but two ships were commissioned by the Marine and Fisheries Department in 1904. For a summary of the argument, see W. Glover, 'The RCN: Royal Colonial or Royal Canadian Navy?', in M. Hadley, R. Huebert and F. Crickard (eds), *A Nation's Navy. In Quest of Canadian Naval Identity* (Montreal, 1996), pp.73, 365.
49 J. Tomes, *Balfour and Foreign Policy. The International Thought of a Conservative Statesman* (Cambridge, 1997), p.74.
50 For reports of Wyatt's mission, see 'Navy League Envoy', *NLJ* (October, 1904); 'The Navy League Dinner', *NLJ* (November, 1904); 'The Navy and the Empire', *NLJ* (January, 1905).

meagre proportion of the total cost from the colonies.[51] Is this a tenable position? While it may be for the closing decades of the nineteenth century, it becomes much harder to support thereafter. In the years immediately prior to 1914 the Dominions could not be completely confident of the support of the Royal Navy.[52] The growth of rival foreign fleets, the policy of concentration, and the preponderance of battleships over battle cruisers, all cast reasonable and real doubt on Britain's capacity to honour its overseas defence commitments. It is important not to overlook these anxieties when assessing the appropriateness of Dominion contributions. They weighed so heavily upon the 'official mind' in Australia that by 1907 its government had decided it could no longer rely upon the Royal Navy to provide an adequate system of defence, despite the fact that the alternative policy – a separate colonial navy – would be far more costly to pursue.

The concept of a centralised fleet was ditched by the Admiralty at a specially convened defence conference in July–August 1909. It was replaced by the concept of a Royal Navy supported by colonial fleet units. These units were to consist of a battle cruiser, smaller cruisers, destroyers and submarines. They were to be large enough to offer a career structure and to attract quality recruits, maintained by the Dominion governments, and placed under colonial control. Collectively they would comprise a reconstituted Pacific fleet with four units: one based at Vancouver (Canadian fleet), a second at Sydney (Australian fleet), a third at Hong Kong, and a fourth at Singapore. The China unit was to be partially subsidised by New Zealand, and in return the Admiralty was to station several modern light cruisers and destroyers at Auckland. Each unit was expected to cost £3.7 million to build, and £600–700,000 a year to run and maintain. The Pacific fleet was to stay in the region regardless of changing defence requirements elsewhere in the Empire.[53]

Thinking in Britain about the viability of colonial fleet units has so far received little attention from historians. Most standard texts barely mention the agreement to proceed with the formation of separate Australian and Canadian navies.[54] Yet if historians have regarded the decision as uninteresting, this is no reflection on its contemporary significance. At the Imperial Press Conference in 1909 the naval defence of the Dominions was the leading issue. As speaker after speaker proclaimed, the fundamental question facing the Admiralty had ceased to be the best means by which the Dominions could contribute to

51 L.E. Davis and R.A. Huttenback, *Mammon and the Pursuit of Empire: The Political Economy of British Imperialism, 1860–1912* (Cambridge, 1986), Chapter 5.
52 This point is also argued cogently by Avner Offer in 'The British Empire, 1870–1914: A Waste of Money?', *EcHR* (1993), pp.227–31.
53 At the 1907 Colonial Conference, Captain Creswell, Australia's Director of Naval Forces, had pushed proposals for a separate Australian navy. It was to comprise 3 cruiser destroyers, 16 torpedo boat destroyers, and 15 torpedo boats, costing an estimated £2.3 million. However, the CID rejected the proposal to establish a 'local flotilla' as strategically unsound. See C. Kinloch-Cooke, 'The Imperial Conference, 1907', *The Empire Review* (May, 1907), p.312.
54 N. Lambert, 'Economy or Empire? The Fleet Unit Concept and the Quest for Collective Security in the Pacific, 1909–14', in Neilson and Kennedy (eds), *Far Flung Lines*, pp.55–83.

the naval security of the Empire. It was more a matter of fitting whatever the Dominions were prepared to do into a workable scheme of defence for the Empire as a whole.

On the second day of the conference, the subject of naval defence was discussed in distinguished company – McKenna presided, and Grey, Cromer and Lyttelton participated. McKenna, as First Lord of the Admiralty, spoke the language of partnership, but also acknowledged the difference in perspective between the United Kingdom and the colonies in the sphere of defence. He assured the overseas delegates that the Admiralty would not force its strategic views upon the Dominions.[55] If any Dominion asked for Britain's opinion about imperial defence, the Admiralty would be ready with an answer, but it was recognised that the colonies would have their own views as to the proper development of their defensive forces.[56] At the same session, Alfred Lyttelton identified two formidable objections to money contributions from the colonies: they failed to provide a nucleus upon which to base the future 'organisation of armaments', and economists in all parties tended to attack such payments. Amery, too, opposed such subsidies on the grounds that they ignored the constitutional position of the Empire, which was not a single unitary state but a partnership of autonomous states. It was inappropriate for the whole Fleet to be based in the home waters. Regardless of strategic theory, sea power had to have its roots in every part of the Empire: 'we want our naval power to be based not only at Portsmouth, but at Vancouver, at Sydney, at Durban, and at Simonstown. Then, if we ever have to fight in the Pacific, we shall still be fighting in our home waters.'[57]

At the third session – with Balfour presiding, and Haldane and Roberts present – discussion was supposed to focus on the army, but more than once returned to the navy. Balfour was a strong advocate of the subordination of local to imperial defence. He provided a robust justification of the policy of demonstrating naval superiority in the 'home waters' rather than dissipating the strength of the Fleet across the globe.[58] Yet whatever the optimal relationship between local and imperial defence in theory, Balfour was forced privately to concede that creating local navies was the only realistic way of extending colonial co-operation. Like Amery, he recognised that Britain had to adapt its military system to 'what is the ultimate constitutional necessity of the Empire'.[59] An adjourned debate on 26 June, under the chairmanship of Lord Esher, with Beresford attending, also dealt at length with naval questions. In an imaginative and inspired speech, Esher expounded his idea of an 'Imperial navy'. In order to harness the 'patriotic impulse' of the Dominions, he argued, the navy's function could not be conceived simply in terms of destroying the enemy's fleet in the first few days of a maritime war. The navy

55 Hardman, *A Parliament of the Press*, p.153.
56 'The Press Conference', *The Times*, 9/6/1909, p.4.
57 Hardman, *A Parliament of the Press*, p.166.
58 'The Press Conference', *The Times*, 9/6/1909, p.6.
59 Tomes, *Balfour and Foreign Policy*, p.75.

had to take responsibility for defending the coasts of the Empire, protecting its overseas trade, and policing the seas in time of peace.[60]

In these debates, the delegates of the Australian and Canadian press expressed strong sympathy for the idea of developing local navies. For Australians, national security had long been the primary focus of concern in their overseas relations. From its inception, the Australian Imperial Federation League had regarded naval defence as the key issue in external policy, upon which other issues, such as the protection of trade and the preservation of a 'white' Australia, ultimately depended.[61] Thus although E.S. Cunningham of the *Melbourne Argus* spoke at the press conference of a growing sentiment in favour of relieving Britain of some of the burden of imperial defence, he also emphasised the importance of Australia first securing its own frontiers, which meant building an Australian navy.[62] Similarly, Theodore Fink, proprietor of the (Melbourne) *Herald*, endorsed Australia's move towards a localised fleet, though he thought it should put itself under the Admiralty in time of war.[63]

For Canada, the position was more complex. Determined to resist Conservative calls for an 'emergency' contribution to the Royal Navy, Laurier declared himself in favour of a Canadian navy, and held it ready to assist Britain in the event of any international dispute which a Canadian government considered critical. But he rejected the Admiralty's original offer of fleet units, arguing that Canada required two squadrons – one for each of its coasts – rather than a single fleet unit.[64] This policy was broadly supported by J.S. Brierley, managing director of the (Montreal) *Daily Herald*, a prominent independent journal. Brierley stressed Canada's determination to maintain a dual position in the business of imperial defence. It was her duty to share in the responsibilities of empire, but without in any way relinquishing control over any money spent, ships built or troops raised. He did, however, add that he could not imagine the circumstances in which, when the needs of the Empire demanded, Canadian ships would not go to help the Fleet. J.A. MacDonald, of the influential Liberal (Toronto) *Globe*, took the argument about Canadian control a stage further. He insisted that a Canadian fleet must be 'an integral part of an Imperial Navy'. This call was echoed in the Canadian House of Commons by the Conservative leader, Borden, who stated that Canadian ships should automatically pass under the charge of the Admiralty in the event of war.[65]

The Navy League's response to the idea of fleet units was in line with colonial thinking. Most Navy Leaguers accepted that if Britain could not

60 Hardman, *A Parliament of the Press*, p.230.
61 L.Foster, *High Hopes. The Men and Motives of the Australian Round Table* (Melbourne, 1986).
62 Hardman, *A Parliament of the Press*, p.176.
63 Ibid., p.255.
64 The original proposal was for Canada to situate a station in the Pacific while a British fleet controlled the Atlantic waters. The subsequent proposal provided for a force of armoured cruisers (but no battleships) to be stationed in the Atlantic and divided between Canada's two coasts. Laurier agreed to the modified version, although on the eve of the war Canada had purchased only two ageing cruisers, which were 'utterly inadequate' for the protection of its coastline: Hadley and Sarty, *Tin-Pots and Pirate Ships*, p.viii.
65 Hardman, *A Parliament of the Press*, pp.170, 183.

provide adequate assurances to the colonies, then it would have to bow to the colonies' decision to take more responsibility for their own defence. On the eve of the special Defence Conference, a leading article in *The Navy* stated the time was ripe for a great step forward in the organisation of imperial defence, provided that in planning for local security the British and colonial governments had regard for the whole. The journal's editor had prepared the way for a new departure in League policy by publishing a number of letters recommending schemes similar to the fleet unit concept.[66] In particular, a letter from a Canadian Navy Leaguer had claimed (somewhat tenuously) that the principle of colonial navies was by no means a new theory, but had received legislative sanction from the British parliament over forty years previously *vide* the Colonial Naval Defence Act.[67] The letter was from H.J. Wickham, former Royal Navy officer, and honorary secretary of the influential Toronto branch of the Navy League. In 1897, the Toronto branch had drawn up a memorandum on naval defence recommending an armed merchant cruiser scheme, jointly subsidised by British and Dominion governments, and a Canadian naval militia (trained to Royal Navy standards) to operate these cruisers against European sea raiders on the Atlantic.[68] The memorandum provided the basis for proposals submitted by the Navy League to the 1907 Colonial Conference. These proposals argued in favour of the development of local fleets. The ships for colonial squadrons were to be supplied by the United Kingdom and manned and maintained by the colonies. Vessels and personnel were to be interchangeable between the colonial and imperial naval services. And colonial militias were to serve occasionally with the Royal Navy on various stations. Finally, colonial squadrons were to be put under the supreme control of the Admiralty in time of war.[69]

Although often portrayed as sticking rigidly to the formula 'one fleet, one flag', Lambert's reappraisal of Edwardian naval policy demonstrates that official attitudes to naval strategy were more flexible than hitherto allowed. The Admiralty was neither hidebound by the precepts of Mahan, nor was it completely opposed to the creation of colonial navies.[70] For example, in 1907–8, the majority of senior Admiralty officials accepted the Dominions' desire to build local naval forces in the form of small torpedo flotillas.[71] They also supported Fisher's subsequent rejection of torpedo flotillas in favour of full-scale colonial fleet units to be stationed in the Pacific. They did, however, insist that these local fleets were not to be mere 'sentimental' navies, but real

---

66 For details see 'The Naval Defence of Australia', *NLJ* (October, 1908), pp.213–14; L. Loraine, 'Proposals for an Imperial Navy', *The Navy* (April, 1909), p.110; 'The Navy and the Empire', *The Navy* (May, 1909), p.121.
67 H.J. Wickham, 'The Navy and the Empire', 23/11/1909, *The Navy* (December, 1909), pp.361–2.
68 Hadley and Sarty, *Tin-Pots and Pirate Ships*, pp.9–11.
69 'The Navy League and the Colonial Conference', *NLJ* (April, 1907), p.89; 'The Empire and the Navy', *NLJ* (May, 1907), pp.117–18.
70 Lambert, 'Economy or Empire?', pp.55, 62–3.
71 Hadley and Sarty, *Tin-Pots and Pirate Ships*, pp.19–21.

fighting forces which could be combined in wartime to serve as components of a multi-national Pacific fleet. Hence when the new scheme of fleet units was finally introduced, the response from within the Admiralty was generally positive. Officials explored how the new Dominion navies could remain closely linked with the Royal Navy, while attention was drawn to the importance of the standardisation of equipment, tactical doctrine, discipline and training.

In Lambert's (as in Beresford's) view, the villain of the piece was not the Admiralty but Churchill, who as First Lord continued to recall ships to the home waters from 1911 to 1914, constantly citing Mahan's doctrine of concentration in justification.[72] Churchill made no secret of his feeling that the Admiralty's decision to establish local navies had been a mistake. He believed that as long as the British navy was supreme in Europe then even the safety of the Australasian colonies was not at risk.[73] In so far as he did anything to maintain naval strength in the Mediterranean it was by encouraging the Canadian premier, Robert Borden, to send additional ships to supplement the 'Imperial' fleet. However, Borden's generous offer of three ships was thwarted by the opposition of the Canadian Senate in May 1913. Writing later that year in *The Empire Review*, Beresford described the First Lord as 'one of the crudest and most cynical opportunists of modern times'.[74] Lambert is almost as scathing:

> Winston Churchill displayed little sympathy towards the 'colonials'' defence worries; it could be argued that he appeared interested in the Dominions only for what he could get out of them. To save a comparatively trifling sum . . . [he] dismantled a highly imaginative and surprisingly popular system of collective security designed to protect imperial interests in the Pacific. . . . His high-handedness had tilted the balance of overseas opinion some distance away from the ideal of broad imperialism thought to be achievable in 1909, towards the separatism and self-reliance in naval and military affairs many had so strenuously tried to avert.[75]

In the years following the Naval Defence Act of 1889 an influential and informed body of naval opinion – drawing support from inside and outside the Admiralty – explored various ways of furthering the principle of imperial unity in the field of defence. The culmination of this process was the concept of the colonial fleet unit. Even though colonial navies were still very much at an embryonic stage by the outbreak of the Great War, the fleet unit concept is important because it represents a recognition of the need to strike a balance between the requirements of colonial and imperial defence. Defence was to be localised in the sense that individual colonies would begin developing their own naval forces; equally, it was intended that those forces would fit

72 Ibid., pp.68–70.
73 R. Quinault, 'Churchill and Australia: The Military Relationship, 1899–1945', *War and Society* (1988), p.44.
74 Beresford, 'The Naval Outlook', p.224.
75 Lambert, 'Economy or Empire?', pp.75–6.

into a global defensive framework, directed from Britain. Yet this still left unresolved the problem of who controlled the Royal Navy. Was the Empire evolving into a loose-knit alliance of friendly but essentially independent states, or was it to function as an integrated military unit? And if it was to operate as an integrated military unit, what part would the Dominions play in deciding naval tactics and strategy? The early-twentieth century was a time when the machinery of British defence planning was in the process of being overhauled. This process presented an opportunity for consulting the colonies more regularly and extensively upon matters of imperial defence and foreign policy.

DEFENCE PLANNING AND THE COMMITTEE OF IMPERIAL DEFENCE

The importance of systematic defence planning was emphasised by the Carnarvon Commission of 1879–82,[76] although it took three more years before the Salisbury government revived the then defunct Colonial Defence Committee. An inter-departmental forum for discussion rather than a Cabinet committee proper, the CDC's broad aim was to promote uniformity and continuity in imperial defence. It was responsible for providing memoranda on local defence for the Colonial Conference in 1887, and for reviewing the results of the defence planning of colonial governments.[77] The idea that the CDC might provide the basis for co-ordinating the two services, and possibly equipping them with a general staff, was soon scotched by the Admiralty. In 1888, the Hartington Commission[78] continued to identify the lack of co-operation between the services as a major cause for concern, concluding pessimistically that the requirements of imperial defence had outrun the existing machinery of planning, and reiterating the need for some co-ordinating body.

It took the British army's lacklustre performance in South Africa to catapult the issue of military administration towards the top of the political agenda.[79] The South African War underlined the necessity of correlating the defence plans of the Empire with those of the home government.[80] For instance, a forcefully argued article published in the *Quarterly Review* observed how the military system of the Empire had been strained to the utmost by the work of defeating the two Afrikaner Republics and was in need of immediate and

76 The Carnarvon Commission was appointed 'to make enquiry into the condition and sufficiency of the means of the naval and military forces provided for the defence of the more important sea-ports within our Colonial possessions and dependencies'.
77 In 1902, the CDC became a sub-committee of the Committee of Imperial Defence. In 1911, it was renamed the Overseas Defence Committee. See N.H. Gibbs, 'The Origins of Imperial Defence', in J.B. Hattendorf and R.S. Jordan (eds), *Maritime Strategy and the Balance of Power. Britain and America in the Twentieth Century* (Basingstoke, 1989), pp.27–8; F.A. Johnson, *Defence by Committee. The British Committee of Imperial Defence, 1885–1959* (1960), pp.19–20.
78 The Hartington Commission was asked 'to enquire into the Civil and Professional Administration of the Naval and Military Departments and the relationship of those Departments to each other and to the Treasury'.
79 Gibbs, 'The Origins of Imperial Defence', p.32.
80 M. Beloff, *Britain's Liberal Empire, 1897–1921* (1969), pp.77–80.

comprehensive reform.[81] It recommended the summoning of an imperial conference to establish the nature of participation of the different self-governing colonies in the business of defence. If any of the colonies pledged themselves to participation, they were to be given a proportionate share in the control of imperial defence and foreign policy.[82] The article also publicised a report of the Imperial Federation Defence Committee. The IFDC was a splinter group of the Imperial Federation League, formed by a group of navalists in 1893 in order to secure an adequate system of maritime defence for the Empire as a whole.[83] The IFDC's report proposed a new body, 'an Imperial Council', upon which the Dominions would be represented, and which would have general supervisory control over the funds voted by the parliaments of Britain and the self-governing colonies for the purpose of general defence.

While the IFDC's suggestion came to nothing, the lessons of the South African War did in fact give rise to a new piece of machinery for co-ordinating the military, naval and foreign policy of the Empire. The Committee of Imperial Defence first met on 18 December 1902, and was provided with a permanent secretariat in 1904 on the recommendation of the War Office Reconstitution (or Esher) Committee. A purely advisory body, the CID's task was to formulate plans for imperial defence, which would then be referred to the Cabinet for approval and implemented by the relevant department(s). The Prime Minister was the only permanent member and had the power to summon whoever he wished to its meetings. Regular attenders included the Secretary of State for War, the First Lord of the Admiralty, the Directors of Naval and Military Intelligence, the Commander-in-Chief of the army, and the First Sea Lord. Colonial representatives could be present on an equal footing with British ministers, but their representation was *ad hoc*.

The CID certainly marked a step forward in the quest for co-operation in imperial defence. However, it fell far short of the goal to which many imperial navalists aspired,[84] having 'little of a concrete nature to do with the Dominions'.[85] No sooner had the CID been put on a permanent footing than a small group of influential academics, civil servants and politicians – known as the Pollock Committee – set about discussing how the machinery of defence planning could be further improved. The membership of the Pollock Committee overlapped with the IFDC. It included Sydenham Clarke, Drage, Milner,

81 'Domestic Parties and Imperial Government', unsigned, *The Quarterly Review* (July, 1900), pp.241–68.
82 Ibid., pp.262–3.
83 Many Navy Leaguers belonged to the IFDC, including its president Robert Yerburgh. On the IFDC, see W.D. Worsfold, 'Past and Present I. The Imperial Federation League: 1884–1893', *United Empire* (April, 1915); A.H. Loring, 'Kindred Societies – Past and Present II. The Imperial Federation Defence Committee: 1894–1906', *United Empire* (May, 1915); IFDC pamphlet collection, nos 1, 2, 5, 6, 8–14, Rhodes House Library, Oxford University.
84 The Admiralty's withdrawal from CID deliberations in 1905 posed particular problems as far as imperial defence planning was concerned: see J. Gooch, 'The Chiefs of Staff and the Higher Organisation for Defence in Britain, 1904–84', in Hattendorf and Jordan (eds), *Maritime Strategy and the Balance of Power*, p.38.
85 d'Ombrain, *War Machinery and High Policy*, p.226.

Parkin, Wyndham and, of course, Frederick Pollock himself. Pollock was Professor of Jurisprudence at Corpus Christi College, Oxford, and had a keen interest in the Empire's constitutional arrangements and legal systems. By 1905, he and other members of the Committee had come to regard a revamped Colonial Conference system as the best way to promote imperial co-operation. The despatch of the Colonial Secretary, Lyttelton, to the self-governing colonies prior to the 1907 Colonial Conference incorporated many of the Pollock Committee's recommendations, and the conference system was placed on a permanent basis as an advisory institution. Yet no effective secretariat was formed, and it would seem that preparation for gatherings in 1909 and 1911 continued to suffer from lack of adequate organisation.[86]

Neither the CID nor the Colonial Conference system had the capacity to transform imperial defence planning. Colonial politicians were suspicious of bodies primarily responsible to the British Cabinet, just as they were unlikely to be bought off by purely consultative organisations which gave them no real say in policy-making. Thus while Borden may have castigated Laurier's proposals for a 'tin-pot navy' as damaging both to Canada's prestige and to imperial unity, he was adamant that Canadian help in maintaining naval supremacy would come at a price – shared control over defence and foreign policy.[87] This view was shared by other important figures in Canadian public life. The President of the Victoria-Esquimalt branch of the Navy League, Captain Clive Phillips-Wolley, is a good example. Phillips-Wolley was prominent in literary and newspaper circles in British Columbia, and later knighted for his services in organising branches of the Navy League in western Canada. Like Borden, he believed that financial contributions had to be contingent upon some degree of control. He proposed that the CID be turned into a body upon which all governments of the Empire would be granted representation according to the value of the contribution they made to its defence.[88] This idea was supported by Wyatt, who spoke strongly in favour of reforming the CID so as to secure for the colonies a 'fair share' of influence over naval policy. To this end Wyatt recommended that the CID sit alternately in the different capitals of 'Greater Britain': 'It should be as much the Navy of South Africa, the Navy of Australia, the Navy of Canada, as it is the Navy of Great Britain.'[89]

Aware of the British government's reluctance to grant the CID any power to impose an obligation upon it, imperial navalists turned their attention to reforming the organisation of the Admiralty instead. In *The Command of the Sea*, Archibald Hurd floated the idea of an 'Imperial Naval Committee', comprising the First Lord of the Admiralty, the First and Second Sea Lords, and

86 J.E. Kendle, *The Colonial and Imperial Conferences, 1887–1911. A Study in Imperial Organisation* (1967), Chapter 4.
87 K. McNaught, *The Penguin History of Canada* (1988), p.209; H. Horden (ed.), *Robert Laird Borden. His Memoirs. Vol. I: 1854–1915* (Toronto, 1969), pp.126, 165.
88 C. Phillips-Wolley, 'Canada and the Navy', *The Navy* (March, 1909), p.57.
89 Speech of Harold Wyatt reported in the *Rand Daily Mail*, 17/5/1904, reprinted in *NLJ* (August, 1904), p.206.

representatives from the Dominions, acting in an advisory capacity to the Admiralty, and responsible for superintending the finance and general well-being of an 'Imperial Service Squadron' based in Gibraltar and covering the Atlantic.[90] Sympathy for reforming the Admiralty was expressed from within the Service too. In an article entitled 'Federation and the Navy', published in *The Empire Review*, Lieutenant L.H. Horden advocated the appointment of a Royal Commission to decide the best way to 'federalise' the navy as a stepping stone towards the ultimate ideal of an 'Imperial Parliament'.[91] The Commission's task, he ventured, would be to ensure the colonies played a part in administering the navy. More specifically, it was suggested that colonial representatives be incorporated as new civilian members upon the Board of the Admiralty. They were then to reside in England for a period of two to three years, thereby increasing the number of colonial statesmen acquainted with the Empire's naval and defence requirements.

Of course, before 1914, neither the CID nor the Admiralty were reorganised along such lines. It was not until the First World War that the patterns of governance of the Empire were significantly, albeit temporarily, transformed. The establishment of the Imperial War Cabinet by Lloyd George in 1917 succeeded for a while in bringing the British and Dominion governments into a much closer working relationship, and prompted Cabinet members like Amery and Milner to think afresh about the prospects for a more institutionalised form of imperial unity (see Chapter 7).

CONCLUSION

The late-nineteenth and early-twentieth centuries are recognised as a period when Britain struggled to meet the combined challenge of the older navies of France and Russia and the new navies of Germany, America and Japan. Rather than thinking of Britain narrowly maintaining a margin of naval supremacy during the Edwardian era, it is more accurate to speak of Britain's seapower giving her regional (as opposed to world-wide) superiority. The indefensibility of Britain's sprawling frontiers was acknowledged as early as 1881–82 by the Carnarvon Commission. The rise of Germany in Europe and the emergence of Japan as a Pacific power only exacerbated the problem, making it necessary to resort to a formal alliance with Japan, and to rely increasingly upon an informal alliance with the United States, in order to defend Britain's imperial interests.

This gradual contraction of Britain's ability to defend her imperial possessions provoked a vigorous debate among journalists, academics and backbench MPs, as well as intermittently causing concern to a wider public. Technology was as much of a factor as foreign rivalry here. The revolution in naval architecture and weaponry which took place during the third quarter of the

90 A. Hurd, *The Command of the Sea. Some Problems of Imperial Defence Considered in the Light of the German Navy Act of 1912* (1912), pp.84–7.
91 Lieut. L.H. Horden, 'Federation and the Navy', *ER* (January, 1904), pp.601–10.

nineteenth century had profound consequences for Britain's defensive capabilities, especially in relation to its empire. In some senses the transition from sail to steam had a liberating effect, but in other respects it was debilitating, tying ships to coal depots and also reducing their range. It was not until the 1880s, when steam technology had settled down and the essentials of pre-dreadnought battleship design had been realised, that long-term defence planning became possible.[92] Yet at precisely this time, the tempo of foreign naval rivalry stepped up, raising a whole new set of problems for British defence planners, and polarising political debate on the navy between two schools of thought.

First, there were those for whom defending the Empire was but an aspect of a grander naval strategy. The Royal Navy had responsibilities to the colonies, but it also existed to protect the United Kingdom from invasion, to guarantee the freedom of international trade for all nations, and to settle disputes (and thereby preserve the balance of power) across Europe. To this way of thinking, maintaining the 'command of the sea' had to remain chiefly if not solely the responsibility of the mother country; only then would it be possible to reconcile the competing and often conflicting demands upon Britain's naval forces. Second, there were those who wanted to see naval policy subordinated to imperial policy. To this way of thinking, Britain's imperial interests were fundamental to debates upon the size, composition and distribution of the navy. Developing the military resources of the Empire as a whole was understood to be of paramount necessity, partly because it would help to keep the sea lanes open and to deter foreign powers from aggression, but also because the achievement of a more united Empire was linked directly to the organisation of imperial defence. Leading exponents of this idea of a *Kriegsverein* (defensive union) included the NL and the IFDC, as well as a range of individual critics and commentators. Rejecting cut-and-dried schemes of federation, these imperial navalists espoused an essentially Whiggish view of empire development, looking towards a gradual, organic and evolutionary restructuring of Anglo-Dominion relations, primarily in the sphere of maritime defence. They were convinced that the defensive argument for closer unity was stronger than the economic one. George Parkin, for example, made no secret of his hostility to attempts to make preference the main item in the imperialist platform. Trade policies, he claimed, were inevitably divergent owing to the heterogenous nature of empire, whereas the necessity of open sea routes was an ongoing and permanent condition.[93] Similarly, Carlyon Bellairs believed the Unionist party to have made a vital error in 1903 by committing itself to a campaign claiming to be truly imperial but in practice proving 'purely sectional' in character. He wished to see an 'alternative system of preference' based upon transport rather than trade.[94]

92 Beeler, 'Steam, Strategy and Schurman', pp.40–5, and his book, *British Naval Policy in the Gladstone–Disraeli Era, 1866–80* (Stanford, CA, 1997), Chapter 1, 11.
93 G.R. Parkin, *Imperial Federation* (1892), Chapter 3.
94 C. Bellairs, *A New System of Preference* (1912), pp.2–5.

With some significant exceptions, imperial navalists espoused a different (and more limited) notion of the British state than that championed by Chamberlainites. Constructive imperialists did not accept that the cost of imperial defence could be met from existing resources, which were thought to be inelastic, nearing exhaustion and unable to support an adequate margin of naval supremacy.[95] Their solution was to increase indirect taxes – tariffs – to make good the shortfall. The Navy League took a different view. There was a strong strain of economic liberalism underpinning many of the policies it put forward, especially in relation to the funding of the Fleet. For many years the League argued that increases in the naval estimates could be financed by a more efficient use of existing resources. When real increases in expenditure were required, rather than resort to extra taxation, the League urged the Liberal government to meet the 'national emergency' by bringing in a new Naval Defence Act to be financed by public debt (in the form of a naval loan). The advantage of this proposal, it was claimed, was that it involved 'no violation of Free Trade'.[96] In this way, imperial navalists were to play an important role in defining and developing what might be called a doctrine of 'free trade imperialism'. This doctrine of 'free trade imperialism' was intended to be a coherent and credible alternative to the policy of preference.

In the next chapter on empire migration we shall turn our attention to a political campaign animated by both of these tendencies. The Royal Colonial Institute's Emigration Committee favoured an extension of state aid, but many of the individual societies it represented reacted suspiciously to proposals for increased government activity which might then encroach upon the voluntary sphere.

95 This was the position adopted by H.W. Wilson, who in 1908 resigned his editorship of the *Navy League Journal* after clashes with the rest of the executive over the fiscal question.
96 'The Need for a New Naval Defence Act', *NLJ* (August, 1908), p.250.

CHAPTER 6

Populating the Empire: Overseas Migration

BRITISH OVERSEAS MIGRATION IN THE LONG NINETEENTH CENTURY

Alongside mortality and fertility, migration is one of the three main demographic trends of the long nineteenth century.[1] At least fifty-two million migrants left Europe for overseas destinations between 1815 and 1930, a figure equivalent to approximately a quarter of Europe's natural population increase.[2] Britain led the way, supplying a staggering 10 million migrants or 23 per cent of the total. The sheer scale of overseas migration would suggest that it had a profound impact upon British society. It is estimated that about 4 per cent of the population of England and Wales emigrated in the 1880s, while in each successive year from 1910 to 1913 Scotland is thought to have lost over 1 per cent of its population through emigration. Indeed, there was net emigration from Britain in every decade from the 1860s to the 1930s, so that many families were caught up in the process in one way or another.[3]

The late-Victorian and Edwardian years witnessed three significant developments in migratory trends. The first was a marked increase in the total number migrating, as shown by figures for outward-bound passengers (see Table 3) – these figures provide the best proxy for overseas migration in Britain's case since migrants were not counted separately until 1912. Emigration increased substantially towards the end of the nineteenth century. From 1875 to 1880, approximately 797,000 outward-bound passengers left Britain; thirty years later (1905–10), the figure stood at 2.5 million.[4] The second development was a change in the destination of British migrants. Migration from Britain was a voluntary process. Most people travelling overseas did so as

1 D. Baines, 'Population, Migration and Regional Development, 1870–1939' in R. Floud and D. McCloskey (eds), *The Economic History of Britain since 1700. Vol. 2: 1860–1939* (1994), p.46.
2 D.Baines, *Emigration from Europe, 1861–1900* (Cambridge, 1991), pp.9–11.
3 F.M.L. Thompson (ed.), *The Cambridge Social History of Britain, 1750–1950. Vol. 2: People and Their Environment* (Cambridge, 1990), p.8.
4 C.J. Erickson, 'Who were the English and Scots Emigrants to the United States in the Late Nineteenth Century?', in D.V. Glass and R. Revelle (eds), *Population and Social Change* (1972), p.349.

Table 3   Outward movement from the British Isles, 1880–1925

	America	British North America	South Africa	Australasia	All other places
1880	166,570 (73%)	20,902 (9%)	9059 (4%)	24,184 (11%)	6,827 (3%)
1885	137,687 (66%)	19,838 (10%)	3,268 (1%)	39,395 (19%)	7,456 (4%)
1890	152,413 (70%)	22,520 (10%)	10,321 (5%)	21,179 (10%)	11,683 (5%)
1895	126,502 (68%)	16,622 (9%)	20,234 (11%)	10,567 (6%)	11,256 (6%)
1900	102,797 (61%)	18,443 (11%)	20,815 (12%)	14,922 (9%)	11,848 (7%)
1905	122,370 (47%)	82,437 (31%)	26,307 (10%)	15,139 (6%)	15,824 (6%)
1910	132,192 (33%)	156,990 (39%)	27,297 (7%)	45,701 (12%)	35,668 (9%)
1915	37,763 (36%)	19,434 (19%)	11,699 (11%)	14,907 (14%)	21,116 (20%)
1920	90,811 (26%)	134,079 (38%)	29,019 (8%)	49,357 (14%)	49,545 (14%)

Source: I. Ferenczi and W.F. Willcox, *International Migrations. Vol. I Statistics* (New York, 1929), pp.636–7. The country-based figures in brackets are percentages of total outward migration.

families or individuals, and made their own decision where to go. During the nineteenth century the majority of British migrants did not make the Empire their first choice. The United States provided the greatest attraction, mainly because opportunities for advancement appeared greater there than elsewhere. From 1861 to 1900 the number of migrants going to America is estimated at between 5 million and 7.5 million, compared to 1.1 million to Australasia and 0.8 million to Canada. After the turn of the century, however, the number of migrants travelling to Britain's colonies increased. Whereas in the 1890s, less than a third of migrants went to places within the Empire, from 1901 to 1910, nearly a half of migrants chose the 'white' Dominions as their new home. The peak period of migration to the Empire came in the years immediately prior to the First World War.[5] Canada accounted for a large slice of the cake. Of the 49,149 people arriving in the Dominion in 1901 only 11,810 were British; but in 1914, 142,622 British migrants entered Canada (compared to 107,530 from the United States). The third trend relates to the identity of British migrants. In the first half of the nineteenth century the vast majority of Britain's outflow of population was of a settler type: farmers and artisans left the country

5 J.A.R. Marriott, *Empire Settlement* (1927), pp.9, 67; G.F. Plant, *Overseas Settlement. Migration from the United Kingdom to the Dominions* (Oxford, 1951), p.174.

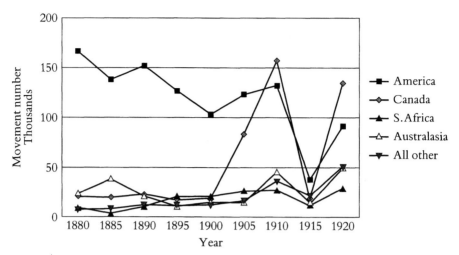

Figure 4   Outward movement from the British Isles, 1880–1925

intending the move to be permanent, and took their families with them.[6] From the mid-nineteenth century, and especially from the 1880s, emigrants were more likely to be drawn from urban areas, and to be unskilled, single and male. It appears that many of these young men left Britain either expecting to return, or subsequently decided to do so as the relative fortunes of the American and British economies oscillated over time. It would probably surprise most people to learn that the exodus of single males as a result of migration during the Edwardian era was more than double the number of British soldiers killed during the First World War.

THE BENEFITS OF EMPIRE MIGRATION

The Victorians regarded emigration as the most rewarding mode of expansion. This was because it created the conditions most favourable to 'progress': comparatively stable governments; legal systems which protected persons and property; and a demand for the products of British industry.[7] However, as already noted, many of the people leaving Britain at the end of the nineteenth century were not destined for the Empire but for America. This 'foreign' migration was criticised for sapping Britain's stamina and strength. Even when migration to the 'white' Dominions began to increase in the early 1900s, imperialists continued to insist 'there was a huge leeway to make good'.[8] Of

6 T.J. Hatton and J.G. Williamson, *The Age of Mass Migration. Causes and Economic Impact* (Oxford, 1998), p.11.
7 R. Robinson and J. Gallagher, *Africa and the Victorians. The Official Mind of Imperialism* (2nd edn, Basingstoke, 1981), p.8.
8 H.A. Gwynne, 'The Proper Distribution of the Population of the Empire', in J.L. Garvin (ed.), *Compatriots' Club Lectures*, First series (1905), p.211.

course, efforts to encourage a greater flow of migrants to the Empire were long-standing.[9] In the 1830s and 1840s, the philosophic radicals – in particular Edward Gibbon Wakefield – had championed a 'scientific' theory of colonisation, whereby the colonies were to soak up Britain's surplus population and to alleviate unemployment.[10] From the 1880s onwards, the issue of state-aided empire migration enjoyed an even higher political profile with the campaigning of the National Association for Promoting State Directed Emigration and Colonisation.[11] The impetus for the formation of this organised political lobby was partly a change in grass-roots thinking on the question of overseas migration. In the late-nineteenth and early-twentieth centuries many of the voluntary organisations which assisted people to settle overseas became more imperially-oriented. Chapter 2 situated the formation of Royal Colonial Institute's Emigration Committee in this broader social context.

At the heart of the political philosophy of the Emigration Committee lay the belief that migration had a key role to play in consolidating the Empire economically, defensively and socially. A steady stream of British migrants to the Dominions, it was argued, would help these states to exploit their natural resources more effectively, to improve their external security, and to maintain a predominantly British sentiment. Even so, some scholars have located the roots of the Edwardian emigration movement in Britain's own social and political structure.[12] They argue that at a time of intensifying labour unrest, unburdening the economy of the long-term under- and unemployed was one of the few safety valves available to the British ruling classes. On the face of it, this would seem a plausible motivation. By the 1880s there was a growing governmental concern with the problem of pauperisation and the ineffectiveness of urban philanthropy. However, there are real problems in presenting migration as a syphon for domestic poverty. That is not to say that empire migrationists did not argue that the state had a moral duty to relieve the social distress caused by rapid urban growth and downswings in the trade cycle. Yet they were equally aware of the need for their schemes to be acceptable to colonial opinion.[13] Because the Dominions were implacably opposed to Britain dumping its unwanted population upon them, it was essential not to approach the question of assisted migration purely from a British perspective. Moreover, the commitment of Edwardian imperialists was to a 'Greater Britain', which

9 S. Constantine, 'Empire Migration and Social Reform, 1880–1950', in C.G. Pooley and I.D. Whyte (eds), *Migrants, Emigrants and Immigrants. A Social History of Migration* (1991), pp.63, 67.
10 W. Thomas, *The Philosophic Radicals. Nine Studies in Theory and Practice, 1817–1841* (Oxford, 1979), pp.379–80.
11 H.L. Malchow, *Population Pressures: Emigration and Government in Late Nineteenth Century Britain*, (Berkeley, CA, 1979), Chapters 4–5.
12 K. Williams, ' "A Way Out of Our Troubles": The Politics of Empire Settlement, 1900–22', in S. Constantine (ed.), *Emigrants and Empire. British Settlement in the Dominions between the Wars* (Manchester, 1990), pp.23–4.
13 A.S. Thompson, 'Thinking Imperially? Imperial Pressure Groups and the Idea of Empire in Late-Victorian and Edwardian Britain', University of Oxford D. Phil (1994), pp.232–4, 237. Cited hereafter as *Thesis*.

meant that migrants had to be an asset rather than a liability to the societies receiving them.

Enthusiasts for empire migration saw military strength, physical health and rural life as mutually dependent. They regularly contrasted the high population density of Britain with the lack of population in the Dominions. As H.A. Gwynne put it, 'the vulnerability of the Empire' was 'in exact proportion to its lack of population'.[14] Gwynne believed unoccupied land to be a continual temptation to other powers, and argued that the Empire would be more capable of fending off aggressors if its population was more evenly distributed. Likewise Richard Jebb claimed that the additional twenty million people which Australia required to defend herself would never be found while emigration from Britain remained sporadic, individual and disorganised.[15] Jebb's sentiments were echoed by Richard Arthur, the president of Australia's Immigration League. In an enquiry into the problem of imperial demography printed in *The Empire Review*, Arthur noted how Australia's population remained fringed on its eastern and southern coasts, leaving the vast territory of the north virtually unpopulated. With the Russo-Japanese War, and the 'roar of guns around Port Arthur', he claimed, Australia's feeling of security had vanished and its inhabitants had 'awoken to the reality of things'. Japan was rapidly establishing itself as a Pacific power, while China was shaking off the sleep of centuries. As long as both territories were overfilled and periodically ravaged by famine, 'the great fertile tract' of northern Australia would be vulnerable to Asiatic expansion. Arthur concluded by recommending a 'white Australia' policy with immigration from Britain on a huge scale.[16]

In the social sphere, enthusiasm for empire migration stemmed from a belief that the Dominions would only evolve in Britain's image if migrants were redirected away from 'foreign' lands and towards the Empire. Probably the most striking analysis of the social benefits of migration came from the pen of the Tory-Radical historian and influential imperial publicist, J.A. Froude. Froude was a great writer of prose, with a talent for dramatic presentation and picturesque description. His most popular work, *Oceana or England and her Colonies*, was published in 1886 after a journey around the Australasian colonies the previous winter. The book fused a deeply-ingrained Protestantism with a more secular faith in the future of the British Empire. Froude felt that late-Victorian society was passing through a crisis of national existence as the physical, moral and spiritual state of people living in England's towns and cities steadily declined. He seized upon overseas migration as the answer to the problem, claiming that it was in the colonies, not in foreign lands, that the nation had the chance to renew itself: 'These islands are small, and are full to overflowing. In the colonies only can we safely multiply, and the people, I

14 Gywnne, 'The Proper Distribution', p.201.
15 Notes for the RCI Migration Committee (undated), *Jebb papers*, G32.
16 R. Arthur, 'Australia and the Empire', *ER* (November, 1906).

137

think, are awakening to know it.'[17] It was Froude's hope that a steady flow of Anglo-Saxon migrants would not only help to raise the colonies to the first rank among nations, but bind them ever closer to Britain. In the same year as *Oceana* was published, Froude joined the National Association for Promoting State Directed Emigration and became directly involved in the campaign for a comprehensive programme of colonisation.[18]

That Froude's legacy was vitally important to the Edwardian emigration movement is apparent from the continuing importance of the bucolic motivation for imperial settlement – the belief that rural life was healthier than urban life was very deep-rooted within British society before the First World War. It is also apparent from the reports which the Emigration Committee's leading members submitted to the Dominions Royal Commission. A recurring theme in these reports was the value of migration in maintaining a predominantly British population in the colonies.[19] The ethnic complexion of Canada and South Africa was of particular concern. In Canada, an increasingly assertive community of French-speaking Canadians, and an influx of migrants from across the border, presented a challenge to Britain's privileged position.[20] In South Africa, the hardening of Afrikaner national sentiment among the Boers of the Transvaal and Orange Free State presented a serious threat to Britain's position in the Cape and Natal. In their evidence to the DRC, the leading figures of the Emigration Committee highlighted the importance of migration in diffusing and sustaining a state of political feeling sympathetic to Britain in each of the self-governing Dominions. Gwynne was adamant on this point: 'the Empire is founded on race and . . . would cease to be if the large majority of its population in Great Britain and the Dominions ceased to be British. Cosmopolitanism in the British Isles and the Dominions would inevitably lead to the destruction of the Empire.'[21] Nor was this perspective peculiarly metropolitan. At the third day of the Imperial Press Conference, Sir Hugh Graham of the *Montreal Star* moved a resolution in regard to migration which stated that:

> It is nothing new to say that Canada is the keystone of the Imperial arch. If the keystone were to fall the arch would be in peril. The steadfastness of Canada in this position depends upon the sentiment of the majority of her people. Today that majority is overwhelmingly British . . . but the immigration of foreigners is threatening that majority.[22]

17 J.A. Froude, *Oceana or England and her Colonies* (1886), p.338.
18 J.W. Burrow, *A Liberal Descent. Victorian Historians and the English Past* (Cambridge, 1981), pp.231–85.
19 *Royal Commission on the Natural Resources, Trade and Legislation of Certain Portions of His Majesty's Dominions: Evidence and Appendices, Part I, Migration* (1912–23): 123, 138–9, 141–2, 148, 173. Cited hereafter as *Report from the Commissioners.*
20 Canadian hostility appears mainly to have been directed towards immigrants from central and Eastern Europe and China. See H. Palmer, *Patterns of Prejudice. A History of Nativism in Alberta* (Ontario, 1982), pp.17–24.
21 H.A. Gwynne, 'Profession of Faith' (unsigned and undated), *Gwynne papers*, dep. 22.
22 T.H. Hardman, *A Parliament of the Press. The First Imperial Press Conference, 1909* (1909), p.226.

VOLUNTARY EFFORT VERSUS STATE INVOLVEMENT

It is a commonplace that Victorian society was imbued with a Smilesian doctrine of self-help. By the end of the century, *Self-Help*, published in 1859, had clocked up a quarter of a million sales. It came to sum up an age of Victorian middle-class values: 'help from without is enfeebling', its author declared, 'but help from within invariably invigorates'.[23] The philosophy of *laissez-faire* individualism with which Samuel Smiles is now associated pulsed through the veins of the Victorian voluntary sector. Each of the societies affiliated to the Emigration Committee was inclined to think of its own work as being of the utmost importance, just as each resisted any suggestion of amalgamating with rival organisations or of surrendering some of its responsibilities to the state. Having said that, the majority of these societies received many more applications for help than they had the funds to support.[24] Thus they could not ignore the fact that without the injection of government capital, large-scale schemes of emigration to the Empire were very unlikely to emerge.

It was the task of the Emigration Committee to prevent unnecessary overlapping of the work of voluntary emigration societies, and to pave the way for closer collaboration between them and the state.[25] Its advantage as a representative body was that it was not itself actively engaged in the work of emigration, and could therefore avoid the charge of having a vested interest to promote or defend. From the outset, the EC was at pains to reassure voluntary emigration societies that in recommending the establishment of an official government body to redirect migrants within the Empire the intention was to facilitate the work of the voluntary sector, not to replace it with state-run machinery. For example, its deputation to the Prime Minister in May 1911 did not argue that emigration was work which the government itself should undertake. Rather, it recommended an officially-recognised central body to co-ordinate (and in some cases subsidise) the activities of voluntary emigration societies, to liaise with UK and colonial agencies concerned with emigration, and to speak with authority on broader aspects of emigration policy.[26]

Yet the government did not respond enthusiastically to these proposals. Demands for state-aided migration had previously been made in the 1870s and 1880s at a time when the Dominions were establishing emigration agencies in Britain. The demands were by and large ignored. An Emigration Information Office (EIO) was established within the Colonial Office in 1886, but it was an advisory body which operated on a shoestring budget and which refused to be drawn into a more active role. This chapter cannot examine in detail why the government did not get directly involved in overseas migration.[27] Commonly

---

23 S. Smiles, *Self-Help. With Illustrations of Character and Conduct* (1860), Chapter 1.
24 N.L. Tranter, *Population and Society, 1750–1940. Contrasts in Population Growth* (1985), p.132.
25 Thompson, *Thesis*, pp.229–31.
26 J.R. Boose (ed.), *The RCI Year Book* (1912), p.195.
27 For a fuller account, see Plant, *Oversea Settlement*, pp.45–54.

expressed reservations included: fears of state assistance undercutting work being carried out by the voluntary sector; the danger of appearing to favour one colony at the expense of others; the refusal to further subsidise the internal development of the colonies; the futility of overriding the laws of the free market; and the palpable failure of privately organised schemes of colonial emigration in the recent past. In fact, the belief that emigration was best left to private enterprise was common across Europe in this period. It was also shared on both sides of the party-political divide in Britain.

Neither did the upheaval and anguish of the South African War much affect the situation. To be sure, the poor health of working-class recruits for the army provoked a wide-ranging debate about racial decline and national efficiency. Yet after the war only female migrants were offered state assistance by the South African authorities (see below). Furthermore, the report of a departmental committee set up in 1906 under the chairmanship of Lord Tennyson was distinctly unfavourable to the grant of state aid to any scheme of colonial colonisation.[28] Thus when the question of Colonial Office representation at the Royal Colonial Institute's 1910 conference was raised, officials in the department, while feeling it necessary to attend, were determined not to be committed to a 'government emigration policy'. Sir Charles Lucas, present on the EIO's behalf, took no part in the discussions and did not vote on any of the conference's resolutions.[29] In the years prior to the First World War, the government's role remained regulatory. It was widely feared in Whitehall that overseas migration might undermine the industrial strength of Britain by syphoning off its reservoir of skilled labour and removing the most active and able elements of the population. This view was expressed forcefully at the early meetings of the DRC.[30]

The question of whether there was a surplus of persons available for emigration to the Empire was tackled head-on in a report which the Emigration Committee submitted to the DRC.[31] The report's main premise was that the large number of under- and unemployed people in Britain would make ideal colonists if only they could be helped to migrate before a long period of idleness had undermined their self-reliance and industry. Particular types of person (which the Dominions were known to favour) were singled out as being especially suitable for government support, such as farmers and agricultural labourers.[32] Hence the approach of the EC was to present empire migration as a policy which could be defended from both a national as well as imperial standpoint.

---

28 It recommended that grants-in-aid (for the purpose of emigration) be allocated to committees formed under the Unemployed Workmen's Act. These committees were to follow the EIO's advice as to where colonists should be sent. The actual work of emigration was to be carried out by societies approved by the EIO.
29 Colonial Office memorandum on the RCI's conference of emigration societies, April–June 1910, PRO CO 323/531–33.
30 *Report from the Commissioners* (1912), 155, 166, 190–4, 236.
31 Ibid., 296.
32 T.R. Reese, *The History of the Royal Commonwealth Society* (Oxford, 1968), pp.162–3.

MIGRANT PERSONALITY

For many years the history of European migration focused upon its causes. Only more recently have historians begun to explore the meaning of migration for those caught up in the process. Closer attention is now being paid to the 'personality' of migrants – their age, gender, occupation, and family situation. The following section examines in detail three of the social groups which empire migrationists targeted: single women, children and ex-servicemen.

In the late-eighteenth and early-nineteenth centuries, local authorities and central government used forced and assisted forms of migration as a penal policy and a pauper strategy. After the American revolution, 160,000 convicts were transported by magistrates to Australia (1788–1868), while over 25,000 paupers left Britain for Australia from 1834 to 1860.[33] Not surprisingly, colonial governments objected strenuously to such migrants. By the end of the century they had successfully evolved mechanisms for excluding the unwanted and prioritising the kind of immigrants they did want. The specific categories of migrants singled out for favoured treatment were: the small capitalist (experienced in farming, and thus likely to stay on the land);[34] agricultural labourers; single women (particularly those qualified for domestic service); and children (mostly those in state care). Inducements for such migrants took the form of cheap passenger schemes, grants of free land, agricultural improvement loans, and the so-called 'bonus' system for third parties recruiting settlers.[35] Thus the governments of the overseas Dominions had strong opinions as to what type of people made good colonists and were most easily integrated into the host society. In formulating schemes of overseas migration, Edwardian imperialists had to bear these preferences in mind. It was equally necessary for empire migrationists to distance themselves from a long-standing tendency to think of emigration simply as a solution to overcrowding and poverty in Britain.[36] The first and foremost aim of the Emigration Committee, therefore, was to help British and Dominion authorities to find common ground. To this end, the Committee corresponded widely and regularly with a whole range of official agencies involved with the migration process.[37] It also accepted that the final word in the selection of migrants had to rest with the colonies themselves.[38]

33 W.S. Shepperson, *British Emigration to North America: Projects and Opinions in the Early Victorian Period* (Oxford, 1957).
34 C. Kinloch-Cooke, 'Emigration and Colonisation', *ER* (May, 1905), pp.306–7.
35 Inducements were strongest in the case of Australia, where the length, expense and hazards of the journey required an elaborate official and commercial apparatus to attract and transport migrants. This included a network of migration agents, based in Britain and responsible for identifying and exploiting reservoirs of suitably skilled migrants. See E. Richards, 'Voices of British and Irish Migrants in Nineteenth-century Australia', in Pooley and Whyte (eds), *Migrants, Emigrants and Immigrants*, pp.19–20.
36 C. Kinloch-Cooke, 'Emigration and the Poor Law Report. A Conference Required', *ER* (August, 1909).
37 See the evidence collected in the *Emigration Letter Book* (1910–14).
38 The report of the RCI's conference held in May 1910 was circulated among Dominion prime ministers, agents-general, high commissioners, and leading colonial newspapers: Boose, *The RCI Year Book*, p.195.

(i) Single women

From the beginning of the nineteenth century emigration to the Empire had represented different things to different women.[39] For some working-class women it was an alternative to unemployment, destitution and even starvation. However, for another constituency – prostitutes arrested under the Contagious Diseases Act and confined to the notorious 'lock hospitals' – emigration was a penalty rather than a preference, something inflicted upon women by the state. This ambiguity was still present at the turn of the century. For some upper-middle-class women, emigration to the Dominions offered an escape from a 'steadily narrowing field of employment' and a 'rigid code of gentility' at home.[40] But for many other women life in the colonies simply reinforced long-established constructions of gender roles, whether as wives, mothers or domestic servants.[41]

Another category of women caught up in the migration process were those involved in selecting and assisting other women to settle overseas. Voluntary work did as much as any other profession to broaden the horizons of Victorian women.[42] Its attractions were several: an escape from boredom; a reflection of virtue; an opportunity to put organisational talents to good use; an expression of Christian faith; and even as a stepping stone to other careers. By the 1870s and 1880s, women's emigration societies had become an important part of the voluntary sector.[43] These societies were responsible for finding suitable migrants, supervising their voyages overseas, arranging for their reception and protection on arrival, and helping some of the more 'worthy' cases with repayable loans. They helped to make emigration a more respectable and less dangerous experience than it had been earlier in the century.[44] A leading organisation was the Female Middle Class Emigration Society, formed in 1861–62 to find occupations for educated middle-class women in the colonies, mainly as governesses.[45] The FMCES reappeared in 1884 as the British Women's Emigration Association, its interests having widened to include the recruiting and transfer of domestic servants. Rooted in Christian philanthropy and imperial patriotism, the BWEA and other similar bodies assisted approximately 20,000 women to migrate between 1884 and 1914.[46] The biggest single restriction

39 J. Trollope, *Britannia's Daughters. Women of the British Empire* (1983), esp. pp.32–3; J. Bush, ' "The Right Sort of Woman." Female Emigrators and Emigration to the British Empire, 1890–1910', *Women's History Review* (1994), p.386.
40 A.J. Hammerton, *Emigrant Gentlewomen. Genteel Poverty and Female Emigration, 1830–1914* (1979), pp.187–8.
41 Constantine, 'Empire migration and social reform', p.65.
42 F.K. Prochaska, *Women and Philanthropy in Nineteenth Century England* (Oxford, 1980), pp.223–7.
43 Plant, *Overseas Settlement*, p.48.
44 Hammerton, *Emigrant Gentlewomen*, Chapter 7.
45 C.E. Snow, 'Emigration from Great Britain', in W.F. Willcox (ed.), *International Migrations*, Vol. 2 (1931), p.257.
46 'Report of a Conference on the Voluntary Co-operation of Societies Concerned in the Emigration of Women', 13/1/1910, in *The Imperial Colonist* (official organ of BWEA and SACS) (February, 1910), pp.18–19.

upon their activities was not financial – it arose from the difficulty of finding 'appropriate' women to come forward in large enough numbers.[47]

The South African War marked a turning point in the history of female emigration. Some of the British women who worked as teachers and nurses in the Boer camps stayed on when the war ended.[48] Moreover, after the war the emigration of single women came to be regarded as a way of strengthening the loyalist community by reducing the risk of intermarriage with Afrikaners. It was widely feared that such intermarriage would lead to British immigrants (and their children) adopting the Dutch cause.[49] Another spin off from the war was a heightened women's involvement in imperial affairs. The contribution of women to political campaigns inspired by the Empire was touched upon in Chapter 2, which showed how long-established extra-parliamentary organisations (like the RCI) and newer groups (like the Victoria League) promoted women's activism at a time when the structures of formal party politics remained resistant to female participation. The Victoria League was actually formed during the war in 1901; it was closely linked to the Guild of Loyal Women in South Africa (the Cape temperance worker, Katie Stuart, being a founder member), received annual grants from the Rhodes trustees, and was primarily an educational body working among children, teachers and working-men's clubs.[50]

A key figure in the Edwardian emigration movement was Louisa Knightley. A devout Anglican, Knightley was interested in a wide range of social and political questions, especially those affecting the well-being of women. She was the first president of the Conservative and Unionist Women's Suffrage Society, edited the *Imperial Colonist* from 1902 (the official organ of the BWEA), and sat as a representative of the South African Colonisation Society on the RCI's Emigration Committee. The SACS was a splinter group of the BWEA,[51] which became nominally independent in 1903, and was one of the more prominent female imperialist associations of the Edwardian era. Counting around 1,000 members, the SACS helped approximately 4,000 people to emigrate to Southern and East Africa between 1901 and 1910. Knightley herself became involved in the SACS in the spring of 1901. As an experienced philanthropist, gifted organiser and imperial enthusiast, she was well-suited to emigration work. Before the South African War, the SACS had been a proponent of highly selective and heavily protected migration, and averse to widening the

47 C. Swaisland, *Servants and Gentlewomen to the Golden Land. The Emigration of Single Women from Britain to Southern Africa, 1820–1939* (Oxford, 1993), pp.5–7, 15, 27, 43.
48 Ibid., p.41.
49 B.L. Blakeley, 'Women and Imperialism: The CO and Female Emigration to South Africa, 1901–10', *Albion* (1981), pp.131, 148; J.J. Van-Helten and K. Williams, ' "The Crying Need of South Africa": The Emigration of British Single Women to the Transvaal, 1901–10', *JSAS* (1983), p.23.
50 J.M. Mackenzie, *Propaganda and Empire. The Manipulation of British Public Opinion, 1880–1960* (Manchester, 1986), pp.152–3; K. Schoeman, 'A Public Life: The Career of Katie Stuart (1862–1925)', unpublished paper, kindly supplied to the author by the South African Library, Cape Town.
51 It was initially known as the South African Expansion Committee.

field of choice beyond those qualified as teachers and nurses. But in 1901 the SACS suddenly found itself the focus of government attention. As part of a policy of post-war reconstruction, Chamberlain, Milner, Rhodes and other mining magnates, rapidly developed an interest in emigration. The SACS became the government's preferred agency for assisting female migrants. It received financial assistance in the form of a £1 capitation grant for each woman sent to the Women's Immigration Department of the Transvaal. In return, the SACS was required to prioritise the emigration of much sought-after domestic servants.[52] Between May 1901 and early 1904, 2,164 women were sent to South Africa under the auspices of this scheme (1,024 arrived in the Transvaal). Thereafter figures decreased to approximately 200 per year, and the programme was stopped in June 1907.[53] From that date onwards, the SACS had to bear the full cost of assisted emigration to South Africa, although it continued to enjoy the financial support of some of the Transvaal mineowners.[54]

In the spring of 1911, the Emigration Committee produced a controversial report on the emigration of women which criticised the treatment of female migrants in certain Australian states and called for greater subsidies for the work of the women's emigration societies.[55] The report emerged from a conference on women's emigration held in London the previous December, and from a series of meetings of an EC sub-committee (chaired by Knightley). In making the case for a programme of state-supported female migration, the report claimed that the British character of the colonies was being imperilled by a want of women to 'build up homes'.[56] It asserted that there was a superabundance of women in Britain and a deficiency of them in the Dominions. This imbalance was to be rectified by a scheme of assisted passages to Canada and Australia for young women aged from 20 to 35, and by an extension of the nomination system – already in force in Australia and New Zealand – to South Africa and Canada.

Much of the report was devoted to discussing the need for greater care to be taken in protecting female migrants after their arrival in the colonies. Moral surveillance was a long-standing concern of female emigrators.[57] The process of screening began with the interviewing of individuals applying to voluntary societies for assistance, and continued with the employment of matrons to accompany female migrants during their voyages overseas. However, the

52 The SACS also had to admit four representatives of the Colonial Office to its executive.
53 Blakeley, 'Women and Imperialism', p.140.
54 Van-Helten and Williams, ' "The Crying Need of South Africa" ', pp.26, 32–3.
55 'Report for the Standing Emigration Committee of the RCI on the Emigration of Women', 1/4/1911, *Emigration Letter Book* (1910–14). In the Canadian case, female migrants appear to have enjoyed higher standards of safety, largely because of an elaborate network of hostels established by women's emigration societies and the Salvation Army. See here the detailed report of W.B. Paton, an EIO official, who visited Canada on its behalf in June–July 1913: copy contained in PRO CO/323/618.
56 'Report of the Standing Committee on Emigration of the RCI – Memo on the Emigration of Women', in *The Imperial Colonist* (July, 1910), p.103.
57 Swaisland, *Servants and Gentlewomen*, pp.24–6; Bush, ' "The Right Sort of Woman" ', p.396.

safeguarding of female migrants after arrival fell mainly to the colonies. After reviewing the regulations affecting the supervision of female migrants in each of the Dominions, the EC's sub-committee singled out for severe criticism the absence of 'proper precautions' at Sydney (New South Wales) and in the northern ports of Queensland.[58] It claimed that female migrants arriving in these ports, and then travelling to the 'up-country' districts of Australia, were constantly subjected to 'moral dangers' – a shorthand either for sexual relations outside marriage or for prostitution. The evidence upon which the EC based its claims was partly from the press – the *Daily Mail* and *Morning Post* had published letters expressing concern about the care of female migrants – but also from correspondence with the officials of women's emigration societies. Many of the reports from these societies were very alarming in tone. For example, a mother superior of the Girls' Friendly Society forwarded the following missive from Queensland:

> I regret to say that there are stations in the bush where no girl's virtue is safe. . . . I can, without exaggeration, say that Queensland and especially Central Queensland, are far more glaringly and audaciously immoral than the Southern States. I have heard more horrors in my five years here than in fifteen years working in the Melbourne slums, and as a gaol visitor for the Church of England.[59]

Anxiety relating to the sexual morality of female migrants was not merely a matter of tender evangelical consciences. The physical dangers to which some women were exposed were actually very serious – abduction and organised prostitution was not unknown.[60] Moreover, for domestic servants found guilty of sexual or social 'deviance' in Canada, the threat of deportation loomed large.[61] In order to protect these women properly, the EC's report recommended a raft of reforms, mostly targeted at colonial authorities. These included: abolishing the system of bonuses for agents (which was thought to tempt them to take 'less respectable girls'); the need for good hostels or lodgings at every port of arrival to welcome female migrants and to accommodate them during intervals of service; a register of unsuitable employers of female domestic servants; and a system of voluntary inspection during the first year of service. Not surprisingly, Australian officials did not take kindly to being lectured at by British emigrationists. The RCI received a batch of strongly worded letters of complaint from the Agents-General for New South Wales, Western Australia and Tasmania, objecting to the way in which the EC had conducted its business, inviting it to inspect existing arrangements, and suggesting

58 *The Imperial Colonist* (July, 1910), p.103; 'Conference on the Inadequate Protection in the Ports of Australia', Imperial Institute, 16/11/1910, *The Imperial Colonist* (December, 1910), pp.199–203.
59 'Report of Meetings of Ladies Sub-Committee', Prince of Wales Hotel, 8/12/1910, *Emigration Letter Book* (1910–14).
60 Swaisland, *Servants and Gentlewomen*, p.24.
61 B. Roberts, *Whence They Came. Deportation from Canada, 1900–1935* (Ottawa, 1988), pp.56–7.

that the British government should shoulder more of the cost of the proposed reforms. It reacted apologetically by suspending the women's sub-committee while expressing regret at some of its procedures. Thus the consensus which enthusiasts for empire migration had been so eager to achieve proved elusive in the sphere of female migration.

(ii) Child migration

From 1900 to 1914 there were approximately 70–80,000 poor law children in residential care in Britain. There were many different forms of care.[62] Some children became general wards of workhouses. Others attended large district schools run by Poor Law Unions. Others were boarded-out, either in cottage homes (again run by Poor Law Unions), or by fostering them in ordinary homes, a practice which became more popular after 1870. Others were cared for in voluntary homes paid for by the Poor Law Unions. Finally, some children emigrated, often under the auspices of societies dealing with the problem of juvenile vagrancy. Before 1888 there was widespread prejudice against child migration in Britain, but in that year the Local Government Board prepared a new code of regulations, which resulted in a large number of pauper children being sent to Canada by various non-governmental organisations. Legislation introduced in 1891 (the Reformatory and Industrial Schools Act), replaced by the Children's Act of 1908, further extended state involvement, allowing for a small number of assisted passages under the authority of the Home Office. There were 3,097 such cases from 1900 to 1914.

The experience of overseas migration is widely understood to have been a very traumatic one for young children in state care. Child migrants were aged from five to seventeen. Some were orphans, but many had simply been neglected or abandoned by their parents, or had parents so poor as to be unable to provide for them.[63] It is understandable if historians have been critical of the policy. The children were torn from family, friends and familiar surroundings to be settled as apprentices in strange lands thousands of miles away from home. They were also placed in situations which were far from ideal. The absence of adequate inspections resulted in many children being deprived of a decent education, and being made to work extremely hard at a very early age.[64] Hendrick's account of the meaning of migration for children paints a particularly bleak picture of late-Victorian and Edwardian child-care policy. Among its failures are counted: the absence of mothering and family affection; poor clothing, food and hygiene; physical cruelty and sexual abuse; and the 'weary routine of institutional life'. In short, children are portrayed as the hapless victims of a policy of empire migration.[65]

62 H. Hendrick, *Child Welfare. England, 1872–1989* (1994), pp.74–6.
63 G. Wagner, *Children of the Empire* (1982), p.xi.
64 J. Parr, *Labouring Children. British Immigrant Apprentices to Canada 1869–1924* (1980), pp.11–12.
65 Hendrick, *Child Welfare*, p.77.

There is, however, another side to the story, even if it is rarely presented in today's media.[66] It should be remembered that the problem of orphaned and destitute children pressed very heavily upon the Edwardian state. By 1914, there were 44,000 juveniles maintained wholly by the public purse. Private philanthropy was also struggling to cope with the numbers of children arriving on its doorstep. Part of the attraction, then, of migrating children was that it was much cheaper than maintaining them in institutions in Britain. Yet it would be wrong to see child migration simply in fiscal terms. The voluntary sector persuaded itself that it was doing its best for these children;[67] only later did it come to realise the many dangers to which the children were exposed, and just how damaging an experience migration could be. Thus the motivations behind child migration were more complex than often allowed. Probably many proponents of the policy were fearful of a growth of juvenile delinquency. But this does not mean they were totally lacking in compassion. Most of those supporting the policy of child migration began with the assumption that children who continued to live in Britain's urban slums would become mentally, morally and physically weak, whereas in the colonies they had a chance of becoming sturdy and independent farmers. Migration was also believed to have the advantage of freeing children from years spent in state care – by the end of the nineteenth century, children's institutions were widely believed to have a corrupting effect upon the young. Emigration, then, was the lesser of two evils; not an ideal solution, but certainly preferable to the provision being made for such children at home. If this seems rather cold and calculating, it is worth recalling the mind-set of later-Victorian and Edwardian philanthropy. There was a hard edge to charity in this period when social workers were dispassionately passionate about improving the lot of the urban poor.

Moreover, what is easily overlooked in debates about juvenile policy at the end of the nineteenth century is that it was no longer being debated simply as a domestic problem. Edwardian migrationists regarded children as the bricks from which the edifice of empire was to be built – the future generation of colonists.[68] With their roots in British culture, they would help to preserve the mother country's special relationship with its self-governing Dominions; yet their young age would make them more adaptable to the new environment awaiting them. For example, Barnardo's, the leading society involved in child migration, became much more imperial in its operation towards the end of the century.[69] How far this was the product of imperial idealism or straightforward pragmatism is difficult to say. The policy of 'an ever open door' (no child was to be turned away), and a severe shortage of funds, certainly prompted the organisation to consider alternatives to the traditional matrix of institutional homes and boarding-out experiments. From 1882, partly with the help of the

66 For a recent example of negative press coverage, see 'Empire's Forgotten Children Strike Back', *The Times*, 18/5/1998, p.7.
67 Wagner, *Children of the Empire*, pp.xiii–xv; Tranter, *Population and Society*, p.136.
68 Parr, *Labouring Children*, pp.143–4.
69 Hendrick, *Child Welfare*, pp.79–82.

Liverpool MP and founder member of the NSPCC, Samuel Smith, Barnardo's started sending children to the colonies in larger numbers. It is estimated that almost a third of the 80,000 children who migrated to Canada between 1868 and 1925 left Britain under the auspices of the society.

Another well-known enthusiast for child migration was Kingsley Fairbridge.[70] Fairbridge was the first Rhodesian Rhodes scholar, who studied for a diploma in forestry at Exeter College, Oxford, from 1909 to 1911. From an early age he became convinced of the potential of child migration to further the consolidation of the British Empire. Initially, Fairbridge intended to settle British children in Southern Africa to counter the Boer influence, only to be told by the British South Africa Company that it could not support a scheme of child migration to Rhodesia. During his first year at Oxford, Fairbridge presented a paper to the University's Colonial Club in which he set out the case for migrating homeless or parentless children to farm training schools in the colonies. He went on to found the Child Emigration Society. The CES turned to Dominion governments to provide the necessary land for its schemes. The premier of Newfoundland, Sir Edward Morris, offered a grant of 50,000 acres, but no further financial assistance. Negotiations with the Western Australian government, however, led to an offer of 1,000 acres at a nominal rent, plus £6 per child passage money, and free education. Parties were to be limited to 30–60 children, and only boys were to be included. In return, the CES agreed to find the children and provide for their care in Western Australia. With money from the Rhodes trustees, Fairbridge set sail with a small group of poor East End children. He arrived in Western Australia in 1913, and settled at Pinjarra, a settlement fifty miles north of Perth. At first, Fairbridge's relations with the Western Australian Labour government proved difficult. It took six months for a school teacher to be appointed, and the government refused to erect a permanent school building on the Pinjarra site as it was not owned by the CES and not part of the original state land grant. It was not until after the First World War that the work of the CES really began to grow, when a grant of £15,000 was made by the Oversea Settlement Committee to restart work on a larger Fairbridge farm. The farm opened in 1921.

The idea of offering children practical training in the colonies appealed to other migrationists too. According to Kinloch-Cooke, there were two categories of children to whom the state stood *in loco parentis* – 'Home Office children' and 'Poor Law children'. Either category could be migrated without encroaching any further upon parental responsibilities, or putting more pressure upon the exchequer.[71] It was suggested that a start be made with the class of

---

70 The major study of Fairbridge's migration work is that by G. Sherington and C. Jeffery, *Fairbridge. Empire and Child Migration* (1998). But see also K.O. Fairbridge, *The Autobiography of Kingsley Fairbridge* (1927), esp. pp.173–4.
71 C. Kinloch-Cooke, 'A State-aided and State-directed Scheme of Emigration and Colonisation: Suggested Departmental Inquiry and Board of Emigration', *The Empire Review* (August, 1905), pp.2–6, and 'Emigration and Colonisation', p.309.

poor law children known as the 'orphans and deserted'. Boards of Guardians in Britain were to undertake to hand over these children at the age of ten. The children were then to be sifted and selected by representatives of colonial governments, and put in agricultural farms in the colonies until they reached the age of fourteen. Colonial governments would receive an agreed sum for bringing up and placing out these child migrants (for a maximum four-year period), and for the cost of inspecting them. In 1903–4, Kinloch-Cooke put these proposals to the Local Government Board and Clerks of the Metropolitan Boards of Guardians. But some Boards of Guardians objected on the ground that this category of juvenile included many of the 'best' children in state care, for whom it was easy to find situations at home.

The subject of child migration was raised at the RCI's conference in May 1910,[72] and the following year a sub-committee was formed to consider specifically poor law children.[73] It included Kingsley Fairbridge as well as representatives of Barnardo's, the Salvation Army and the Charity Organisation Society. After consulting the relevant societies, a draft report was produced and circulated among High Commissioners and Agents-General in the spring of 1912. The report suggested that the time was ripe 'to seriously consider the best system by which a steady flow of child emigration of both sexes could be ensured with regard to the future welfare of the Empire'.[74] Home and colonial authorities were to share responsibility for child migrants. The British government was to facilitate the emigration of suitable orphan, deserted and adopted children by paying a subsidy to voluntary societies for each child migrated; by encouraging the Local Government Board to make more use of its powers to emigrate children; by modifying existing statutory requirements relating to child consent; and by extending the powers of Poor Law Guardians over adopted children. Dominion governments were to undertake to improve the facilities for the reception, supervision and after-care of approved child migrants, to establish receiving homes and farm schools, and to co-operate with emigration societies in Britain by giving free or assisted passages to nominated children. At the age of eighteen, boys were to go into farming, girls into domestic service.

The response of Dominion governments to child migration schemes, including that of the RCI, was guarded. Aware of the public hostility to migrants becoming a burden on the taxpayer, the Immigration branch of the Interior department of Canada was constrained in what it could do.[75] Steps were taken to expand its supervisory role regarding the larger rescue homes, and to regularise the medical certificates which were required pre-embarkation. But proposals for training homes were not supported. Ellinor Close tried to start one

72 *The Imperial Colonist* (July, 1910), p.101.
73 J.R. Boose to Colonel Rawson, 22/1/1912, *Emigration Letter Book* (1910–14).
74 J.R. Boose to Colonel Rawson, 13/4/1912, and Boose to the Secretary of the Departmental Committee of Poor Law Boys, 10/6/1912, *Emigration Letter Book* (1910–14); 'Report of the Sub-Committee on Child Emigration', copy in *Emigration Migration Committee Minute Book*.
75 Parr, *Labouring Children*, p.149.

such home for child migrants at Nauwigewauk in New Brunswick. In 1912, the RCI's secretary reported that, after an eight-year trial period, the New Brunswick farm had reached the 'highest expectations'.[76] However, the Canadian Interior department decided that Close's scheme was too costly to be practical and the farm subsequently fell into disuse.[77] Meanwhile in Australia a 'Dreadnought' migration scheme was set up in 1911, whereby the money raised for an Australian battleship during the naval scare of 1909 was diverted to the training of British boys for Australian farms.[78] The Western Australian government was especially eager to encourage immigration from Britain, and used its own training farms to prepare children for agricultural life.[79] After the War, in response to the Empire Settlement Act of 1922, the New Zealand government and several Australian states instituted a system of apprenticeship whereby child migrants were placed with selected farmers who were subject to state supervision.

The British government was co-operative but cautious. The Imperial conferences of 1907 and 1911 had commended child migration, and the Colonial Office later endorsed the findings of an EIO official who, after visiting Canadian children's emigration homes, concluded that child emigration was 'the most economical and the most successful of all methods of emigration.'[80] In February 1912, the Emigration Committee's Secretary, James Boose, secured an interview with Sir James Davey, the official in charge of emigration work at the Local Government Board.[81] Partly in response to the lobbying of the State Children's Association, the Local Government Board had already declared emigration as 'one of the best means of providing satisfactorily for the orphans and deserted children under the care of Guardians'.[82] Davey asked the Emigration Committee to put its views on the question to a departmental committee on the employment of poor law boys. The Emigration Committee's representatives argued that the emigration of poor law children to the Dominions was the best way to provide for their future. Further contact with government followed in January/February 1913, when a deputation met with John Burns, President of the Local Government Board, and another with a group of poor law guardians gathered together for a national conference in London.[83] As a result of these meetings it became clear that there was no definite limit upon what government could spend on the emigration of poor law children. However, the EC also discovered that nothing could be spent upon the maintenance of these children

---

76 J.R. Boose to Colonel Rawson, 13/4/1912 and 4/4/1912, *Emigration Letter Book* (1910–14).

77 Parr, *Labouring Children*, p.145.

78 Sherington and Jeffery, *Fairbridge*, pp.29–30, 108.

79 Agent-General for Western Australia to J.R. Boose, *Emigration Letter Book* (1910–14).

80 Colonial Office memorandum on the report of Mr W.B. Paton regarding British emigration to Canada, August 1913, PRO CO 323/618.

81 J.R. Boose to Marlborough, 15/2/1912, and J.R. Boose to Davey, 27/2/1912, *Emigration Letter Book* (1910–14).

82 Parr, *Labouring Children*, p.144.

83 John Burns to J.R. Boose, 25/1/1912, and Boose to Sir William Chance, 24/1/1913, *Emigration Letter Book* (1910–14).

after they had left Britain, and that there were at least 411 Poor Law Unions not then sending children to the colonies.[84] Although each of these Unions subsequently received a circular stating the benefits of child migration, Boards of Guardians appear to have become increasingly sceptical about the merits of child migration from 1910–14. This was particularly true of northern England where socialist representation in municipal government was strong, and where Guardians felt children in the colonies to be poorly protected.[85] Yet despite this growing hostility, the enthusiasm of the voluntary sector for child migration did not diminish, and several new agencies entered this field of emigration work during the Edwardian era.

(iii) The migration of ex-servicemen

The South African War undermined confidence in British military efficiency and the organisation of imperial defence. In so doing, it pushed the question of army reform up the political agenda. Among the many proposals for improving the effectiveness of Britain's armed forces were those relating to the welfare of discharged soldiers.[86] To ease the return of ex-servicemen to civilian life, a number of imperial social reformers and philanthropists urged the benefits of subsidised migration to the Dominions. Milner led the way, but his policy of settling demobilised troops in South Africa after 1902 failed miserably. The inefficiency of the Transvaal's Land Settlement Department meant that fewer than 2,000 troops were attracted into official resettlement programmes.[87] Following Milner's departure from South Africa, lobbying for soldier settlement continued. This lobbying tended to be sporadic and ill-organised, though the work of the Imperial South Africa Association's land settlement committee and the Central Emigration Board did help to keep the subject alive.

The debate upon soldier settlement received a renewed impetus in 1909–10 with the formation of the Naval and Military Emigration League, the only British emigration society to deal exclusively with former military personnel.[88] The NMEL boasted Lord Roberts as its president. It tried to find jobs in the Dominions for ex-servicemen (especially those unemployed) and to advance (by way of a loan) the money necessary for their emigration. Men had to be of 'good character' and 'sound physique', and to display 'an aptitude for colonial life'. They also had to be unable to obtain permanent employment at home.[89] The NMEL's publicity played upon two themes. Most obviously, the emigration of ex-servicemen would help to improve the defence of the

84 J.R. Boose to W.A. Evans, 5/12/1913, *Emigration Letter Book* (1910–14).
85 Parr, *Labouring Children*, pp.144–5.
86 K. Fedorowich, 'The Migration of British Ex-servicemen to Canada and the Role of the Naval and Military Emigration League, 1899–1914', *Histoire Sociale–Social History* (1992), pp.75–80.
87 K. Fedorowich, 'Anglicization and the Politicisation of British Immigration to South Africa, 1899–1929', *JICH* (1991), p.223.
88 For a fuller discussion of the NMEL, see Fedorowich, 'The Migration of British Ex-servicemen', pp.87–99.
89 'Emigration for Ex-Service Men' (unsigned), *The Navy* (May, 1912), p.134.

Empire, but it would also assist military recruiting in Britain by assuring those who joined the armed forces of secure employment when they left. Although Colonial Office officials refused to assist actively emigration work, a network of support was built up among regimental associations at home and sympathetic individuals in the colonies. By the outbreak of the First World War the NMEL had assisted approximately 2,400 men, women and children to migrate. Canada was the favoured destination, partly because of its proximity, but also because the Canadian authorities took the greatest interest in assisting British veterans.

After August 1914, the NMEL's secretary, E.T. Scammell, joined other RCI members in urging the Colonial Secretary to initiate a joint scheme for settling ex-soldiers and sailors after the War on selected Dominion lands.[90] In fact, Scammell had spoken to the EC on this very matter in February 1914, and as a result a representative of the NMEL (Colonel Barnett) had been invited to attend its meetings. From these discussions an Empire Land Settlement Committee emerged, which despatched the adventure novelist, Henry Rider Haggard, to the Dominions to discuss possibilities and prospects. Thus by 1915 a major campaign was under way for the intervention of the British government in soldier resettlement. This campaign is discussed in greater detail in the next chapter.

TESTING THE SUITABILITY OF MIGRANTS

As early as 1886 Froude wrote of the colonies' need for immigrants 'of the right sort'. Private philanthropy likewise placed great importance upon the careful recruitment and selection of migrants.[91] For voluntary societies, the most popular method of testing the suitability of migrants was the 'home' or 'farm' colony.[92] The system of home or farm colonies was designed to rescue men from the poverty trap and to equip them as prospective colonists with the necessary agricultural skills. Victorian and Edwardian political society was inclined to view the problem of poverty as a vicious circle. A worker was dismissed from his trade; the weary search for alternative employment then began; the search continued day after day, week after week, as the man was sapped of his energy and spirit; the qualities of self-reliance and individual self-help finally destroyed, the man became unemployable. Empire migration was to be the virtuous spiral whereby such a man was lifted out of the hopelessness of urban metropolitan life and provided with a fresh start in one of Britain's colonies.

Farm or home colonies had first begun to attract public attention in the 1880s.[93] Experiments organised by the Salvation Army, Church Army, Christian

90 E.T. Scammell's speech at the RCI's May 1910 conference was reported in *The Imperial Colonist* (July, 1910), p.103.
91 Plant, *Overseas Settlement*, p.50.
92 Minutes of the Emigration Committee, 18/4/1910, 20/10/1910 and 25/10/1910.
93 J. Marsh, *Back to the Land. The Pastoral Impulse in England, from 1880 to 1914* (1982), Chapter 8.

Social Service Union, and the Home Colonisation Society, generated a great deal of interest in these establishments as a way of reducing unemployment and preparing men for emigration. The Central Unemployed Body for London had gone so far as to recommend the system for all would-be emigrants, but the Local Government Board refused to sanction the necessary expenditure either from the rates or a parliamentary grant.[94] Two figures associated with the Emigration Committee had first-hand knowledge of the farm colony system. Walter Hazell (of the Self-Help Emigration Society) had set up such a colony under the auspices of the Salvation Army at Hadleigh in Essex, inspired by General Booth's celebrated book *Darkest England and the Way Out*. Men for whom the local labour bureau could not find work were sent to this 3,000-acre farm and required to observe its disciplinary codes and perform the tasks of work imposed. Many politicians and social reformers spoke positively about the experiment as an example of what could be achieved in rehabilitating the unemployed and saving them from the evils of drink and other urban vices. The colony's superintendent was D.C. Lamb, a member of the EC, who had travelled to Canada in 1901 in connection with the work of the Salvation Army's emigration department. Lamb was a strong advocate of the extension of the farm colony system.[95] He believed that the existing laws of vagrancy lacked a reformative element and argued that if the current rise in vagrancy was to be halted, the state must equip itself with the powers necessary to detain 'unemployables' and compel them to work. The Hadleigh colony was later moved to a larger farm at Great Hundridge near Chesham. Walter Hazell's memoir candidly records its 'failures' as well as 'successes' – one man showed his gratitude by setting fire to the farm's buildings! He estimated, however, that nearly 50 per cent of those attending Great Hundridge had emigrated to the Empire.[96]

The founder of the Central Emigration Board, Clement Kinloch-Cooke, was another powerful proponent of the farm colony system.[97] Men could not be expected to follow an agricultural life in the colonies, he argued, without some recent form of training in Britain. Although a significant number of men were being sent to work on farm colonies, he regretted that it was seldom with a view to emigration.[98] According to Kinloch-Cooke, the day was past when a successful 'back to the land' policy could be pursued in Britain. The temptations of town life were such that the majority of men soon gave up agriculture and returned to urban centres to swell the ranks of the unemployed.

94 J. Harris, *Unemployment and Politics: A Study in English Social Policy, 1886–1914* (Oxford, 1972), pp.186–7.
95 'Land Colonies', a report to General Booth (February, 1904), reprinted in W. Leal, *D.C. Lamb. A Memoir* (1912), pp.24–33.
96 W. Hazell, *The Australasian Colonies* (1887), pp.23–4.
97 Kinloch-Cooke, 'A State-aided and State-directed Scheme of Emigration and Colonisation', pp.7–8.
98 The poor law guardians from Poplar in East London had established a farm colony at Laindon in Essex in 1904, but this institution was not transitional – it aimed to get families 'back to the land' in Britain.

The idea of smallholdings near towns was likewise impractical – most of the best plots were already cultivated by market gardeners or by people of some means. A recent study of rural resettlement supports Kinloch-Cooke's analysis, showing how the high price of land hindered all attempts to create more smallholdings.[99] It is not surprising, then, that the prospects for land settlement in the Dominions were considered by emigrationists to be much better than those at home. Moreover, the colonies themselves preferred migrants intending to work on the land rather than in the towns. In industry, teaching and clerical occupations, the demand for labour was restricted, and in all of these spheres trade unionists offered strong opposition to migrant labour. As agricultural labourers, migrants had a far greater chance of obtaining work.

CONCLUSION

The poverty and degradation of urban life in later-Victorian and Edwardian Britain was both visible and potentially dangerous. It would be naive, therefore, to think that the spectre of labour demonstrations and industrial strikes did not hang over the Edwardian emigration movement. However, to describe emigration simply as a safety-valve which protected Britain from the serious social and political dislocations which affected parts of the European continent during these years would be seriously wide of the mark. In fact, many of those migrating from Britain were not from the poorest classes, skilled workers being just as likely to migrate as the unemployed.[100] More importantly, the policy of empire migration was never projected purely as a strategy for coping with domestic poverty. To be sure, the men and women discussed in this chapter were all deeply involved in private philanthropy. Yet they were equally concerned about the development and consolidation of the Empire – indeed, they considered the two to be closely linked. Writing about unemployment, Kinloch-Cooke declared:

> It is not on the United Kingdom alone that the future of the British race depends; it is on the development and consolidation of the Empire. Accordingly it is folly to expect that everyone who is born a Britisher must necessarily find work in the home-land; to discourage emigration to the British colonies . . . is against the policy of Empire, detrimental to our progress as a nation and fatal to the most effective solution of the unemployment problem.[101]

Migration was advocated by imperialists precisely because of its capacity to transform the Empire into a stronger, stabler and more cohesive unit. It was also felt to be the most practical policy of 'federation'. While politicians continued to argue about the impact of a preferential tariff, a properly organised scheme of overseas settlement appeared unlikely to increase the cost of living.

99 Marsh, *Back to the Land*, pp.133–5.
100 Erickson, 'Who were the English and Scots Emigrants?', pp.363, 371.
101 C. Kinloch-Cooke, 'Unemployment: Causes and Remedies', *ER* (February, 1909), p.18.

For these reasons, migration became an important strand of imperial political activity during the late-nineteenth and early-twentieth centuries. In the years after the South African War, a number of imperialist associations began to make the issue of overseas migration a part of their political platform. After 1910, the campaign for state-supported empire migration was put upon a more organised footing, largely through the efforts of the RCI. In drawing together the different agencies which were involved in this sphere of social policy, the RCI's Standing Committee on Emigration marked a qualitative advance upon previous lobbying for empire migration. It was a well-organised and sustained agitation, which represented a substantial body of informed opinion, articulated its ideas forcefully, put forward specific policy suggestions, and prepared the ground for a shift in official policy between 1914 and 1918.

Where, then, did the movement for state-supported empire migration fit into the overall framework of imperial political activity? Did empire migrationists possess a coherent doctrine of the state and its responsibilities in relation to restructuring the Empire? A central theme in recent British historiography has been the relationship between the state and civil society. While the example of imperial political economy (Chapter 4) points to imperialists as state-builders, and the example of naval defence (Chapter 5) points to imperialists as supporters of a small government, the arguments explored in the present chapter suggest yet another conception of the state. As we have seen, the empire migration movement harnessed the energies and expertise of the voluntary sector while at the same time lobbying for an extension of government activity. The state and the voluntary sector were to work in unison. If the voluntary sector was in itself incapable of securing a steady stream of British migrants for the colonies, there were also genuine doubts about the state's capacity to take over the voluntary sector's work. Thus while the constructive imperialism of tariff reformers mirrored the *etatist* regimes of Britain's continental neighbours, and the free trade imperialism of navalists aimed to contain the sphere of state activity, many of the leading figures associated with the campaign for empire migration occupied an intermediate position. They allocated the state a greater role in reorganising the Empire, but argued that this role was to galvanise private effort and individual initiative, not to erect large bureaucratic structures.

The ideology of empire migration can best be characterised as a synthesis of individualism and collectivism. The British state was to continue to function as 'a great delegator',[102] and power was to be devolved to a range of non-official bodies. With the benefit of government recognition and state subsidy, these bodies would then be able to expand their operations and generally improve the efficiency of their work. In this way, private philanthropy and state welfare would be yoked together in a state-sponsored and supervised programme of empire migration. This combination of state and voluntary activity was quite common in late-Victorian and Edwardian Britain. As recently

102 M. Daunton, 'Payment and Participation: Welfare and State-formation in Britain 1900–51', *P&P* (1996), pp.170–2.

recognised, there was a pragmatic strain to the politics of this period, a pragmatism which held the ring between the individual and the state. Before 1914, a localised and amateur voluntary sector continued to function alongside a rational, centralised bureaucracy;[103] certainly, there was no wholesale movement to collectivism.[104] Indeed, the DRC proved sympathetic towards the programme put forward by the migration lobby precisely because it was based upon a belief in the complementary rather than competing roles of the voluntary sector and the state. Moreover, the Emigration Committee's proposals had the added advantage of striking a delicate but necessary balance between 'domestic', 'colonial' and wider 'imperial' needs. Put forward as a sensible solution to the major social and economic problems Britain was facing, empire migration was also shown to be of great importance to the future stability, security and prosperity of the Empire.

103 For an example of the links forged between the state and the voluntary sector, see Brian Harrison's account of the RSPCA in *Peaceable Kingdom: Stability and Change in Modern Britain* (Oxford, 1982), pp.83–4, 108–9.
104 J. Harris, 'Society and the State in Twentieth Century Britain', in Thompson (ed.), *The Cambridge Social History of Britain*, pp.83–4, 108–9.

CHAPTER 7

The First World War and its Imperial Aftermath

Britain did not take up arms in August 1914 simply to safeguard its security in Western Europe. To be sure, many of the First World War's most famous battles took place in France and Belgium. Yet fighting also took place in German Togoland, the Cameroons, South West and East Africa, while Turkey's entry into the War on the side of the Central Powers added a Middle Eastern dimension to the conflict. An Austro-German victory was thus recognised to be a threat to the whole of the British Empire, not just to Britain's survival as an independent island nation. Furthermore, the entire British Empire went to war against Germany in 1914. The extent to which Britain was able to draw on the resources of its colonies is evident from the rapid mobilisation of their troops (see Table 4 below). Within a matter of months, 30,000 Canadians had been recruited, trained and sent to Western Europe, and shortly thereafter a combined Australian and New Zealand force arrived in Egypt, ready for the ill-fated attack on the Turks at Gallipoli in April 1915. Twenty-two per cent of Britain's male population served overseas in its army; the figure for Canada and Australia is 14 per cent, and for New Zealand almost 20 per cent. Neither should South Africa's contribution to the War effort be minimised. As well as clearing the Germans out of South-west Africa, some 76,000 South Africans fought outside the Dominion in Egypt, East Africa and France.

Unlike the South African War, when the War Office rejected Curzon's offer of Indian troops,[1] it proved impossible to keep the First World War white. The British Expeditionary Force's first reinforcements came from India, and from 1914 to 1916 Punjabi Muslims, Sikhs and Gurkhas were to fight and die in many of the major battles of the Western Front. Indigenous troops were also recruited elsewhere in the Empire. Something in the region of 50,000 Africans were mobilised to combat von Lettow-Vorbeck's legendary force

---

1 Earl of Ronaldshay, *The Life of Lord Curzon* (1928), pp.68–9.

Table 4 The contribution of colonial troops to the war effort, 1914–18

	Nos recruited	Nos serving overseas	Nos killed
Canada	628,964	458,218	56,639
Australia	412,953	331,814	59,330
New Zealand	128,525	112,223	16,711
South Africa	136,070	76,184	7,121
India	683,149[a]	1,096,013[b]	65,056

[a] The total strength of the Indian army on the eve of the War was 155,423 men; 414,493 non-combatants were also recruited from 1914 to 1918.
[b] The figure is for Indian soldiers only; 285,037 British soldiers were also despatched overseas from India.
Sources: C.E.Carrington, 'The Empire at War, 1914–18', in E. Benians (ed.), *The Cambridge History of the British Empire*, Vol. 3 (Cambridge, 1959), pp.641–2; India's Contribution to the Great War (Calcutta: Government of India, 1923) quoted in D. Omissi, *Indian Voices of the Great War: Soldiers' Letters, 1914–18* (Basingstoke, 1999), p.514; and D.C. Ellinwood and S.D. Pradhan (eds), *The Indian Army and the First World War* (Manohar, 1978), pp.54–5.

in East Africa, and many more were conscripted as carriers.[2] Similarly, New Zealand Maoris, prevented from despatching a contingent to South Africa in 1899, were used in 1914 for garrison duties and subsequently for armed combat.[3] This readiness of Britain's colonies to rally to its side had important implications for public perceptions of the Empire.[4] Previously, imperial unity and solidarity had largely been conceived in terms of the 'white' colonies. But from 1914–18 the machinery of wartime propaganda projected images of a multi-racial empire utterly united in a common crusade against Prussian militarism.[5] We need, therefore, to consider carefully the effect of wartime propaganda upon the imperial consciousness of the British public.

In the War's early stages, propaganda was discreet, selective and aimed mainly at neutral and allied countries. The organisation responsible for its production was the secretive War Propaganda Bureau, set up in August 1914, and better known by the name of its headquarters, Wellington House.[6] In 1917, Wellington House was upgraded into a Department of Information, led by John Buchan, the popular adventure novelist and acolyte of Milner. Propaganda organisation was overhauled again in February–March 1918 when the Department was turned into a Ministry, directed by Lord Beaverbrook. It was intended that this new Ministry would bring all official propaganda activity within the control of a single institution. The success of Beaverbrook's

2 B. Waites, 'Peoples of the Underdeveloped World', in H. Cecil and P. Liddle (eds), *Facing Armageddon. The First World War Experienced* (1996), pp.607–8.
3 W.H. Oliver and B.R. Williams (eds), *The Oxford History of New Zealand* (Oxford, 1981), p.297.
4 W.J. Reader, *At Duty's Call. A Study in Obsolete Patriotism* (Manchester, 1988), pp.38–9.
5 M.L. Sanders and P.M. Taylor, *British Propaganda during the First World War, 1914–18* (1982), pp.50, 152.
6 M.L. Sanders, 'Wellington House and British Propaganda', *HJ* (1975), pp.119–43.

Ministry rested partly with its exploitation of the power of visual imagery. From very early on in the War there was a move away from purely literary efforts as it was discovered that photography and film fired the public imagination in a way which the printed word could not.[7] Official photography was used in illustrated magazines, pamphlets and official photographs sold directly to the public. A favoured technique was the shot of troops on the march. For example, when reporting fighting in the Dardanelles, pictures of the Anzacs published by British newspapers conveyed very powerfully the contribution made by Australian and New Zealand troops to the campaign.

Although cinema attracted little attention from politicians prior to the War, by 1917 its importance as a tool of propaganda was not in doubt. As Minister of Information, Beaverbrook greatly accelerated the expansion of film propaganda. 'With Indian troops at the Front, Part I' was the first official film, released in January 1916; its sequel was premièred the same year.[8] The majority of these films have disappeared and so our knowledge of their content is sketchy. But a number of films had an imperial motif: 'The Building of the British Empire' (1917) contained historical information on the acquisition of the colonies; 'The World's Greatest Story' stressed the War's significance in solidifying the Empire; and 'The Life of Lord Kitchener' (1918) reconstructed the general's career in Egypt, South Africa and India, with the aim of emphasising the military strength of the Empire. Historians of wartime propaganda testify to the popularity of the major films released between August 1916 and June 1917. In 1918, cinemotor tours expanded the audience still further. Lorries equipped with generators and projectors travelled the country. Wales was first in February 1918, and such was the success of the tour that much larger excursions were arranged in April–May and September–October, when 140 constituencies were covered by thirty vehicles. Up to 20,000 people could see a cinemotor film at any one time, and the estimated weekly attendance was in the region of 160,000 people.[9]

If the written word was not a particularly powerful tool of wartime propaganda, the spoken word most definitely was. In 1915, an imperial studies campaign was organised by the Royal Colonial Institute. It recruited many well-known journalists and academics to travel around the country to preach the superiority of the British concept of empire over that of Germany, and to draw attention to the contributions of the colonies to the war effort.[10] Of even greater importance in publicising the Empire were the speeches of Dominion war leaders. The Australian Prime Minister, Billy Hughes, led the way here, visiting the major industrial centres of England in 1916 to argue for a more

7 J. Carmichael, *First World War Photographers* (1989), pp.16–21; N. Reeves, *Official British Propaganda during the First World War* (1986), pp.1–7.

8 Reeves, *Official British Propaganda*, pp.147, 150.

9 A twenty-five foot screen was mounted at a height of 100 feet from the lorry. Ibid., p.226.

10 P. Greenlee, 'Imperial Studies and the Unity of Empire', *JICH* (1979), pp.328–33; R. Aldrich, 'Imperialism in the Study and Teaching of History', in J.A. Mangan (ed.), *'Benefits Bestowed': Education and British Imperialism* (1988), pp.27–9.

vigorous war policy.[11] Hughes's speeches were likened by Lloyd George to shells which consistently hit their target and had a 'detonating quality of the highest order'.[12] An indication of his popularity is provided by the sales figures for a selection of his speeches – over 34,000 copies were sold to the British public. Patriotic speeches aimed at lifting Britain's sagging morale were also delivered with great gusto by Joseph Ward and William Massey – coalition leaders in New Zealand from 1915 – and by Robert Borden, the Prime Minister of Canada. But it was Jan Smuts, the Boer 'poacher' recently turned imperial 'gamekeeper', who had the biggest impact. After helping to conquer South-West Africa from the Germans, Smuts joined Lloyd George's War Cabinet in 1917. He rapidly became something of a celebrity in Britain. Municipal councils, universities and other public bodies showered distinctions upon him. Smuts, in turn, championed the cause of British imperialism. 'The British Empire', he was apt to declare, 'is not founded on might or force, but on moral principles – on principles of freedom, equality and equity. . . . Our opponent, the German Empire, has never learnt that lesson yet in her short history.'[13] Coming from a Boer general who in 1899–1902 had 'fought against British imperialism and everything it then stood for',[14] we should not underestimate the arresting effect of these words on British audiences. Indeed Smuts's speeches often played upon this apparent paradox:

> The cause I fought for fifteen years ago is the cause for which I am fighting today. I fought for liberty and freedom then, and I am fighting for them today. You are a large-hearted people, and I am sure you will bear with me if I express the view that fifteen years ago you were wrong. For a brief moment in your national history you got off the track and you came to grips with a small people. . . . You returned to wiser counsels in handing back to us the liberty which we had thought would be jeopardised under the British flag. You made us free. . . . As the result of the policy you adopted after the Boer War, a small nation that fought against you not so many years ago is today fighting in the common cause with you.[15]

Yet if Smuts joined the British Establishment during the War it was very much on his own terms. His speeches were to expose the British public to the Dominion (or at least, South African) view of imperial development. For example, in 1917 Smuts visited the South Wales coalfields at the War Cabinet's request. Industrial relations in the region had begun to deteriorate as early as July 1915 during a ten days' stoppage. The following year, Welsh miners spoke out so strongly against conscription that the (national) Miners

11 L.F. Fitzhardinge, *The Little Digger, 1914–52. William Morris Hughes. A Political Biography*, Vol. II (1979), pp.73–94.
12 D. Lloyd George, *War Memoirs*, Vol. I (1938), p.1046.
13 S.G. Millin, *General Smuts. The Second Volume* (1936), p.13.
14 I. Smith, 'Jan Smuts and the South African War', paper given to the Unisa Library Conference, 'Rethinking the South African War, 1899–1902', 3–5 August 1998.
15 Millin, *General Smuts*, p.14.

Federation was almost persuaded to oppose it.[16] The disaffection in 1917 resulted from a so-called 'combing-out' policy whereby the government turned to the mines for military recruitment. This policy provoked a bitter dispute among South Wales miners. Thus Smuts was sent to South Wales to avert a strike. Speaking at Tonypandy, he came face to face with thousands of angry miners. Folklore has it that they were won over by being challenged to prove their singing prowess.[17] After an emotional rendition of 'The Land of My Fathers' all was apparently forgiven. Press coverage of the episode suggests a different story.[18] Prior to Smuts's arrival the ground had been carefully prepared. About a quarter of a million reprints of his speeches were distributed, his portrait was displayed in local shops, and articles describing his war achievements were published in the local press.[19] Moreover, in facing the Welsh miners Smuts had to draw deeply upon his rhetorical skills. His strategy was to appeal to their pride and patriotism, to stress their affinity with the Boers as one of the world's 'small peoples', and to offer a vision of the United Kingdom and the Empire based upon the recognition of 'national ideals'. In this way, Smuts was able to present the War as a 'great moral crusade' in which Wales and South Africa had a special stake. Soon after his departure a strike ballot was held – the vast majority of miners accepted the government's decision and returned to work. In a fit of hyperbole, *The Times* hailed the results as the most remarkable demonstration of working-class patriotism during the War.[20]

THE EMPIRE IN THE AFTERMATH OF THE WAR

By 1919, the British Empire appeared to have defied Germany's prediction that it would fall apart under the strains of a world war. Indeed, the Empire emerged from the Paris Peace Conference not only intact but greatly extended, with the establishment of the League of Nations mandates ushering in a new phase of expansion. Yet all was not a bed of roses for British imperial policy-makers after the War. At home, reductions in public expenditure led to severe problems in military manpower, so that post-war demands on the British army came far to exceed its actual capabilities.[21] Further afield, the rise of violent anti-colonial movements in Ireland, Egypt and India constituted a new challenge to the imperial relationship in the dependent empire, while the emergence of a more assertive form of Dominion nationalism increased the pressure for a redefinition of Britain's relationship with these regions. We now need to explore the implications of these developments for the domestic politics of imperialism during and after the War.

16 K.O. Morgan, *Rebirth of a Nation: Wales 1880–1980* (Oxford, 1981), pp.173–5.
17 The source for this story seems to be a local official. See W.K. Hancock, *Smuts. The Sanguine Years, 1870–1919* (Cambridge, 1962), pp.455–6.
18 See the reports of the correspondent of *The Times* 29/10/1917, p.9, and 30/10/1917, p.4.
19 W.K. Hancock and J. Van der Poel (eds), *Selections from the Smuts Papers*, Vol. III (Cambridge, 1966) pp.566–7.
20 *The Times* 12/11/1917, p.8.
21 K. Jeffrey, *The British Army and the Crisis of Empire, 1918–22* (Manchester, 1984).

Responses to expansionist imperialism in the Middle East

With the collapse of the Ottoman empire, the Paris Peace Conference offered the opportunity for a 'new partition of the world' which Britain was not slow to seize.[22] Palestine, Mesopotamia (Iraq), Syria and Persia (Iran) all fell under its sway, with well-worn platitudes regarding the safety of the Raj yet again providing the pretext for territorial expansion. At first sight, then, it would seem that Britain's pre-war preference for consolidation over enlargement had been abandoned, as a new phase of empire-building enveloped the Middle East. However, the British public had little appetite for further colonial involvement after 1919. Rather, as Keith Jeffrey argues, the First World War resulted in Britain gaining an empire which it could not – and did not wish – to afford.[23]

When in 1920–21 communal riots broke out in Jerusalem, and a serious anti-British uprising erupted in Mesopotamia, it was the army's responsibility to re-establish control. Yet so strong was public pressure upon the Treasury for a reduction in the cost of the armed services, and such was the depth of public feeling against conscription, that the War Office struggled to meet its new military obligations in the Middle East.[24] As the Director of Military Operations had later to confess, 'we ran things too fine and a great disaster was only narrowly avoided'.[25] Neither could Britain rely upon that traditional 'imperial fire-brigade', the Indian army, to put down uprisings in the region. More than ever, the Indian army was needed for domestic use. With politicians falling over each other to reduce troop levels, the Treasury bent on radical economies and Trade Unions demanding more spending on social services, Britain's new Middle Eastern empire was rapidly down-sized. In December 1920, the decision was taken to evacuate troops from Persia and in August 1921, Britain opted for indirect rule in Mesopotamia by installing a friendly Arab ruler, Prince Faysal ibn Husayn, as king, rather than bankroll an expensive military regime or an elaborate civilian administration. Clinging on to territory in the Middle East by direct methods of rule would have meant either a redistribution of Britain's armed forces or an increase in military spending. The former would have left too few troops to police Ireland, Egypt and India, while the latter would have met with strong domestic opposition from Labour MPs and from pressure groups like the Anti-Waste League. Neither was to happen. A rapid retreat from the dizzy heights of 'war imperialism' safeguarded Britain's position in its old empire, and removed its League of Nations' mandates from the arena of political controversy. Thus the first major change to the British imperial system which was a consequence of the

---

22 J. Gallagher, *Decline, Revival and Fall of the British Empire. The Ford Lectures and Other Essays*, edited by Anil Seal (Cambridge, 1982), p.87.
23 Jeffrey, *The British Army and the Crisis of Empire*, pp.159–60.
24 D. Silverfarb, *Britain's Informal Empire in the Middle East. A Case Study of Iraq, 1929–41* (Oxford, 1986), pp.7–8.
25 Sir Percy Radcliffe quoted in K. Jeffrey (ed.), *The Military Correspondence of Field Marshall Sir Henry Wilson 1918–22* (1985), p.144.

War did not give rise to any new or powerful strand of imperial politics. If anything, the public reaction to Britain's involvement in the Middle East was rather muted.

Diehardism: attitudes towards colonial nationalism in Ireland, Egypt and India

The First World War provided a major stimulus to the forces of colonial nationalism in Britain's existing Empire. Open insurrection in Ireland, Gandhian non-co-operation, and nationalist unrest in Egypt emerged simultaneously to test Britain's power and influence in these regions. Britain responded to this 'general crisis' of empire[26] by trying to place its paramountcy on a firmer footing, either by identifying and encouraging new collaborators, or by shoring up alliances with old ones. For example, in India, the Montagu-Chelmsford reforms (1919), while not aiming at a systematic transfer of power, did extend Indian involvement in provincial administration under a new system of dyarchy. In Ireland, a treaty was signed (1921) which effectively conceded independence to the South by stretching the language of 'dominion status' to the point where it ceased to have any real meaning beyond the swearing of oaths of allegiance to the British Crown and the unwelcome presence of a few British naval stations. In Egypt, which had been made a protectorate in 1914, the Allenby declaration (1922) attempted to reach a political accommodation with the traditional ruling class. Egypt was no longer to be ruled as a Crown Colony, even if Britain was to hold on tenaciously to its rights as paramount power.

How, then, did parliament and the public react to this loosening of the bonds of political control in regions of long-standing imperial importance? Unlike the expansion and rationalisation of Britain's presence in the Middle East, the concessions extracted by nationalist movements in Ireland, Egypt and India were to have significant domestic political repercussions. A new strand of imperial politics emerged in the form of 'Diehardism' – arguably the only easily identifiable Conservative faction in the 1919–22 parliament.[27] Estimated at about fifty to sixty in strength, Diehard MPs came mainly from the landowning classes and the armed forces, and a high percentage were Irishmen or had Irish connections. They tended to have more parliamentary experience than the average MP, but very few held a ministerial post. For publicity, Diehards relied upon Fleet Street: Maxse's *National Review*, Lady Bathurst's *Morning Post*, and *The Spectator* all opened their columns to Diehard attacks on the Lloyd George Coalition. In the country at large, however, Diehard organisation was weak. MPs were heavily concentrated in London, especially in its residential West End, and although Rothermere's Anti-Waste League may have given a new impetus to Diehard activity in 1921,[28] there is little evidence

26 J. Gallagher, 'Nationalisms and the Crisis of Empire, 1919–22', *Modern Asian Studies* (1981), pp.355–68.
27 The rest of this paragraph is based primarily on M. Kinnear's, *The Fall of Lloyd George: The Political Crisis of 1922* (1973), pp.71–87.
28 K.O. Morgan, *Consensus and Disunity: The Lloyd George Coalition Government, 1918–22* (Oxford, 1979), p.243.

of constituency parties rallying to the cause. In so far as the Diehards achieved any level of constituency organisation it was not until after April 1921, when the thirty-five branches of Henry Page Croft's National party were absorbed into its ranks.[29]

Although Diehardism drew strength from the hardships of post-war depression,[30] home affairs were not at the core of its creed. In fact, Diehards were divided over aspects of domestic policy (such as protection), while over other issues (such as the treatment of 'aliens') there was little to distinguish their position from that of mainstream Conservatism. Fundamental to the political mindset of Diehardism was the notion of imperial weakness – the feeling that the British Empire might be living on borrowed time. Diehards believed Britain to have 'providentially sanctioned imperial obligations',[31] and insisted that challenges to imperial authority had to be resisted. Revolutionary extremists, it was argued, would not be bought off by concessions – they would simply become all the more determined to boot the British out. Negotiations with Sinn Fein came in for the strongest criticism;[32] but Diehards also took up the cudgels for General Dyer, an Indian army officer forced in 1920 to resign for ordering troops to fire on an unarmed crowd which had gathered in the Punjab city of Amritsar. Through the efforts of Howell Gwynne at the *Morning Post*, over £15,000 was collected for a Dyer Fund.[33] The historian Maurice Cowling judges the moral defence of Dyer by the Diehards to have been their 'most remarkable success'.[34]

It is unlikely that Diehards exercised much influence over the imperial policies of the Lloyd George Coalition. In the exclusion of Northern Ireland from Home Rule, it was Ulster which proved decisive. With respect to Egypt and India, Diehard pressure may have affected the presentation of policy, but it did little to alter its substance. If the Diehards had a finest hour, it was probably the removal of Edwin Montagu as Indian Secretary of State. In March 1922, Sir Robert Sanders, the Conservative party's Deputy Chairman, reflected in his diary that 'a Conservative at the India Office would do a lot to pacify our Diehards'.[35] It is unclear whether Sanders was involved in the selection of Montagu's successor or whether he was simply gazing into his political crystal

---

29 W.D. Rubinstein, 'Henry Page Croft and the National Party, 1917–22', *JCH* (1974), pp.136–8.

30 J. Darwin, 'Fear of Falling. British Politics and Imperial Decline since 1900', *TRHS*, 5th series (1986), p.34.

31 G. Studdart-Kennedy, 'The Christian Imperialism of the Diehard Defenders of the Raj, 1926–35', *JICH* (1990), pp.342–35.

32 J. Darwin, *Britain, Egypt and the Middle East: Imperial Policy in the Aftermath of War, 1918–22* (1981), pp.40–1; Jeffrey, *The Military Correspondence of Field Marshall Sir Henry Wilson*, pp.218–21.

33 D. Sayer, 'The British Reaction to the Amritsar Massacre, 1919–20', *P&P* (1991), pp.158–60.

34 M. Cowling, *The Impact of Labour, 1920–24: The Beginning of Modern British Politics* (Cambridge, 1971), p.87.

35 J. Ramsden (ed.), *Real Old Tory Politics: The Political Diaries of Sir Robert Sanders, 1910–35* (1984), p.174. Entry for 10/3/1922.

ball. Either way, Montagu, a well-known Indian sympathiser, and *bête noire* of the Diehards, was to be replaced by the Conservative, Viscount Peel. Peel lost no time in pouring cold water on a Government of India scheme for the Indianization of the army.[36]

The part played by Diehards in the collapse of the Lloyd George Coalition also merits investigation. Although the real danger of Diehardism was always that it would 'ignite a wider explosion' in the Conservative party,[37] Diehard MPs account for only a fifth of the anti-Coalition vote at the famous Carlton Club meeting. Thus the main fault line in 1922 was between Coalition ministers and the rest of the Conservative party. Diehardism remained a minority, if passionately held, view. It petered out soon after Lloyd George's resignation, and was not resuscitated until debates on the Government of India Act in the early-mid 1930s. The new strain of imperial politics it represented certainly made an imprint upon post-war Conservative politics. But it did little to alter in any lasting or fundamental way the political consciousness of empire in Britain.

From 'Empire' to 'Commonwealth': new conceptions of the Anglo-Dominion relationship

The third major change to Britain's imperial system resulting from the First World War was a redefinition of the Anglo-Dominion relationship. Just how far it was redefined is a matter of dispute. An older historiography portrays the War as the major staging post on the road to Dominion independence.[38] It claims that the Dominions emerged from the Paris Peace Conference with a new international status, proud of their military achievements, intolerant of British administrative inefficiency and military incompetence, and increasingly assertive in their dealings with the outside world. The Balfour Declaration of 1926 was thus merely an *ex post facto* recognition of a profound transformation in Anglo-Dominion relations which had taken place during the previous decade. This Whiggish teleology has not gone unchallenged. Rejecting the idea of an inescapable march towards Dominion independence, other historians have emphasised the complexity of the changes stemming from the War, while continuing to insist upon a 'general devolutionary drift' in Anglo-Dominion relations up to 1926.[39] Finally, some take up a more sceptical position, arguing that the assertion of independence after 1918 was largely rhetorical. Partnership with Britain – or 'Dominionhood' as it has been called – is the

---

36 S.R. Mehrotra, *India and the Commonwealth, 1885–1929* (1965), p.164.
37 Darwin, 'Fear of Falling', p.34.
38 R.M. Dawson (ed.), *The Development of Dominion Status, 1900–1936* (1937), Part I; N. Mansergh, *Survey of British Commonwealth Affairs. Problems of External Policy, 1931–1939* (Oxford, 1952), Chapter 1; W.D. McIntyre, *The Commonwealth of Nations. Origins and Impact, 1869–1971* (Minneapolis, MN, 1977), Chapter 11.
39 P. Wigley, *Canada and the Transition to Commonwealth*, pp.1–3, 230.

maximum to which the Dominions are thought to have aspired.[40] The market provided by the British economy, the investment provided by the City of London, and the protection provided by the Royal Navy, all these factors meant the Dominions had every incentive to remain part of Britain's imperial system.

The older nationalist historiography was certainly right to recognise how the War brought to the fore some of the difficulties and tensions already evident in the Anglo-Dominion relationship. In South Africa, the War was particularly damaging to national unity,[41] and posed profound problems for the sense of 'white South Africanism' which became a feature of the Dominion's politics after 1904.[42] In October 1914, a rift opened in Afrikaner society as certain disaffected Afrikaners rebelled against conscription (introduced to raise troops for service in South-West Africa). The revolt took three months to suppress and contributed to the rapid growth in support for Hertzog's National Party. In the general election of October 1915, the National Party gained votes at the expense of Botha's moderate South African party.[43] By 1917, Hertzog had sufficient faith in the cultural and political appeal of Afrikaner nationalism to declare republican independence as his party's goal. Meanwhile in Canada the decision of the federal government to join the War was welcomed with 'an unforeseeable degree of unity' in 1914.[44] However, by 1917 anti-war feeling and loyalist opposition to it were widespread. It was well known that Quebec had played an inadequate part in recruiting: French Canada constituted about two-fifths of the population, but accounted for only 5 per cent of the forces supplied by Canada.[45] As Robert Borden remarked to Lady Bathurst, 'about forty per cent of our population are of non-British origin and they are not generally sympathetic with Canada's participation in the war'.[46] Yet in May 1917 Borden's government pressed ahead with the introduction of compulsory military service. Resistance to the measure culminated in anti-conscription riots in Quebec in 1918, forcing the Canadian authorities to suspend the arrest of army deserters.

In addition to a hardening of ethnic sentiment among Afrikaners and Canadiens, the First World War is widely recognised by historians to constitute a crucial phase in the development of Australian and New Zealand nationalism through the making of the so-called 'Anzac legend'. Anzacs were Australian and New Zealand soldiers who fought as volunteers on the Western Front, and as part of the ill-fated Mediterranean Expeditionary Force

40 J. Darwin, 'The Third British Empire. The Dominion Idea in British Politics', *Oxford History of the British Empire* (forthcoming).
41 B. Nasson, 'War Opinion in South Africa, 1914', *JICH* (1995), pp.248–76.
42 S. Dubow, 'Colonial Nationalism, the Milner Kindergarten and the Rise of "South Africanism", 1902–10', *HWJ* (1997), p.76.
43 N.G. Garson, 'South Africa and World War I', in N. Hillmer and P. Wigley (eds), *The First British Commonwealth* (1980), pp.71, 78–9.
44 R.M. Bray, ' "Fighting as an Ally": The English–Canadian Patriotic Response to the Great War', *CHR* (1980), p.142.
45 E.H. Armstrong, *The Crisis of Quebec, 1914–18* (1937), appendix.
46 R.L. Borden to Lady Bathurst, 13/2/1918, *Glenesk–Bathurst papers*, 1990/1/2806.

which landed at Gallipoli in April 1915, only to be evacuated the following December after suffering tragic losses. Nearly 8,000 Australians[47] and some 2,700 New Zealanders[48] died in the campaign. However, if the plan to seize the Dardanelles strait and to knock Turkey out of the War ended in abject failure, it did not prevent Gallipoli from being invested with a special status by Britain's Antipodean allies. For Australians and New Zealanders, commemoration of the War, a 'universal preoccupation'[49] after 1918, was to be synonymous with the 25 April, the day their troops landed on the Turkish peninsula.

Not surprisingly, perhaps, the significance of Gallipoli for Anglo-Dominion relations is hotly contested. Some suggest it provided the 'focus for a specifically nationalist sentiment' which undermined the imperial attachment of Australians.[50] Others present it as proof that Australian nationalism could still 'reside within the Imperial bond', and that there was 'no incompatibility between Empire loyalty and Australian nationalism' after 1915.[51] Here it is worth pausing for a moment to reflect upon the making of the Anzac legend. The publicity given to the exploits of the Anzacs owed a great deal to the work of two journalists – the Australian, Charles Bean, who wrote the campaign's official history, and the colourful British war correspondent, Ellis Ashmead Bartlett.[52]

A leading critic of the Dardanelles campaign, Ashmead Bartlett shared with many members of Lloyd George's War Cabinet their anxieties regarding its repercussions in Australia and New Zealand. Much of his reporting sought to persuade Australians and New Zealanders that their sacrifices had not been in vain, as did his lecture tour of Australia and New Zealand in 1916. Declared bankrupt in 1914, and with a journalist's eye for self-publicity, it is easy to be cynical about Ashmead Bartlett's motives for undertaking the tour. Nevertheless, press reports of the speeches he delivered in Sydney and Melbourne point to a genuine concern about Gallipoli's impact on recruiting and empire relations.[53] There was, admittedly, an element of playing to the gallery. Public interest in the Dardanelles campaign was riding high in 1916; we should not be surprised if a leading war correspondent chose to exploit it. But Ashmead Bartlett's speeches did more than pander to popular sentiment. They were carefully calibrated responses to the failings of British military leadership, which aimed to prevent a hardening of anti-British feeling. What had hurt Australians and New Zealanders most regarding Gallipoli was not so much

47 M. Clark, *A History of Australia* (Pimlico edn, 1995), p.461.
48 M. McKinnon, 'New Zealand in the World', in K. Sinclair (ed.), *The Oxford Illustrated History of New Zealand* (Oxford, 1996), p.239.
49 J. Winter, *Sites of Memory, Sites of Morning: The Great War in European Cultural History* (Cambridge, 1995), p.248.
50 B. Gammage, *The Broken Years. Australian Soldiers in the Great War* (Harmondsworth, 1975), p.277.
51 J. Robertson, *Anzac and Empire. The Tragedy and Glory of Gallipoli* (1990), pp.248, 261.
52 K. Fewster, 'Ellis Ashmead Bartlett and the Making of the Anzac Legend', *Journal of Australian Studies* (1982), pp.17–30.
53 *The Age*, 14/2/1916, p.8, and 23/2/1916, pp.9–10; *Sydney Morning Herald*, 14/2/1916, pp.10–12, and 16/2/1916, pp.14–16; *The Argus*, 22/2/1916, p.8, and 23/2/1916, pp.10–12.

withdrawal from the peninsula but the lack of recognition of their troops. Determined that the achievement of the Anzacs should not go unnoticed, Ashmead Bartlett did all he could to draw attention to the significance of their contribution to the campaign.

That a British war correspondent played a key part in the forging of the Anzac legend is testimony to the complex allegiances and multiple loyalties which were characteristic of Dominion societies at this time. Even after 1919, Dominion nationalism and imperial patriotism were far from incompatible feelings. Of course, it is arguable that in the inter-war years self-interest continued to rule out Dominion separation from Britain just as it had prior to 1914. Yet the Empire's ideological appeal, which Ashmead Bartlett's speeches had so skilfully played upon, also acted as a powerful incentive towards co-operation. As Milner suggested in 1919, the League of Nations had the advantage of a 'regular constitution' over the Commonwealth, but it lacked the 'moral ties which made for unanimity'.[54] Neither Hughes, Borden nor Smuts would have disagreed.

How, then, did British and Dominion statesmen conceptualise the nature of imperial loyalty after the War? For imperialists in Britain, the Dominions' response to the outbreak of war was taken as further proof that they were in the Empire voluntarily. Yet it also deepened their conviction that the national aspirations of the Dominions needed to be more fully recognised. Indeed, by 1917–18 many politicians were rethinking the correct terminology for describing the relationship in which the Dominions now stood to Britain. Although it had no legal validity, the phrase 'British Commonwealth of nations' gained a much wider currency in the 1920s.[55] It was an expression which seemed best to capture the liberal and progressive aspect of relationships within the British world.[56] It was approved by Smuts, who felt the need for a 'real appropriate name' for the 'system of states' which was the British Empire in order to distinguish it from empires founded on assimilation rather than freedom and liberty.[57] And it was approved by Borden, who had first raised the question of the future status of the Dominions at the Imperial War Conference in 1917, and who saw in a new imperial nomenclature an opportunity to dispel any idea of subservience to Britain.[58] Amery, too, favoured the term 'Commonwealth', arguing that the ideal which the self-governing colonies aimed at could not be stretched to include 'Nigeria, or India, or Malta'.[59]

Even towards the end of the War, then, the tendency was to keep the discussion of Britain's dependencies separate from the discussion of Anglo-

54 'Lord Milner on the British Commonwealth', speech to the Oxford University Summer School, reported in *The Oxford Times*, 8/8/1919, p.5.
55 S.R. Mehrotra, 'On the use of the term "Commonwealth"', *JCPS* (1963), p.10.
56 R. Koebner and H.D. Schmidt, *Imperialism. The Story and Significance of a Political Word, 1840–1960* (Cambridge, 1964), p.233.
57 Hancock and Van der Poel, *Selections from the Smuts Papers*, Vol. III, pp.510–11.
58 H.H. Borden, *Robert Laird Borden: His Memoirs* (Toronto, 1938), p.670.
59 Hancock and Van der Poel, *Selections from the Smuts Papers* Vol. III, p.517; L. Amery, *My Political Life. Vol. II: War and Peace, 1914–1929* (1953), pp.389–90.

Dominion relations. True, an attenuated form of the 'Dominion model' was applied to India by Lionel Curtis, the Round Table's constitutional expert and former Beit Lecturer in Colonial History at Oxford. During a lengthy stay in India from 1916 to 1918, Curtis championed constitutional reform. His scheme of dyarchy, actively publicised in Britain, represented a 'half-way house' towards self-government, designed to give Indians more control over aspects of their own affairs.[60] However, few others thought Britain's relationship with India could evolve in this way. Even the Round Table veteran, Philip Kerr, regarded talk of self-government for India as meaningless and premature. In its initial incarnation, therefore, the term 'Commonwealth' continued to refer to a particular group of nations within the Empire; only later would it be stretched to embrace the Empire as a whole.

IMPERIALISTS IN THE LLOYD GEORGE COALITION

The War, then, produced subtle shifts but no radical transformation in the meaning of imperialism. There were, however, important structural changes in imperial politics which resulted from Lloyd George's accession to the premiership in December 1916. Impatient with traditional methods of administration, Lloyd George placed himself at the centre of a complex web of cabinets, committees, conferences and personal advisers. In the process of reconstructing the machinery of government, he rescued Milner from political oblivion and appointed many of Milner's acolytes to positions in his administration. For a while the centre of gravity of imperial politics shifted away from the extra-parliamentary sphere as imperialists strutted the corridors of power.

Milner joined the War Cabinet as Minister without Portfolio, and later took up departmental responsibilities at the War Office (1918) and Colonial Office (1919–21). Despite long years in the wilderness, his talent for self-dramatisation had not deserted him. The erstwhile 'civilian soldier of the British Empire' now described himself as an 'emergency man' – a politician called upon to play a vital part in conducting the Empire's affairs at a moment of world crisis.[61] Neither had Milner forsaken the preoccupations of his earlier career. He continued to cling to the essentials of the constructive imperialist doctrine which had conditioned his political thinking prior to 1914. He also remained passionate about 'imperial unity', eager to carry the wartime spirit of Anglo-Dominion co-operation into the period of peace which would follow the defeat of Germany.

Milner's standing in the War Cabinet is a matter of dispute. Some argue he was second in importance only to Lloyd George,[62] while others believe

60 On this point, see P. Woods, 'Lionel Curtis, the Round Table Movement and the Montagu–Chelmsford Reforms', in A. Bosco and A. May (eds), *The Round Table, the Empire/Commonwealth and British Foreign Policy* (1997), pp.369–79.
61 J.E. Wrench, *Alfred Lord Milner. The Man of No Illusions* (1958), p.333.
62 Ibid., p.351; V. Halperin, *Lord Milner and the Empire: The Evolution of British Imperialism* (1952), p.165.

this place belonged to Bonar Law.[63] It is probably closer to the truth to say that both men were important, but in different ways. Milner's skills lay in administration, Bonar Law's in parliamentary and party management. Either way, Milner's membership of the War Cabinet certainly gave him considerable political clout, as did the appointment of many of his supporters to non-ministerial positions in the Coalition government. Amery joined the Cabinet Secretariat as a Political Secretary in 1916, and subsequently served Milner as Parliamentary Under-Secretary at the Colonial Office; Philip Kerr worked closely with Lloyd George as his Private Secretary (1916–21), paying particular attention to the Dominions, India and the United States; Kerr was succeeded in this post by the former colonial editor of *The Times*, Edward Grigg; the tariff reformer, William Hewins, was Under-Secretary to Walter Long at the Colonial Office (1917–19); and Lionel Curtis played a part in shaping the Montagu-Chelmsford reforms (1919).

The question of how far the political objectives of these men were shared by the Prime Minister is also disputed. In his study of Lloyd George's Secretariat, Turner emphatically rejects the idea that the leading Milnerite in the Coalition, Philip Kerr, was 'able to make any great use of his position to advance the policies dear to him or to the Round Table'.[64] This view has some merit, for there is little doubt about the pronounced authority of the Prime Minister over decision-making. Members of the War Cabinet definitely felt this to be the case. Prior to the Paris Peace Conference, Curzon complained that 'things are being done, for which we shall bear the responsibility but of which we are not aware';[65] and the labour leader, Arthur Henderson, recollected that 'Lloyd George was the War Cabinet, and nobody else really counted'.[66] Nevertheless, the political philosophy of the Milnerites had much in common with that of Lloyd George. This is not to argue that Lloyd George suddenly became a convert to imperial causes in 1916–17; quite the opposite. Even before 1914 there was little difference between him and Milner on the principle of imperial consolidation.[67] To be sure, their viewpoints had been diametrically opposed during the South African War. Lloyd George, like Smuts, believed that British imperialism had been derailed in 1899–1902, betraying everything it then stood for. But the Union of South Africa in 1910 had reinforced Lloyd George's conviction that white colonial freedom could be reconciled with imperial unity.

The real problem for imperialists in the Coalition was not a clash of their political philosophy with that of the Prime Minister, but Lloyd George's short-termism and expediency. While Lloyd George wished to consult with the Dominions, he was not inclined to think about imperial questions in any great

63 Darwin, *Britain, Egypt and the Middle East*, pp.16–17; A.M. Gollin, *Proconsul in Politics. A Study of Lord Milner in Opposition and Power* (1964), p.369.
64 J. Turner, *Lloyd George's Secretariat* (Cambridge, 1980), p.138.
65 Ronaldshay, *Life of Lord Curzon*, Vol. III, pp.259–60.
66 C.A. Repington, *The First World War, 1914–18*, Vol. II (1920), p.278.
67 J. Grigg, *The Young Lloyd George* (1973), pp.295–7.

detail. So much is evident from his attitude towards the Imperial War Cabinet (IWC). Organised by the Cabinet Secretariat, the IWC met in London during March–May 1917, and again in June–August 1918. Its permanent membership comprised the British Prime Minister and War Cabinet, the Foreign Secretary and the Secretary of State for the Colonies, the Dominion Prime Ministers, the Secretary of State for India (along with three advisers) and the chiefs of the military and naval services. Two sub-committees were convened. One examined territorial questions (chaired by Curzon), the other dealt with economic issues (under Milner). At the Paris Peace Conference, the IWC metamorphosed into the British Empire Delegation.

THE IMPERIAL WAR CABINET AND IMPERIAL FOREIGN POLICY

The IWC epitomised Lloyd George's approach to wartime government – both his preference for by-passing traditional institutions and his penchant for creating new ministries of a temporary (Munitions, Reconstruction) and permanent (Labour, Health, Transport) nature.[68] Lloyd George later claimed to be the originator of the IWC,[69] yet Milner is also given the credit for its formation.[70] Undoubtedly, both Lloyd George and Milner had their own particular reasons for promoting a new consultative body. It is likely that Lloyd George saw in the leaders of the Dominions an opportunity to strengthen his own hand against the British High Command.[71] Milner's adversary, meanwhile, was the Colonial Office, which he felt to be unfit to manage Anglo-Dominion relations. By placing the organisation of the IWC in the hands of the Cabinet Secretariat, Milner was to clip the wings of the Colonial Office, much to the chagrin of Walter Long.[72] Of course, both Lloyd George and Milner were also reacting to events in 1916–17, and it could be argued that, in view of their sacrifices, the fuller political involvement of the Dominions in the management of the War was inevitable by this time.

It is vital to consider how far the IWC advanced the agenda of imperialists in the Lloyd George Coalition. Some argue that the Coalition produced no effective instrument of imperial government,[73] and dismiss it as a 'glorified public relations exercise'.[74] Such views contrast sharply with the opinion of *The Times*, which in the summer of 1917 declared that of all the constitutional developments set in train by the War, by far the most important was the

68 R. Lowe, 'Government', in S. Constantine, M. Kirby and M. Rose (eds), *The First World War in British History* (1995), pp.30–1.
69 Lloyd George, *War Memoirs*, Vol. I, p.1026.
70 Gollin, *Proconsul in Politics*, pp.396–7, 533. Milner, of course, had long talked of a new organ of empire government, and as recently as 1916 had set out the case for such a body in a speech to the Empire Parliamentary Association.
71 G.L. Cook, 'Sir Robert Borden, Lloyd George and British Military Policy, 1917–18', *HJ* (1971), p.374.
72 Turner, *Lloyd George's Secretariat*, p.126.
73 J. Bourne, *Britain and the Great War* (1989), p.236.
74 P. Rowland, *Lloyd George* (1975), p.400.

creation of a supreme executive authority for the Empire.[75] Nor was it only *The Times* which pinned such high hopes upon this body. Philip Kerr, for example, felt the IWC to be a real step towards imperial federation,[76] while Leo Amery saw in Lloyd George's invitation to the Dominion premiers an opportunity to secure greater continuity of consultation.[77]

From the British point of view, the IWC marked the culmination of a concept of imperialism which substituted for metropolitan ascendancy the principles of partnership and mutual co-operation. As Amery explained, part of its attraction was that it did not raise the 'almost indissoluble' problem of how to devise some federal or quasi-federal machinery for the conduct of imperial affairs.[78] Similarly, from the perspective of Dominion leaders the IWC's appeal was not just that it enhanced their status as war leaders, but that it avoided federalism. Billy Hughes welcomed the fact that its decisions required the assent of the various governments of the Empire before they could be translated into action.[79] Smuts hoped the IWC could inject a stronger sense of unity into the imperial system without interfering with the executive functions of Dominion governments.[80] And Borden identified in the IWC a way of improving imperial co-operation while respecting the national autonomy of the Dominions. As he explained to Lady Bathurst:

> Each Prime Minister will represent his Dominion and will act for it; but his action will be subject to his own Parliament; responsibility to the people will be maintained; no Dominion will lose its autonomy or right of self-government; and yet it is hoped that unity of action after necessary deliberation and consultation can be secured.[81]

Thus, conceived as a 'Cabinet of Governments rather than of Ministers', the IWC was perfectly consistent with contemporary conceptions of imperial development. Yet when considering how far the IWC enabled the Dominions to press their own views on how the War should be fought, a distinction must be made between its 1917 and 1918 sessions. In 1917, Dominion leaders had very little input into the policy-making process. They were not even consulted about the Flanders offensive.[82] In 1918, the atmosphere was decidedly different. Borden, in particular, was highly critical of the 'terrible blunders' on the Western Front.[83] In order to appease him and the other Dominion premiers, Lloyd George set up an 'inner Imperial War Cabinet' – a committee

75 *The Times*, 10/7/1917, p.5.
76 J.R.M. Butler, *Lord Lothian (Philip Kerr) 1882–1940* (1960), pp.64–5.
77 Amery, *My Political Life*, Vol. II, pp.105–7.
78 Ibid., pp.109–10.
79 W.M. Hughes, *The Splendid Adventure* (1929), pp.49–51.
80 Hancock, *Smuts. The Sanguine Years*, pp.514–15; Borden, *Memoirs*, pp.674–5.
81 Borden, *Memoirs*, p.692; R.L. Borden, *Canadian Constitutional Studies. The Marfleet Lectures. University of Toronto, October 1921* (Oxford, 1922), pp.110–11.
82 Cook, 'Sir Robert Borden, Lloyd George and British Military Policy', p.394.
83 Hughes, *Splendid Adventure*, pp.62–3; Wigley, *Canada and the Transition to Commonwealth*, p.29.

of Prime Ministers – charged with the task of preparing a new strategic plan. This committee appears to have worked as a real partnership, and its draft report is said to have contained a 'genuinely common imperial military policy'.[84]

The IWC also discussed the terms of the peace settlement. This gave the Dominion premiers an opportunity to commit the British government to the pursuit of their own war aims. Yet it has been suggested that what passed for consultation on the peace settlement was little more than Dominion ratification of British conclusions.[85] The sub-committee dealing with territorial questions is a case in point. Although it accepted that the peace settlement should leave in the Empire's hands German and Turkish territory captured by Britain during the War, the full IWC added the proviso that the Empire's demands would have to be correlated with those of its Allies. This was to cause great problems at the Paris Peace Conference when South Africa's contribution to the war effort was readily acknowledged by the award of the mandate for German South-West Africa, but Australia's claims to territory in the Pacific were vigorously opposed by the American President, Woodrow Wilson.[86] Bitterly disappointed on the reparations question, Hughes was all the more determined to safeguard Australian security in the Pacific. The crucial issue was that of New Guinea. Wilson resolved to make acceptance of the mandate system a test case for his principles, while Hughes held out for outright annexation of the island. After heated debate, a compromise was reached in the form of the 'C' class mandate, whereby Wilson secured the formal recognition of his principles but Australia gained control over immigration and prevented the application of an 'open door' policy. Yet if Australia had secured its position in New Guinea, it was mainly due to the tenacity and courage shown by the 'Little Digger', rather than any prior commitment entered into by the IWC.

The possibility of institutionalising the IWC – of making it a regular annual event – was taken seriously in 1918. Amery actually prepared a memorandum, 'The Future of the Imperial Cabinet System', which argued that it should be maintained as a permanent body. A copy of the memorandum was sent to Smuts.[87] As already noted, Hughes, Smuts and Borden had been drawn to the IWC as a way of pressing their own conception of Dominion status. Their desire to improve the channels of imperial communication, and to promote consultation in the field of foreign policy, suggested that it might have a future after the Armistice. But with the collapse of Lloyd George's government in 1922, and the revival of the old party system, the IWC suffered a serious setback. The end of the Coalition signalled a return to the *status quo ante* and a preference for the old ways of governing. Like the Coalition, the IWC had come into being because of a manifest national emergency. As with

84 Hughes, *Splendid Adventure*, pp.65–7; Cook, 'Sir Robert Borden, Lloyd George and British Military Policy', p.395.
85 Wigley, *Canada and the Transition to the Commonwealth*, pp.35–6.
86 Fitzhardinge, *The Little Digger*, p.378.
87 Hancock and Van der Poel, *Selections from the Smuts Papers*, Vol. III, pp.664–5.

the other pieces of administrative apparatus introduced by Lloyd George, the odds were stacked against it surviving into peacetime.

The most likely post-war function for the IWC was to co-ordinate imperial foreign policy. However, Churchill's handling of the Chanak crisis in 1922–23, when the Canadian premier, Mackenzie King, first heard of the Colonial Office's request for Canadian troops through the press, hardly gave the impression that Britain took the business of prior consultation very seriously. Mackenzie King's riposte came at the 1923 Imperial Conference when he made a critical distinction between 'imperial foreign policy' and his country's external affairs.[88] The former would encompass issues of 'overwhelming and enduring common interest'; the latter implied that in all other areas of policy Canada would take responsibility for its own foreign relations. The Foreign Office was quick to read the writing on the wall. Recognising that the IWC had not developed into a co-ordinating body for imperial foreign policy, and unwilling to restrict its freedom of action by promising full and continuous consultation, each Dominion was granted the right to negotiate and sign its own bilateral treaties.

It is tempting to mark the 1923 Imperial Conference as the moment when the idea of a unified Commonwealth partnership gave way to complete Dominion independence. This view is seemingly reinforced by Britain's ratification of the Locarno treaties in 1925: ratification was not discussed beforehand with the Dominions, and it was not until the following year that Britain's new commitment to European security was aired.[89] The problem with such an argument is that the alternative to joint control of imperial foreign policy was not necessarily to let the Dominions go their own way. At least one of the Dominions – New Zealand – did not wish to go its own way, preferring to follow the lead of the British government. The other antipodean Dominion – Australia – expected to have an influence on policy, but in the event of not being consulted, it lacked the capacity to formulate a distinctive foreign policy.[90] Moreover, efforts to improve inter-imperial communication in the sphere of foreign policy continued after 1923. Kerr, Amery and Austen Chamberlain were key figures in this process. In February 1925, a series of articles was published (anonymously) by Kerr in *The Times*. The articles, later reprinted as a pamphlet, *The Dominions and Foreign Policy*, suggested that the Foreign Office rather than the Colonial Office be put in charge of the consultation process, that Dominion High Commissioners be kept in personal touch with the Foreign Secretary, that Governors-General in the Dominions be given a diplomatic role, and that the Dominions make more use of the British diplomatic service or train experts of their own.[91] From January to April 1926,

88 Wigley, *Canada and the Transition to Commonwealth*, pp.193–4.
89 R. Grayson, *Austen Chamberlain and the Commitment to Europe. British Foreign Policy, 1924–29* (1997), p.66.
90 D. Day, *The Great Betrayal. Britain, Australia and the Onset of the Pacific War 1939–42* (1988), p.7; and *Reluctant Nation. Australia and the Allied Defeat of Japan* (1992), p.314.
91 Butler, *Lord Lothian*, pp.107–9.

officials at the Foreign Office discussed a memorandum entitled, 'Consultation with and Communication of Information to the British Dominions on Foreign Policy'. The memorandum touched upon most of the issues already raised by Kerr. It was written by Percy Koppel, head of the Foreign Office's News Department, and was read and commented upon by a number of senior diplomats.[92] From these exchanges emerged a new plan for improving liaison on foreign affairs which was designed to bring the Dominion High Commissioners into closer touch with policy-making at the Foreign and Dominion Offices. The plan was promoted by Austen Chamberlain (Foreign Secretary) and Amery (Colonial Secretary), initially rejected by the British Cabinet, publicised in the Dominions during Amery's 1927 empire tour, and eventually implemented in 1928.[93]

THE WASHINGTON NAVAL TREATY (1921–22) AND THE SINGAPORE STRATEGY

The only full Fleet action during the War resulted in a tactical victory for the German High Seas Fleet – the Royal Navy suffered greater losses of ships and men. But the battle of Jutland (31 May 1916) was a strategic victory for Britain. For the next two and a half years the German navy rarely ventured beyond the Baltic seas,[94] and with the scuttling of the High Seas Fleet at Scapa Flow, Britain again became the world's strongest maritime power.[95] A new challenger soon emerged, however. By the summer of 1919, America had established itself as the world's second naval power, intent upon building a fleet equal and perhaps even superior to the British Royal Navy.[96] For Britain, a new naval arms race was out of the question. Financially exhausted by the time of the Armistice,[97] deep cuts were made in all of its armed services. Under the so-called 'Ten Year Rule', the Admiralty and War Office were instructed to make their strategic plans on the basis that the nation would not be involved in another great war during the next decade. This stipulation gave the Treasury the whip hand in negotiating the naval estimates for the whole of the 1920s. Neither could the Admiralty rely on extra-parliamentary pressure groups to force the Treasury's hand. Organisations like the Navy League, which prior to 1914 had helped to mobilise public opinion in favour of higher naval spending, were now overshadowed by powerful non-governmental groups, like

---

92 For the memorandum and the debate it provoked, see FO 272/2197, T 5885/5885/384 (16/1/ 1926) and 5886/5885/384 (21/4/1926). I am grateful to Dr Richard Grayson for supplying the references, and for discussing these documents and his own important monograph with me.
93 R. Holland, *Britain and the Commonwealth Alliance, 1918–39* (1981), pp.68–74.
94 B. Ranft, 'The Royal Navy and the War at Sea', in J. Turner (ed.), *Britain and the First World War* (1988), p.53.
95 G. Till, 'Retrenchment, Rethinking, Revival 1919–39', in J.R. Hill (ed.), *The Oxford Illustrated History of the Royal Navy* (Oxford, 1995), p.319.
96 J.K. McDonald, 'Lloyd George and the Search for a Postwar Naval Policy, 1919', in A.J.P. Taylor (ed.), *Lloyd George. Twelve Essays* (1971), p.191.
97 Holland, *Britain and the Commonwealth Alliance*, p.13.

the League of Nations Union and the Union of Democratic Control, which were determined to force a reduction in arms expenditures.[98]

It was, then, in Britain's interest to discuss naval arms limitation at the Washington Naval Conference in 1921. While the German navy was no longer a threat, the United States and Japan possessed large navies, and the gap was widening between Britain's defence resources and commitments, particularly in the Pacific. At Washington, Britain accepted parity with the US navy, and a system of fixed ratios was devised to determine the comparative naval strength of the major powers: 5 (Britain): 5 (US): 3 (Japan): 1.75 (Italy, France). Although this ratio applied to capital ships only – it was not extended to cover cruisers and destroyers until the London Naval Conference of 1930 – it signified Britain's formal abandonment of the so-called 'Two-Power Standard'. In future, Britain would aim to maintain a navy as strong as that of the United States. The Washington Conference also had important implications for the distribution of the British Fleet. In an effort to bring stability to East Asia, Britain conceded naval supremacy to the United States in the eastern Atlantic and to Japan in the Pacific. Henceforth the Royal Navy was to be stationed in British waters and in the Mediterranean, not east of Suez where the centre of gravity of the Empire arguably lay.[99] In some sense, Britain had no choice. Although the German High Seas Fleet had been scuttled after the War, the naval dockyards of the Pacific (Colombo, Hong Kong, Singapore) would have struggled to cope with some of Britain's older battleships, let alone its latest capital ships. Nonetheless, the fact that there was to be no Pacific fleet[100] raised the question of how quickly the main Fleet could be moved to the region in the event of Japanese aggression or some other crisis.

In view of their contribution to the war effort, Australia and New Zealand felt they were entitled to the full protection of the Royal Navy.[101] Yet Britain's new one-power standard meant that the idea of mutual protection came under greater threat in the 1920s than at any time previously. By building a modern naval base at Singapore,[102] Lord Beatty (First Sea Lord), Leo Amery (First Lord of the Admiralty) and Winston Churchill (Colonial Secretary) hoped to reassure the Antipodean Dominions of the empire-wide mobility of the Fleet. If Singapore could harbour a large, modern fleet of capital ships, then Britain would be able to flex its naval muscle in the Indian and Pacific Oceans, should the need arise. For this reason, the Singapore strategy became something of an acid test of Britain's resolve to maintain a truly imperial navy. When the Labour

98 B.J.C. McKercher, 'The Politics of Naval Arms Limitation in Britain in the 1920s', in E. Goldstein and J. Maurer (ed.), *The Washington Conference, 1921–22. Naval Rivalry, East Asian Stability and the Road to Pearl Harbor* (1993), pp.35–9.
99 J. Neidpath, *The Singapore Naval Base and the Defence of Britain's Eastern Empire, 1919–41* (Oxford, 1981), pp.9–10.
100 In 1919, Admiral Jellicoe had recommended a Far Eastern fleet based at Singapore and jointly financed by Britain, Australia and New Zealand, but the British Admiralty rejected the proposal.
101 Neidpath, *The Singapore Naval Base*, p.6.
102 The non-fortification clauses of the Washington Treaty prevented Britain from improving the defences of Hong Kong.

party came into power in 1924, and the MacDonald government stopped all new construction at Singapore, imperially-minded navalists were incensed. In a speech to the Navy League on 28 March, Churchill spoke of a 'supreme issue of principle' involved in the decision:

> [The] moral forces [of the British Commonwealth of nations] would never have achieved their result, would never have found their physical expression, had it not been for the protection given to the whole Empire at all times by the Royal Navy. (Cheers). That protection has been universal and unceasing. . . . Now, for the first time, that naval defence, that practical bond of Empire, is to be withdrawn from the British Dominions which happen to be situated in the Pacific Ocean. Britain is definitely putting it out of her power to go to their aid, no matter how dire might be their distress or how grievous the wrong under which they suffer.[103]

Churchill's stance may have been politically expedient – he was hoping to be returned to parliament as an anti-socialist.[104] Neither should we forget how he had earlier antagonised many navalists by withdrawing ships from the Mediterranean.[105] Nonetheless, when a Conservative government returned to office in 1926 work on the Singapore naval base was resumed. Churchill, now Chancellor of the Exchequer, argued that money should initially be provided for docking but not repair facilities (enabling Singapore to handle a battle cruiser squadron but not the whole war fleet), and that the deadline for the completion of this reduced project should be put back from 1933 to 1937.[106] He did not, however, dispute that Singapore remained the 'pillar of imperial communications' in the Far East. From 1924 to 1930, £4.1 million was spent on the project, including contributions from Hong Kong (£.25 million), the Federated Malay States (£2 million), and New Zealand (£1 million).

In so far as imperial navalists did agitate in the 1920s it was to make sure the Baldwin government did not renege on its political commitment to the Singapore base, and to fight the 'economy school' inside and outside the Cabinet. Up until 1927, they had a powerful and popular advocate in the Admiralty – Lord Beatty.[107] It was an open question whether Britain would be able to measure up to Japan in the Pacific by the end of the 1920s. However, as a recent study of the problem concludes, until the modernisation of the Japanese fleet in the 1930s, and the combined hostility from Nazi Germany and Fascist Italy, the Singapore strategy was at least plausible. Significant steps had been taken to improve imperial security in the region: 'in the financial and political circumstances of the time this was a solid achievement, however inadequate'.[108]

103 R. Rhodes James (ed.), *W.S. Churchill. His Complete Speeches, 1897–1963*, Vol. IV (1974), p.3450.
104 R. Quinault, 'Churchill and Australia: The Military Relationship, 1899–1945', *War and Society* (1988), pp.49–50.
105 See pp.117–18 and p.126.
106 Neidpath, *The Singapore Naval Base*, p.104.
107 S. Roskill, *Admiral of the Fleet Earl Beatty. The Last Naval Hero: An Intimate Biography* (1980), pp.343–4.
108 Neidpath, *The Singapore Naval Base*, p.121.

TARIFF REFORM REDIVIVUS, THE EMPIRE MARKETING BOARD,
AND THE EMPIRE SETTLEMENT ACT

By agreeing to the Bonar Law memorial,[109] the tariff reform movement had apparently signed its own death warrant in January 1913. Bonar Law's act of 'betrayal' was never really forgiven by men like Amery and Hewins, who displayed a very guarded attitude towards the party's new leader. Nevertheless, the Tariff Reform League was far from being defunct on the eve of the War. Vigorous branch activity was evident in Scotland, South Wales, Lancashire, the western Counties and the London area, new literature for local activists was being produced, the ninth annual conference was well attended by regional delegates, and a campaign had recently been initiated to counteract the propaganda of the Free Trade Union at by-elections.[110]

During the War the organisational base of the tariff reform movement was significantly broadened. New sources of support included business pressure groups (especially the Unionist Business Committee, Empire Resources Development Committee, British Empire Producers' Organisation, and British Commonwealth Union),[111] other political pressure groups (strong links were forged with the British Workers' National League and the Imperial Mission, but not with Page Croft's National Party), Dominion premiers (as a spokesman for the 'New Britains', Billy Hughes championed tariff reform during his stay in England in 1916), and influential figures within the Lloyd George administration (Milner, Amery, Hewins and Arthur Steel-Maitland[112]). However, muzzled by Conservative participation in the Coalition government, it was not until after the summer of 1916 that the Tariff Reform League was able to campaign publicly. In response to a renewed campaign by the Free Trade Union and Cobden Club for an 'open door' trade policy, the League organised a series of open-air meetings, targeting the constituencies of 'anti-patriot' MPs. It also staged an exhibition of certain 'key' industries, considered vital to the safety and well-being of the Empire but endangered by 'unfair' competition from Germany.

It is a moot point how far the ideology of tariff reform was changed by the events of 1914–18. Some suggest the objectives of tariff reformers were much narrower after the War than before it.[113] Others claim a greater diversity of purpose within the tariff reform movement by 1917, as the goals of preference and protection were augmented by new schemes of government–industry co-operation, and by the need to restore stable trading conditions in post-war

---

109 The memorial pledged the Conservative party not to introduce a food tax unless approved at a second general election.

110 Information sourced from *Monthly Notes on Tariff Reform* (January–June, 1914).

111 For a recent, detailed account of the origins and objectives of business pressure groups during and after the War, see A.J. Marrison, *British Business and Protection, 1903–32* (Oxford, 1996), Chapter 11.

112 Head of the Department of Overseas Trade (est. October 1917).

113 Marrison, *British Business and Protection*, pp.330–2; and Marrison (ed.), *Free Trade and its Reception 1815–1960*, Vol. I (1998), p.206.

Europe.[114] It is certainly true that the War forced a re-appraisal of the case for tariff reform. The issue of national security came to the forefront of fiscal debate, and reparations and demobilisation were central to the discussion of post-war trade policy. But old habits died hard. When the TRL announced its 'policy of thorough' in 1916 the policy objectives of the movement were very similar to those of 1903: 'Our new Imperial fiscal policy must aim at revenue, but still more at encouraging, supporting and enlarging our agriculture and our manufactures; at the fullest possible employment of our workers; at the freedom from foreign legal shackles of our trading vessels; and at the utmost development of the British Empire.'[115] Tariff reform continued to be regarded as the foundation of empire partnership. Indeed, there was repeated criticism of the Asquith and Lloyd George governments for dragging their feet over preferential trade. The McKenna duties of 1915, Balfour of Burleigh's trade committee, and post-war statements of economic policy – all of these were scrutinised and found wanting in this respect.

Yet if the War did little to reconfigure the constructive imperial ideology of tariff reformers, it did enhance the rhetorical power of their programme. Tariff reformers spoke of a 'new imperial relationship' resulting from the coming together of the Empire in 1914, and the mobilisation of its military and economic strength against the enemy. They argued that the 'unstinting aid' of the Dominions in financing the War would require these colonies to seek extended markets for their goods after victory had been achieved. If the Dominions were not to be drawn into trading arrangements with the United States and other foreign powers, Britain would have to open its market to them.[116] The War also created new possibilities for fiscal reform by calling into question the inviolability of free trade. After 1914, government control over the economy was vastly extended: the state took direct charge of transport; tariffs were introduced to limit imports and free shipping; and restrictions were placed on the production of oil and non-ferrous metals. Yet while these measures undermined the tenets of liberal political economy which had been so widely accepted before 1914,[117] they did not signify a transformation in attitudes towards the British state. Far from it. The climate for economic planning, seemingly so favourable in 1917, was decidedly difficult after Germany's sudden and unexpected collapse in 1918.[118] Industrial, political and bureaucratic factors all militated against interventionist government in the

114 J. Turner, *British Politics and the Great War. Coalition and Conflict, 1915–18* (1992), p.350.
115 11th Annual Meeting of the Northern Federation of the TRL, *War Notes* (15/2/1916), p.11.
116 Sir J. Lawrence, *War Notes*, 1/2/1916, p.170; 'Objects of the TRL', *Tariff Reformer and Empire Monthly*, (March, 1917), p.6; W.A.S. Hewins, *The Apologia of an Imperialist: Forty Years of Empire Policy*, Vol. II (1929), pp.107–8.
117 F. Trentman, 'The Strange Death of Free Trade', in E. Biagini (ed.), *Citizenship and Community: Liberals, Radicals, and Collective Identities in the British Isles, 1865–1931* (Cambridge, 1996), pp.235–6.
118 P.J. Cain and A.G. Hopkins, *British Imperialism. Vol. II: Crisis and Deconstruction, 1914–1990* (Harlow, 1993), p.54; P. Cline, 'Winding Down the War Economy: British Plans for Peacetime Recovery 1916–19', in K. Burk (ed.), *War and the State: The Transformation of British Government, 1914–19* (1982), p.159.

1920s. 'Home rule for industry' was a popular cry among businessmen who feared that the continuation of state production would be to the detriment of private enterprise;[119] Treasury control over public spending was rapidly reasserted (much to the relief of taxpayers clamouring for income tax reductions);[120] and officials outside the Colonial Office voiced grave misgivings about the concept of empire development.[121]

To be sure, after 1918 the tariff reform movement scored some successes. Austen Chamberlain's 1919 budget contained an imperial preference clause (although it covered existing customs duties only). In the summer of 1920 the TRL issued a 'new manifesto' in which the components of its proposed 'British Customs Tariff' were spelt out in greater detail than ever before and protection was introduced for certain 'strategic' industries under the Safeguarding of Industries Act (1922). But, by the same token, it proved very difficult to hold the government to the resolutions passed at the Paris Economic Conference (1916) and Imperial War Conference (1917).[122] Moreover, even after Walter Long's trade committee had obtained the War Cabinet's approval for the inclusion of a preferential tariff as a part of post-war reconstruction, Lloyd George and Bonar Law resisted pressure to define this aspect of economic policy more precisely.[123] Worse still, the Coalition's manifesto for the 1918 election categorically stated that there would be no new taxes on food or raw materials. Despite intense lobbying by the TRL, Bonar Law repeated this message in 1922 when he announced that the Conservative party would not change the country's fiscal system without the sanction of a second general election.

Only in the face of a fourth winter of high unemployment was Baldwin to approach the electorate in 1923 asking for a release from this pledge. He was immediately rebuffed. When Labour came to power in 1924, Philip Snowden (Chancellor of the Exchequer) was quick to dismantle wartime protection and to rescind Austen Chamberlain's preferential tariff. By this time the TRL was as dead as a dodo, although a new organisation, the Empire Industries Association, soon emerged to take its place.[124] The EIA became a powerful pressure group after 1924, forging links with kindred organisations, cultivating the press, and spearheading the opposition from within the parliamentary and constituency party to tariff reform being expunged from the Conservative programme.[125] It also acted as a magnet for the growing body of support for

119 C. Wigley, *Lloyd George and the Challenge of Labour. The Postwar Coalition, 1918–22* (1990), p.7.
120 Lowe, 'Government', pp.36–9.
121 Holland, *Britain and the Commonwealth Alliance*, p.18.
122 These resolutions favoured measures to encourage postwar trade among the Allies and preferential trade within the Empire.
123 R. Murphy, 'Walter Long and the Conservative Party, 1905–21', University of Bristol PhD (1984), pp.305–8.
124 For a fuller account of the EIA, see Marrison, *British Business and Protection*, pp.361–86.
125 'Imperial Trade. A New Association Formed', *The Times*, 28/9/1925, p.11. For positive assessments of the EIA's impact, see R. Self, *Tories and Tariffs. The Conservative Party and the Politics of Tariff Reform, 1922–32* (1986), p.312, and F. Capie, *Depression and Protectionism* (1983), p.74. For a more cautious appraisal, emphasising the EIA's willingness to work within the parameters set by official party policy, see Marrison, *British Business and Protection*, pp.322, 364ff.

protection and preference from within industry and business.[126] Of course, the Ottawa agreements of 1932 – a series of bilateral arrangements between Britain and the Dominions establishing a system of imperial preference – were ultimately a response to world depression. Yet the fact that tariffs were put back on the political agenda by the slump should not be allowed to obscure the way in which the various lobbying and propaganda activity of bodies like the EIA had kept the cause of tariff reform alive in the 1920s. When, in the early 1930s, prices and production collapsed and unemployment began to climb, the idea that a solution to Britain's economic problems lay in the Empire had already been very widely circulated.[127]

Hailed as a triumph for the Chamberlain school of imperialism,[128] the 1932 Ottawa agreements were by no means the only advance towards a policy of planned empire development in the inter-war years. As Chancellor of the Exchequer, Churchill shelved tariff reform during the 1924–29 parliament. Yet under pressure to prove it had not completely abandoned its imperial commitments, the Baldwin government threw its weight behind a number of other initiatives which testify to the growing importance attached to the Empire as a trading bloc. In 1924, a British Empire exhibition was staged at Wembley Park. Sited on 216 acres of farmland, it attracted over 27 million people during its two-year lifespan.[129] The cost came to £12 million, most of the money being raised by private borrowing, although the government guaranteed the event against loss to the tune of £100,000.[130] The exhibition's main aim was to boost trade. Visitors saw a vast array of dominion produce, including a model of the Prince of Wales made from Canadian butter! Two years later Amery squeezed money out of the Treasury to set up the Empire Marketing Board.[131] A wide range of interests was represented on the Board: Liberal and Labour as well as Conservative; Dominion, Indian and colonial as well as British.[132] Described as an experiment in imperial preference with tariffs left out,[133] the EMB conducted a series of high-profile publicity campaigns for imperial goods. These included placing advertisements in the press, launching a nationwide series of public lectures, organising empire shopping weeks, taking over empty shops and letting them to empire governments to advertise the products of

126 W.R. Garside, 'Party Politics, Political Economy and British Protectionism, 1919–32', *History* (1998), pp.63–5.
127 F. Capie, 'The Sources and Origins of Britain's Return to Protection, 1931–32', in Marrison (ed.), *Free Trade and its Reception*, pp.250–6.
128 Self, *Tories and Tariffs*, p.76; A. Howe, *Free Trade and Liberal England, 1846–1946* (Oxford, 1997), pp.274, 283, 288.
129 D. Judd, *Empire. The British Imperial Experience from 1765 to the Present* (1996), Chapter 21.
130 K. Walthew, 'The British Empire Exhibition of 1924', *History Today* (1981), pp.34–5.
131 Originally promised £1 million a year, the EMB was actually granted £3,681,500 during its seven-year existence from May 1926 to September 1933.
132 S. Constantine, 'Bringing the Empire Alive. The Empire Marketing Board and Imperial Propaganda, 1926–33', in J.M. Mackenzie (ed.), *Imperialism and Popular Culture* (Manchester, 1986), p.198.
133 D. Meredith, 'Imperial Images: The Empire Marketing Board, 1926–32', *History Today* (1987), pp.30–5.

their countries, and putting up eye-catching posters on specially constructed hoardings.[134] Efforts to promote the buying and selling of empire goods were therefore a key aspect of inter-war imperial propaganda.

For many imperialists, the corollary of expanding empire trade was state-assisted migration. It was claimed that empire settlement would enlarge the market for British goods in the Dominions, cheapen the mother country's imports, secure supplies of scarce raw materials, and pave the way towards imperial self-sufficiency.[135] Prior to the British government introducing migration legislation in 1922, the Treasury provided free passages for ex-servicemen, women and their dependents who wished to go to the Dominions and who satisfied their entry requirements. Between 1919 and 1924, over 86,000 people were assisted at a cost of £2.4 million. The Royal Colonial Institute had begun to lobby for such a scheme as early as February 1914 by publicising the work of the Naval and Military Emigration League. In the spring of 1915, its Emigration Committee was reconstituted so as to focus solely on the employment of ex-servicemen – in future it was to be known as the Empire Land Settlement Committee. The ELSC twice approached the Colonial Office (in 1915 and 1916) arguing for a policy of soldier settlement, partly to reward fighting men and women for the hardships they had endured, but also to alleviate the problems involved in demobilising soldiers after the War. The initial response was unsympathetic, but a combination of factors helped to change the bureaucratic mindset in 1916–17. These included the surprisingly positive response from official opinion in the Dominions to Henry Rider Haggard's 1915 fact-finding tour, the absence of a large-scale domestic colonisation scheme, and the social and political dangers presented by veterans' discontent and chronic unemployment in 1919.[136] At first, the policy of settling demobilised soldiers in the Empire was impeded by a shortage of shipping – owing to the repatriation of Dominion forces – and thereafter by depressed job markets in the Dominions. However, soldier settlement is recognised by historians to have been a precursor to the Empire Settlement Act of 1922.[137]

The importance of the RCI's lobbying on the issue of empire migration should not be underestimated. Just before the Empire Settlement bill was introduced, Churchill (the Colonial Secretary) welcomed a deputation from the Institute and tried to enlist its services in defending the measure outside parliament.[138] The bill itself drew heavily upon long-standing RCI recommendations: it targeted particular social groups (especially single women and children); it attached great importance to the training of migrants, and to the superintendence of female and juvenile migrants after arrival; it recognised the need for Dominion scrutiny of applications; and it stipulated that the cost was

134 Amery, *My Political Life*, Vol. II, p.352.
135 I.M. Drummond, *Imperial Economic Policy, 1917–39* (1974), pp.65, 137.
136 K. Fedorowich, *Unfit for Heroes. Reconstruction and Soldier Settlement in the Empire between the Wars* (Manchester, 1995), esp. pp.25–6, 53.
137 Ibid., p.192.
138 Rhodes James (ed.), *Speeches of Winston Churchill*, Vol. III, pp.3178–80.

to be shared between the British and Dominion governments. These were key aspects of migrationist thinking before 1914 (see Chapter 6). Moreover, the ideology underpinning the Empire Settlement Act strove for that same synthesis of individualism and collectivism which had been the hallmark of the Edwardian migration movement. In particular, the 1922 legislation aimed to subsidise and stimulate the work of voluntary emigration societies, and to take advantage of their experience in selecting, training and caring for migrants.[139] It also imposed clear limits to state aid. As Amery explained: 'The less that aid was felt to be State given, the more the migrant felt that he, and he alone, was responsible for the success or failure of his adventure, the better.'[140] In short, the Empire Settlement Act was to embody most of what the RCI had been hoping for from a migration policy.[141] Admittedly, annual government expenditure on migration was much less than the £3 million annual allocation – only £6.7 million was spent over the whole period 1922–35. Nonetheless, assisted migration was statistically significant. It accounted for over 31 per cent of total emigration in the period 1923–29, while at the same time probably increasing the ratio of female to male migrants as well as the number of child migrants.[142]

CONCLUSION

A few historians still cling to the idea that the First World War put an end to the British public's interest in empire.[143] Two explanations are offered. Either Britain's imperial pretensions gave way to the 'moral internationalism' of the League of Nations,[144] or the call for imperial unity lost its appeal in the face of difficult domestic problems such as mass unemployment.[145] It is, however, more commonly believed that the strength of the imperial factor in British political thinking did not suddenly subside in 1918. Stirred by the extraordinary mobilisation of imperial resources during the War,[146] those who governed Britain in the 1920s and 1930s were much more favourably disposed to migration and tariff policies than their Edwardian predecessors.[147] Meanwhile the effect of wartime propaganda was probably to spread imperial sentiment more widely in British society, and to reinforce the appeal of empire as a 'living principle'[148] and a bulwark of liberal, democratic values. Far from being a period

139 S. Constantine, 'Empire Migration and Social Reform, 1880–1950', in C.G. Pooley and I.D. Whyte (eds), *Migrants, Emigrants and Immigrants. A Social History of Migration* (1991), pp.74–5; A.G. Scholes, *Education for Empire Settlement. A Study of Juvenile Migration* (1932), p.76.
140 Amery, *My Political Life*, Vol. II, p.208.
141 T.R. Reese, *The History of the Royal Commonwealth Society* (Oxford, 1968), p.165.
142 Constantine, 'Empire Migration and Social Reform', p.75.
143 Greenlee, 'Imperial Studies and the Unity of Empire', p.332.
144 C. Barnett, *The Collapse of British Power* (1972), pp.59–61.
145 Holland, *Britain and the Commonwealth Alliance*, pp.6–7; B. Porter, *The Lion's Share. A Short History of British Imperialism, 1850–1983* (2nd edn, Harlow, 1984), pp.266–7.
146 R.F. Betts, *Uncertain Dimensions. Western Overseas Empires in the Twentieth Century* (Oxford, 1995), p.11.
147 Constantine, 'Bringing the Empire Alive', p.192.
148 The phrase is from Billy Hughes's autobiography, *Splendid Adventure*, p.82.

of popular disillusionment with empire, if anything the inter-war years witnessed a deeper cultural penetration of imperial ideals. Post-war propaganda for the British Empire was bolstered by new institutions (like the Empire Marketing Board) and new media (radio, film), and it is in the 1920s that the apogee of mass phenomena of empire (shopping weeks, empire advertising, empire exhibitions, and Empire Day celebrations) is to be found.[149]

Of course, the political climate of 1919–20 was very different to that of 1913–14. Public pressure for retrenchment and calls for disarmament made the protection of Britain's imperial interests decidedly more difficult. By the summer of 1920 the War Office faced a crisis of manpower – it simply could not find enough troops to garrison the new territories Britain had acquired at the Paris Peace Conference. The next year, at the Washington Naval Conference, Britain gave up the pursuit of naval hegemony and settled for a one-power standard of maritime strength. Moreover, if, during the War, the Empire had shown itself to be surprisingly united and cohesive, after the Armistice it was beset by serious internal unrest. A battery of nationalist revolts in Ireland, Egypt and India added immensely to anxieties about Britain's imperial future. As for the self-governing areas of empire, we have already seen how their participation in the war effort provoked domestic disaffection (in Canada) and an armed uprising (in South Africa). Moreover, while the Dominion governments may have responded readily to the call for help from the 'mother country', the wartime speeches of their premiers made it clear that their future attachment to the Empire would by no means be unconditional or unchanging.

True, Britain's empire survived the First World War, while the empires of other powers – Habsburg, Hohenzollern, Ottoman and Romanov – were destroyed by it. Yet even though it was still intact, the British Empire was a far more fragile structure after the Versailles peace treaty. To a large degree, its survival depended on the absence of a coalescence of challengers. When, in the mid- to late-1930s, Britain was confronted by anti-colonial nationalist movements in Asia and Africa, and by the rise of Fascism in Europe, it began to look as though its empire might be living on borrowed time. Even so, there was no mood of imperial fatalism prior to the depression. Wartime co-operation underscored the benefits to be derived from empire. It also made imperialists determined to find a way of sustaining into peacetime the new sense of partnership generated during the years 1914–18.

The First World War did not, then, put an end to campaigning for imperial unity. Initially, ideas about imperial reform coalesced around the Imperial War Cabinet and the possibility of its continuation as a consultative body. Imperialists also explored the possibilities of regulating and reinforcing other mechanisms of co-operation (foreign policy-making, for instance). Moreover, imperial agitation continued unabated into the 1920s, the War having broadened the basis of the tariff reform movement and enhanced its rhetorical power,

---

149 S. Constantine, *The Making of British Colonial Development Policy, 1914–40* (1984), pp.4–5; J.M. MacKenzie, *Propaganda and Empire. The Manipulation of British Public Opinion, 1880–1960* (Manchester, 1986), pp.8–11.

kick-started state support for migration with the Colonial Office's soldier settlement scheme (1917), and generally advanced the concept of empire development in significant ways. Neither did the events of 1914–18 alter in any lasting or fundamental way the political consciousness of empire in Britain. New strains of imperial politics were introduced by the War – 'war imperialism' in the Middle East and Diehard opposition to constitutional concessions in Britain's dependencies – but they proved superficial or short-lived. Like their later-Victorian and Edwardian predecessors, imperial activists in the 1920s continued to conceptualise Britain's imperial future mainly in terms of greater Dominion involvement in imperial affairs. In fact, much of what imperialists achieved in the inter-war years not only has its origins in, but is partly attributable to, their intensive and unrelenting lobbying and propaganda activity before 1914.

Conclusions

Ever since J.A. Hobson published *Imperialism: A Study* in 1902, the question of which groups in British society were most enthusiastic about empire has been something of a hot potato. The view often expressed is that it was from the ranks of a public school, Oxbridge-educated, male elite that the strongest support for empire emerged. However, some have tried to provide a more precise definition of the social basis of imperialism, most recently, of course, Cain and Hopkins, with their concept of 'gentlemanly capitalism'. The problem with this approach is that it is far too reductive. Imperial politics cannot be confined within a 'gentlemanly capitalist' framework because imperialism appealed to a much wider range of interests, aspirations and enthusiasms than those succoured by the City or the service sector. Within the imperial movements which we have been discussing free traders rubbed shoulders with protectionists, industrialists with financiers, *laissez-faire* liberals with state interventionists, evangelical Christians with agnostics, humanitarians (and even a few pacifists) with the more military-minded, suffragists with anti-suffragists. Thus the plurality of British society was very well reflected in the Empire's capacity to draw people together from different backgrounds in a common political cause. Chapter 2 highlighted the broad church character of various extra-parliamentary imperial campaigns. Possibly the most striking example of the catholicity of imperialism's appeal is provided by the combination of Christian philanthropy, feminist thinking and imperial patriotism evident in some women's emigration societies. However, the issue of emigration was by no means unique, and campaigning for an imperial preferential tariff or for higher levels of defence spending also benefited from the support of a cross-section of society.

The imperial issues which engaged the attentions and excited the imaginations of British politicians were to a surprising degree dominated by the ambition of welding together the English-speaking empire into a great consolidated unit. The late-1870s and early-1880s was a pivotal period here. Previously, political usage of terms like 'empire' and 'imperialism' had been largely pejorative, conjuring up images of foreign, and especially French, rule. Thereafter,

186

imperial language came to signify a feeling of solidarity between British society at home and the overseas British societies in the Empire. This idea of a fraternity of British communities – or a greater British world – constituted the central element of a new public doctrine of imperialism which emerged in the 1880s and 1890s. At this time the belief gained ground that the future lay with large aggregations of states with big populations and vast regions of natural resources. Yet in looking to the youthful and vigorous periphery of empire, imperialists did not hanker for a centralised structure in which Britain predominated over the rest. Rather, their vision was of a free partnership of democracies, whereby the colonies of settlement would eventually achieve a genuine equality of status with the 'mother country'. The place assigned to America in this 'federation' of states changed over time. Among others, Charles Dilke and Cecil Rhodes testify to the tendency during the 1880s and for much of the 1890s for imperialists to turn to the United States to give a new lease of life to 'Anglo-Saxondom' and to share in its 'divinely-ordained' imperial mission. Marriages among Britain's and America's political and social elites have also been taken as evidence of a *rapprochement* between the two countries.[1] But by the early 1900s, the dangers which an expansionist United States presented to Canada, competition from US firms in foreign and colonial markets, and the need to redirect settlers away from the United States and towards the Empire, all conspired to exclude America from imperialists' schemes.

Throughout this book emphasis has also been laid upon the ambiguous place of India, the supposed jewel in Britain's imperial Crown, in later-Victorian and Edwardian conceptions of empire. Chapter 1 explained why imperialists believed the question of Anglo-Dominion relations to be at the heart of the task of reconstructing the Empire. It showed how sympathy and solidarity with the English-speaking empire was expressed in various spheres of British culture, and how emigration and return migration created complex family networks between Britain and the new world. The hard-and-fast distinction which politicians made between Britain's 'liberal' and 'authoritarian' empires was again examined in Chapter 4. Though a few constructive imperialists tried to show that India would be fairly treated by a preferential tariff, the majority turned their backs on Britain's dependent territories. This was because their overriding objective was to forge closer links between Britain and the self-governing Dominions. Recognising this to be so, men like Curzon, Cromer and Meath objected strenuously to the narrowness of their vision of empire and its failure to recognise the enormous economic and military benefits which India especially conferred on Britain.

To stress this point is not to deny that India left a long-lasting impression upon the nation's religious, intellectual, or literary life. Fascination with what Kipling famously described as the 'white man's burden' was part and parcel of British popular culture. But the question of whether, and for how long, a white, protestant, liberal empire could continue to co-exist alongside colonies

---

1 K. Robbins, *Great Britain. Identities, Institutions and the Idea of Britishness* (Harlow, 1998), p.215.

of authoritarian rule was at best fudged, and often ignored, by imperialists. In the political sphere, 'Imperial Britain' was essentially 'Greater Britain', however incomplete and inadequate a construction of empire this may now seem. Neither the *Raj* in India, nor the acquisition of territory in tropical Africa, gave rise to any powerful home-grown political campaigns. It was the self-governing Dominions which were regarded as the bedrock of empire, and the basis of its strength and prosperity. As a result, the sorts of imperial-mindedness which emerged in British politics before the First World War tended to marginalise the dependent parts of the British Empire.

Here, however, it is necessary to sound a note of caution. Many scholars have been content to use the blanket term 'imperialists' to refer to those elements of British political society which displayed a particular and persistent interest in empire. But imperialists can really only be said to be of a like mind in the way in which they conceived empire as a grand alliance of British settler states. Admittedly, there were voices of dissent, and certain of the Empire's proconsuls made it their mission to establish Britain's governance of non-European peoples as an issue of primary political concern. Yet it was not until after 1914 that India's place within the Empire was re-evaluated. This was partly the result of the multi-racial images of empire projected by the machinery of wartime propaganda. But it was also because of the mobilisation of Diehard resistance within the Conservative party at the time of the Montagu–Chelmsford reforms (1919). Even then, the precise place of India in the 'Commonwealth of Nations' cherished by inter-war imperialists was far from clear.

Treating imperialists as a single political entity is misleading for other reasons too. First, there is a need to distinguish between differing types of commitment to empire. Whereas some politicians were intent upon constructing a national political agenda around the Empire, and invested their political ideals in it, others were more opportunistic in the way they invoked imperialism. This book has been mainly concerned with the former, but the latter did exist. The Liberal Imperialists, for example, were ultimately attracted to empire for reasons of electoral expediency – a more positive imperial platform was understood by Rosebery and the Liberal League to be essential to their party's revival, especially among the 'moderate' middle classes.[2] Ulterior motives have also been uncovered in the imperial campaigning of British suffragettes. Their interest in empire seemingly had as much to do with women's struggle for equality at home as it did with the protection of Indian women.[3] Yet historians writing about the politics of imperialism frequently fail to separate politicians for whom empire was a guiding principle from politicians whose commitment to empire rarely progressed beyond the rhetorical sphere. We may question their motives for doing so. For in drawing attention to the partial or incomplete

---

2 H.C.G. Matthew, *The Liberal Imperialists. The Ideas and Politics of a Post-Gladstonian Elite* (Oxford, 1973), Chapter 5.
3 A. Burton, *Burdens of History. British Feminists, Indian Women and Imperial Culture, 1865–1915* (Chapel Hill, NC, 1994), Chapters 1, 7.

hold which the doctrine of imperialism had upon the lives of some politicians it has been much easier to play down the political effects of empire on Britain.

Second, we must be sensitive to the different contexts in which empire was raised as an issue of political concern. Many studies of the domestic politics of imperialism focus exclusively upon the South African War and its aftermath. Our understanding of the subject remains rather blinkered as a result. The war no doubt awakened an interest in imperial affairs, especially among the middle- and upper-class women who joined philanthropic and educational bodies like the Victoria League. Neither should we play down the importance of pro-Boer and pro-war activism during the years 1899–1902 – South African questions were to shake up party, electoral and extra-parliamentary politics at the turn of the century. However, as Chapters 4–7 argued, imperialists became involved in a wide range of public policy debates, relating to the economy, defence and demography. These debates had a long life after the Peace of Vereeniging (1902).

Third, debate about empire did not just revolve around its champions and its critics. Imperial politics was contested terrain, if not in terms of its underlying conception of empire, then certainly in terms of its ideology.[4] As Chapters 4–6 argued, the patterns of political thought surrounding the empire are far too complex to be compressed into a single 'ism'. There were varieties of imperialism, in just the same way that there were varieties of pacifism.[5] Doctrinal disputes among imperialists stemmed primarily from conflicting views about the right strategy for reorganising the Empire. Was it to be economic, defensive or demographic? Above all, there was a diversity of opinion regarding the proper role of the state in imperial reconstruction. The *etatism* of constructive imperialists – a faction within the Edwardian Unionist party – saw the state as a creative and dynamic agency which had a key role to play in the Empire's consolidation. The doctrine of free trade imperialism cut across the boundaries of party organisation and tradition, suggesting that defensive integration could succeed where economic integration had failed. It encompassed attitudes to government which ranged from a Tory individualist belief in the 'minimal' state, to the constrained collectivism of 'Liberal-Imperialists' which regarded the state as an interferer of the last resort.[6] Either way, the stability and security of empire was understood to reside in the informal social ties of sentiment and affection, buttressed by a properly organised system of imperial defence, and not in major programmes of government intervention. In between these two ideologies lay a more pragmatic position taken up by many of the enthusiasts for empire migration. Through state subsidy and support, the efficiency and

4 For an exposition of this argument, see A.S. Thompson, 'Imperial Ideology in Edwardian Britain', in A. Bosco and A. May (eds), *The Round Table, the Empire/Commonwealth and British Foreign Policy* (1997), pp.3–19.
5 M. Ceadel, *Pacifism in Britain 1914–1945: The Defining of a Faith* (Oxford, 1980), Chapter 1, and *Thinking about Peace and War* (Oxford, 1989), Chapters 4–7.
6 For the constrained collectivism of imperially-minded Liberals, see Matthew, *The Liberal Imperialists*, pp.227, 244, 250, 264.

effectiveness of voluntary emigration societies was to be enhanced, Britain's surplus population (re)directed to the Empire, and the British character of the colonies preserved.

Hence we must question the assumption that after 1903 the most committed imperialists were the Chamberlainites, and that those who opposed preference were not in the vanguard of imperial politics. The rejection of the preferential part of the tariff reform programme was not the same thing as the rejection of empire as a whole. Rather, it was a verdict upon a particular type of imperialism, alternative creeds being elaborated by imperial navalists and empire migrationists, and by the Empire's proconsuls. Moreover, situating imperial campaigns in their wider intellectual and philosophical context demonstrates that imperialism was in a very fundamental sense a house divided. Owing to doctrinal differences among imperialists there was little agreement as to how the Empire was to be reorganised. This meant that their energies were dissipated in a number of different schemes. This, in turn, made it easier for successive British governments to ignore their demands.

How powerfully, then, did the Empire impress itself upon the British political scene between the mid-1880s and the late-1920s? If its effects are to be measured narrowly in terms of legislative activity and official decision-making, it is possible to claim that the ideas of imperialists did not 'catch on', and that their achievements, when measured against the full extent of their ambitions came to very little.[7] After all, the Empire was not federated, tariff reform was rejected at the polls in 1906, and only in wartime was the machinery of British government adapted to perform an imperial role. The problem with this line of argument is that it fails to recognise that the political significance of imperialism before 1914 lies not in achievement but in aspiration and expectation. Put another way, politics is about more than office and legislation. In its widest sense, Britain's political process was undoubtedly influenced and modified by its imperial involvement. Yet for this to be fully appreciated we must look beyond Westminster and Whitehall and adopt a broader conception of 'politics' which embraces pressure group and press activity, extra-parliamentary political culture, intra-party allegiances, and the configuration of national political debate. Measured against such criteria, the effects of empire on domestic British politics were much more marked than analyses focusing chiefly upon the realm of high politics seem to suggest.

Imperialism provided a powerful impetus to political mobilisation in Britain. The energies and enthusiasms of later-Victorian and Edwardian imperialists were channelled into the creation of a new and modern extra-parliamentary movement. This movement had a kind of 'Heineken effect': it was able to strike deep roots into society and to embrace areas of the nation's political life which the conventional party caucuses struggled to reach. Imperialism was

7 B. Porter, *Britain, Europe and the World, 1850–1982: Delusions of Grandeur* (1983), pp.63–4, and *The Lion's Share. A Short History of British Imperialism, 1850–1983* (2nd edn, Harlow, 1984), pp.192–5.

not therefore simply the passion of a vocal minority. Indeed, as a result of the campaigning of imperial pressure groups the Empire became more widely discussed; a growing women's interest in Britain's imperial 'mission' was given an organisational outlet and expression; the rhetoric of imperial unity was related to specific policy debates; and public ceremonies celebrating Britain's imperial achievement were organised and observed (Trafalgar Day; Empire Day; Chamberlain Day). The Tariff Reform League was particularly important here. Well-funded, and eager to exploit the latest technologies of the gramophone and cinematograph, the constituency it carried was of real political consequence, so much so that to many people at the time it looked more like an alternative party than a pressure group pure and simple.[8] It might be even argued that the longer-term significance of the techniques pioneered by the League, if not the issue it championed, was to blaze a trail for the great inter-war Conservative achievement: making the party of privilege the popular party. Similarly, the history of the British press in these years cannot be written without paying attention to the imperial commitments of many newspaper owners, editors and journalists. Papers and periodicals were instrumental in circulating ideas about empire among a wider public, and in promoting various imperial causes. Many of the most memorable press campaigns of the late-nineteenth and early-twentieth centuries were inspired by the Empire. And the organisation of an Imperial Press Conference in June 1909 stands out as a major event in the history of Edwardian journalism.

The Empire was also significant in forging an extra-parliamentary political culture, and in providing people with a means of identifying with the British nation. The term 'imperialism' is often used as a shorthand for elitist, authoritarian, and illiberal attitudes. Take, for instance, the concept of social-imperialism, the idea that imperialism acted as an effective system of class conciliation and social discipline. Bernard Semmel interprets imperial ideology in these terms, tracing its roots back to 'the nineteenth century history of the working class' and the fact that from the 1880s 'England at last found itself face to face with the socialist difficulties which were besetting the continent'.[9] But while it is perfectly proper to link domestic to colonial policy, the implication that the main purpose of imperialism was to retard the politicisation of British society, and to make the masses more quiescent, seems doubtful. It is not only that imperial politics was less tainted with jingoism and hysteria than contemporary critics of empire argued. Imperial activists promoted a participatory approach to politics. They challenged the representativeness of the party caucuses. They insisted upon a definition of citizenship which embraced some working-class men and upper- and middle-class women. They pioneered new political techniques and styles of campaigning. And, in the process, they fashioned more

---

8 For a recent discussion of the competition between the TRL and the Unionist party caucus, see G.E. Maguire, *Conservative Women. A History of Women and the Conservative Party, 1874–1997* (Basingstoke, 1998), p.61.

9 B. Semmel, *Imperialism and Social Reform. English Social Imperial Thought, 1895–1914* (1960), esp. pp.13, 19, 22–4.

open and inclusive political structures than they are generally credited for. Nor was a sense of imperial belonging imposed from above. In so far as empire became more important to the British people's sense of their own identity in the late-nineteenth and early-twentieth centuries, it was not so much the result of official policy or elite manipulation as of political pressures emanating from below.

Imperialists were also acutely aware that the progress of their causes depended upon colonial co-operation. They did not fashion their programmes from a narrowly Anglo-centric perspective, but were as concerned with developing and defending the Empire as they were with developing and defending Britain. By visiting the colonies they were able to keep abreast of political developments there, and to seek out allies among local politicians. Mobilising colonial support was especially important to tariff reformers and empire migrationists because they were eager to avoid the charge of putting Britain's interests before those of the Dominions. However, even in the case of naval defence, organised opinion in the colonies had to be taken into account, and was to play a key role in defining the concept of the colonial fleet unit. Thus the level of colonial involvement in the imperial movements studied in this book was much higher than frequently appreciated. Notwithstanding the arguments of some recent commentators,[10] imperialists were not condescending or dismissive towards colonial opinion. Nor were they unable to grasp the significance of those forces propelling colonial societies towards greater independence from Britain.

Neither should we overlook the effects of empire upon intra-party loyalties and rivalries. Many of the fault-lines of late-nineteenth and early-twentieth-century British politics stemmed, in part, from disagreements about empire. As we now know, imperial questions drove a wedge between Liberal-Imperialists and Radical 'Little Englanders' during the 1880s and 1890s, and divided the Liberal party top to bottom during the South African War. Similarly, divergent views of empire were espoused by, and within, the various elements of the Edwardian Labour party – the Fabian Society, the Trade Union movement and even the Marxist Social Democratic Federation[11] were all at sixes and sevens as to how to respond to British military intervention in South Africa.[12] But, above all, the Empire reconstituted allegiances within the Edwardian Unionist party. Joseph Chamberlain's mission to convert Conservatives to the tariff reform programme, and the constructive imperial ideology which underpinned it, split his adopted party wide open. The consensual, quietist and centrist tradition represented by Salisbury and Balfour did not sit comfortably with the reformist, statist and assertive political creed championed by

10 See, for instance, R.G. Moyles and D. Owram, *Imperial Dreams and Colonial Realities. British Views of Canada, 1880–1914* (Toronto, 1988).
11 The SDF's devoted but idiosyncratic leader, H.M. Hyndman, looked to a reconstructed empire to spread 'enlightened' socialist views throughout the world, whereas other SDF members, such as Belfort Bax and Theodore Rothstein, regarded socialism and imperialism as fundamentally incompatible principles.
12 For a recent review of Socialist responses to the war, see P. Ward, *Red Flag and Union Jack. Englishness, Patriotism and the British Left, 1881–1924* (1998), Chapter 4.

Chamberlain and other leading tariff reformers. The enemies of tariff reform – or, more precisely, imperial preference – were hunted down and harassed by organisations like the TRL and the Confederacy. In so doing, 'wholehoggers' plunged the party into a period of civil war from which it did not really begin to recover until 1914.

Finally, imperial issues were part and parcel of domestic political debate, not necessarily in the sense that they were consistently centre stage, but in that they intersected with many of the other major topics of the day. Problems of urban poverty and unemployment were linked to the economic development of empire. High levels of spending on the armed forces were justified by Britain's imperial commitments and not just its own security. The purpose of a large navy was explained in terms of defending the Empire as well as the United Kingdom. The position of women, the welfare of children and the future of demobilised soldiers were all thought to be open to improvement through empire migration. In each case the Empire provided the context in which key domestic issues were debated. Neither did imperial sentiment suddenly peter out after the First World War. To be sure, the idea of imperial weakness was more widely diffused post-1918. Nonetheless, in some ways the War politically strengthened imperialists. Lloyd George's Coalition government placed Milner and many of his strongest supporters in positions of power. The wartime propaganda machine not only raised public awareness of empire, but brought sections of the British public into direct contact with some of its leading statesmen. The experience of shared sacrifice by the component parts of the Empire was capitalised upon by inter-war imperial propaganda. The Imperial War Cabinet idea aroused very high hopes among British and Dominion politicians. And, after 1917, there was an increased official commitment to imperial interests, especially in the economic sphere (tariff reform and empire migration). It also needs to be emphasised that the idea of the 'Commonwealth' which emerged in the 1920s was organically linked to the sorts of imperial-mindedness which were present before 1914.

This study of the meaning and significance of imperialism in domestic British politics makes it clear that the Empire was not just something which happened beyond the British Isles. As well as being a key aspect of international affairs, empire was internal and integral to Britain's own political process. Yet this still begs the question of how far it influenced political behaviour in Britain. Was Britain's imperial enterprise a 'fundamental' and 'constitutive' part of its political culture?[13] Or was the Empire's impact more limited, better understood in terms of it reflecting and reinforcing existing political trends, rather than pushing domestic politics in new directions?[14] Certainly, to suggest that

13 A. Burton, *At the Heart of the Empire. Indians and the Colonial Encounter in Late-Victorian Britain* (1998), pp.7–8, 191–2.
14 P.J. Marshall, 'No Fatal Impact? The Elusive History of Imperial Britain', *Times Literary Supplement*, 12/3/1993, p.10; 'Imperial Britain', *JICH* (1995), pp.392–3; and 'Imperial Britain', in Marshall (ed.), *Cambridge Illustrated History of the British Empire* (Cambridge, 1996), pp.336–7.

British politics was totally remade by its imperial involvement would be seriously to overestimate the effects of empire. On the other hand, to interpret empire simply as a metaphor for domestic politics, or to suggest that there was no genuine or sustained political interest in imperial affairs, would be equally misleading. To be sure, if we think of party as the only vehicle for political argument and conflict, then debate about empire can often, though by no means always, be explained in terms of faction-fighting, electoral pressures, and the struggle for power and status inside the British parliament. Yet, as we have seen, a powerful strand of imperial thought flowed through other channels of British politics between the mid-1880s and the late-1920s. During these years, empire became deeply embedded in extra-parliamentary political culture, a persistent and pervasive sense of imperial Britishness imprinted itself upon the nation's political consciousness, and the goal of closer imperial unity gave rise to a number of large-scale and long-term political campaigns. Nor should we overlook the dynamism of the imperial debate that went on within Britain. After all, empire was as often a matter of political controversy as consensus.

From J.R. Seeley onwards every generation of historians has re-evaluated the British Empire. The early-twentieth century was preoccupied with its Whiggish evolution towards the 'Commonwealth', and bequeathed to us a rather dry and narrow constitutional history of Anglo-Dominion relations. Subsequently, in an attack upon Marxist theory, a post-war generation of historians debunked the idea of a late-nineteenth-century 'new imperialism' in Africa, and emphasised instead the centrality of India to Britain's imperial enterprise. And in the 1980s and 1990s, with the decline of manufacturing industry, and the prominence of the City in national economic policy, the rapid rise of a service sector has been presented as the key to understanding British overseas expansion. As for efforts to reintegrate British and Imperial history, it may well be that they have been spurred by late-twentieth-century anxieties about the future of the United Kingdom. If the major props of a British national identity in the past were religion, wars and empire, then its prospects in an essentially secular society, with a fading memory of the century's two world wars, and virtually no colonies left to govern, can be made to look rather bleak. Yet to argue that Britain's political culture was influenced and modified by its empire is not simply to seek in the past an explanation for problems in the present. Nor is it an argument that is relevant only to the more modern period. New research on the ways in which British people were drawn into the imperial effort in the eighteenth century shows how a popular vision of imperial greatness manifested itself in the press, the theatre and in populist, libertarian notions of the polity.[15] Thus in the same way that Hanoverian political culture is now being recognised to have been permeated by empire, so too historians of the later-nineteenth

15 K. Wilson, 'Empire of Virtue. The Imperial Project and Hanoverian Culture, *c.* 1720–1785', in L. Stone (ed.), *An Imperial State at War. Britain from 1689 to 1815* (1994), pp.128–64.

and early-twentieth centuries must be aware that Britain's political system was not hermetically sealed off from its empire. They must pull down the artificial barriers dividing the 'domestic' from the 'imperial'. And they must be less insular and inward-looking in how they write about the development of the modern British state.

Biographical Appendix

L. Amery: journalist on *The Times* and an author of *The Times History of the South African War*, Unionist MP (1911–45); Parliamentary Under-Secretary to Milner at the Colonial Office (1919–21); First Lord of the Admiralty (1922); Colonial Secretary (1924–29). Amery chaired the TRL's Management Committee.

T.W.A. Bagley: dedicated and energetic secretary of the TRL (from 1907); formerly a Unionist party agent.

V. Brooke-Hunt: social worker and political activist; nursed wounded British soldiers and organised Soldiers' Institutes in South Africa (1899–1902). Brooke-Hunt was the secretary of the WUTRA.

A. Chamberlain: Unionist MP (1892–1937); Civil Lord of the Admiralty (1895–1900); Chancellor of the Exchequer (1903–6; 1919–21); and Foreign Secretary (1924–29).

H. Chaplin: large landowner in Lincolnshire; Unionist MP (1868–1916), and prominent spokesman for the party on agricultural questions; President of the Local Government Board (1895–1900).

J. Ratcliffe Cousins: lawyer; first secretary of the TRL, who resigned in October 1906.

H. Page Croft: renegade Unionist MP (1910–40) who formed the Nationalist Party in 1917. Page Croft succeeded Goulding as Chairman of the TRL's Organising Committee.

Duncannon (Viscount): Member of London County Council (1907–10); Unionist MP (1910; 1913–20); supporter of National Party; Governor-General of Canada (1931–35). Duncannon was Chairman of the TRL from 1913–17.

J.L. Garvin: influential journalist who edited the *Outlook* (1905–6) and *The Observer* (1908–42); author of three volumes of *The Life of Joseph Chamberlain* (1932–34).

E. Goulding: chairman of Rolls Royce Ltd and close business associate of Lord Beaverbrook; Unionist MP (1895–1906; 1908–22). Goulding was a dedicated Chairman of the TRL's main policy-making forum, the Organising Committee (1904–12).

A. Griffith-Boscawen: Unionist MP (1892–1906; 1910–22); Parliamentary Charity Commissioner (1900–6); Minister of Health (1922–23). Griffith-Boscawen was Chairman of the TRL's Literature Committee.

A. Henderson: chairman of the Great Central Railway; Unionist MP (1898–1906; 1913–16); created Lord Faringdon in 1916. Henderson was the TRL's Treasurer.

W.A.S. Hewins: first Director of the London School of Economics (1895–1903); Secretary of the Tariff Commission (1903–17), and Chamberlain's leading economic adviser; Unionist MP (1912–18); Under-Secretary of State for the Colonies (1917–19).

J. Lawrence: pioneer of the Manchester Ship Canal; chairman of a Linotype company; Unionist MP (1901–6); member of the Surrey County Council; later involved in the establishment of the British Commonwealth Union.

F. Leverton Harris: successful shipowner and well-known art collector; Unionist MP (1900–10; 1914–18); Parliamentary Secretary to the Ministry of Blockade (1916–19).

H. Mackinder: founder of the School of Geography at Oxford University, and a pioneer of the study of 'geopolitics'; Director of the London School of Economics (1903–8); Unionist MP (1910–22); Chairman of the Imperial Shipping Committee (1920–45).

L. Maxse: outspoken journalist and political writer; owner and editor of the *National Review* (1893–1932).

H. Gilbert Parker: prolific and popular author, especially of novels about Canada; Chairman of the ISAA (1903–9); Unionist MP (1900–18).

J. Parker Smith: Unionist MP (1890–1906); Parliamentary Private Secretary to Joseph Chamberlain (1901); Deputy-Lieutenant for Renfrewshire and the Corporation of the City of Glasgow. Parker Smith was Vice-President of the Scottish branch of the TRL.

C.A. Pearson: newspaper proprietor and owner of the *Daily Express* and the *Standard*; founder of Dunstan's home for blinded soldiers and sailors (1915). Pearson was the first Chairman of the TRL. He resigned in March 1905 after publishing a series of articles in the *Standard* which deviated from the policy outlined by Joseph Chamberlain, but continued as a Vice-President of the League.

M. Ridley: a Northumberland landowner; Under-Secretary to Lord Aberdeen as Governor-General of Canada (1893–98); Unionist MP (1900–4), then succeeded as 2nd Viscount Ridley. Ridley replaced Pearson as the TRL's Chairman from 1905.

G. Wyndham: Unionist MP (1889–1913); Chairman of ISAA (1896–98); Parliamentary Under-Secretary at the War Office (1898); Chief Secretary for Ireland (1900–5).

THE NAVY LEAGUE

Lieut. C. Bellairs: joined Royal Navy in 1885; became a Lieutenant in 1891; retired in 1902 to become a lecturer on the war course for senior naval officers (1902–5); Liberal MP (1906–9) who defected to the Conservative party in 1909 to protest against the Lloyd George budget. Bellairs was Vice-Chairman of the NL from 1909.

A. Burgoyne: director of a company of colonial merchants; author of volumes on submarines and naval history; Unionist MP (1910–22; 1924–29); Secretary of Parliamentary Air Commission (1918–20). Burgoyne was honorary Treasurer of the NL (1909–13) and editor of *The Navy League Annual*.

Commander W.C. Crutchley: served for thirty-one years at sea, including seven years in command of first-class mail steamers; Secretary of the NL for sixteen years.

H. Cust: editor of the *Pall Mall Gazette* (1892–96; 1902–6); Unionist MP (1890–95; 1900–6). A founder member of the NL.

G. Drage: Secretary of the Royal Commission on Labour (1891–94); Chairman of the ISAA (1898–1900); President of the Central Poor Law Conference (1906); Chairman of the training ship *Exmouth* for periods from 1901 to 1922; Unionist MP (1895–1900).

Lord Elcho: owner of a large landed estate in Scotland; Unionist MP (1883–85; 1886–95); succeeded as 11th Earl of Wemyss in 1914. Elcho was Chairman of the NL's executive from 1909.

G. Fiennes: wrote widely on naval affairs for various papers and periodicals; editor of the *Birmingham Gazette* (1904–5); assistant editor of the *Standard* (1905–7) and *Pall Mall Gazette* (1912–15).

Admiral E.R. Fremantle: Commander-in-Chief of the China fleet (1892–95), who wrote numerous articles on the navy after his retirement in 1901.

B. Ginsburg: Secretary of the Royal Statistical Society; published books on shipping; editor of *The Navy* (1908–10).

P. Hannon: Director of Agricultural Organisation in South Africa (1904–9); Director of the British Commonwealth Union (1918–28); Unionist MP (1921–50). Hannon was a talented organiser who served as the NL's Secretary from 1911 to 1918 and edited *The Navy* (1912–18).

Viscount Helmsley: Assistant Private Secretary to Lord Selborne as First Lord of the Admiralty (1902–4); Unionist MP (1906–15); killed in action in 1916.

A. Jones: head of the world famous shipping firm, Elder, Dempster & Co., which gained the monopoly of West African shipping trade, pioneered the export of bananas to Britain from the West Indies, and inaugurated a new steamship service with Bristol in 1901; helped to found the Liverpool School of Tropical Medicine (1898–99). Leader of the NL's Liverpool branch.

Lieut. H.T.C. Knox: entered the service in 1872; promoted to Lieutenant in 1883; escorted to Australia its first squadron of warships and then worked for the government of Victoria. Knox was the NL's Principal Organising Lecturer.

Miss de Labrosse: honorary Secretary of the NL's Women's Organising Committee; Assistant Secretary of the Navy League.

A. Lafone: Chairman of a leather trading company; Unionist MP (1886–92; 1895–1900). A founder member of the NL.

G. Parkin: Canadian educationist, and principal of Upper Canada College, Toronto (1895–1902); settled permanently in England in 1902; first Organising Secretary of the Rhodes Scholarship Trust; prolific writer on the subject of imperial unity.

F. Pollock: Professor of Jurisprudence at Oxford University (1883–1903); founder member of the Imperial Federation League; author of the NL's widely-circulated catechism pamphlet.

H. Spenser Wilkinson: journalist and military historian; leader writer for *Manchester Guardian* (1882–92) and the *Morning Post* (1895–1914); first Chichele professor of military history at Oxford University (1909–23); co-author (with Charles Dilke) of *Imperial Defence* (1892). A founder member of the NL.

H.W. Wilson: naval historian and leading naval journalist; assistant editor and leader writer for the *Daily Mail* (1898–1938); moving spirit behind the 1909 naval agitation for more battleships. Wilson was editor of the *Navy League Journal* from 1895 to 1908.

H.F. Wyatt: speaker and writer on naval and imperial affairs; NL's envoy to the colonies (1902–4) and honorary Secretary of NL (1905); founder and joint Secretary of the rival Imperial Maritime League (1908); head of Speaking Staff at the Naval Intelligence division of the Admiralty (1917).

R. Yerburgh: Leading spirit of the Agricultural Organisation Society and Vice-President of the Soldiers' Land Settlement Association; Unionist MP (1886–1906; 1910–16); long-serving President of the NL from 1900.

J.H. Yoxall: General Secretary of the National Union of Teachers (1892–1924); Liberal MP (1895–1918).

THE EMIGRATION COMMITTEE OF THE ROYAL COLONIAL INSTITUTE

J.R. Boose: Librarian of the RCI (1881–1910); the RCI's travelling commissioner to the Dominions; Joint Secretary of the EC.

Earl of Dundonald: army officer who commanded the South Natal Field Force during the South African War; commanded and reorganised the Canadian militia (1902–4); retired from the army in 1907, then served on R.B. Haldane's committee for reorganising the Territorial Army. Dundonald was the EC's first Chairman.

H. Rider Haggard: popular adventure novelist and agricultural reformer; Secretary to H. Bulwer as Governor of Natal in the 1870s; member of the Dominions Royal Commission (1912–17); undertook fact-finding mission for the RCI to the colonies in 1916.

W. Hazell: printer and publisher; Treasurer and then Chairman of Peace Society; representative of the Central Unemployed Body for London; founder of the Self-Help Emigration Society; Liberal MP (1894–1900).

R. Jebb: imperial propagandist, and leading thinker on the subject of colonial nationalism; leader writer for the *Morning Post*; at the age of twenty-four, he embarked on a three-year tour of Canada, Australia and New Zealand; later publicised his vision of empire as a 'partnership' of British states in *Studies in Colonial Nationalism* in 1905.

P. Kerr (later Lord Lothian): member of the Settlers' Emigration Society; Secretary to the Transvaal Indigency Commission (1907); editor of *The State* (1908–10) and the *Round Table* (1910–16); Private Secretary to Lloyd George (1916–21); Secretary to the Rhodes Trustees (1925–39). Kerr was a joint Secretary of the EC.

Lady Knightley: experienced philanthropist; member of the Victoria League; President of the South Africa Colonisation Society; first President of Conservative and Unionist Women's Franchise Association. Knightley was the author of the EC's report on the emigration of women.

C. Kinloch-Cooke: Private Secretary to Lord Dunraven as Under-Secretary for the Colonies (1885–87); leader writer for the *Morning Post*; Chairman of the Central Emigration Board; founder and editor of the *Empire Review*; Unionist MP (1910–29).

G. Lagden: long-serving colonial administrator in Africa, whose posts included assistant Secretary for Sierra Leone (1883), Resident Commissioner of Basutoland (1893–1901), and Commissioner for Native Affairs (1901–7). Lagden was the RCI's representative on the EC.

D.C. Lamb: Superintendent of the Salvation Army's farm colony at Hadleigh in Essex; visited Canada on behalf of the Salvation Army's Emigration Department in 1901 and the Emigration Information Office in 1906.

Duke of Marlborough: Assistant Military Secretary to Lord Roberts in South Africa (1900); Paymaster-General (1899–1902); Under-Secretary at the Colonial Office (1903–5). Marlborough succeeded Dundonald as Chairman.

F. Morris: Administrative Commissioner of the Charity Organisation Society (1913–34); Chairman of the Children's Holiday Fund (1912–38) and the Metropolitan Asylums Board (1924–28).

E.T. Scammell: founder and Secretary of the Naval and Military Emigration League, Scammell produced a report on soldier land settlement for the RCI in 1915.

Lady Talbot: social worker and member of the Catholic Social Union; actively involved in the working-class education movement and in settlement work. Lady Talbot (Mary Caroline) was wife of Lord Edmund Talbot, veteran of the South African War, Unionist MP, and party chief whip from 1913.

L. Tupper: member of the Indian Civil Service until 1907 (including Governor-General's executive council in 1905–6), and author of works on Indian government; then devoted himself to the cause of an imperial federation.

F. Young: travelled widely in the Empire, and actively promoted imperial union; prolific writer on imperial affairs, including *A True System of Emigration* (1869), *Imperial Federation* (1876), and *A Senate for the Empire* (1895); Vice-President of the RCI.

Select Bibliography

A. UNPUBLISHED SOURCES

1 Private Papers

Birmingham University Library
Austen Chamberlain papers
Joseph Chamberlain papers

Bodleian Library, Oxford University
Howell Gwynne papers
Alfred Milner papers

British Library
George Curzon papers

Brotherton Library, University of Leeds (Special Collections)
Glenesk-Bathurst papers

House of Lords Record Office
Bonar Law papers
Edward Goulding (Wargrave) papers
Patrick Hannon papers

Institute of Commonwealth Studies, University of London
Ellis Ashmead Bartlett papers
Richard Jebb papers

Northumberland Record Office
Matthew Ridley (Blagdon) papers

Sheffield University Library
W.A.S. Hewins papers

2 *Organisational Records*

Letter books and Minute books of the Emigration Committee of the Royal
  Colonial Institute, Cambridge University Library
Minute books of the Navy League (1895–1914), Sea Cadet Association,
  Lambeth Road, London
Minute books of the Tariff Reform League (1912–13), London School of
  Economics
IFDC Pamphlet Collection, Rhodes House Library, University of Oxford

3 *Official Papers (Public Record Office, Kew, London)*

(i) Foreign Office
FO 371: Foreign Office Political Files
FO 372: Foreign Office Treaty Department Files
FO 800/256–63 Miscellaneous Correspondence of Austen Chamberlain,
  1924–29

(ii) Colonial Office
CO 323: Colonies (General): Original Correspondence

(iii) Carrier, N. and Jeffrey, J., *External Migration. A Study of the Available
  Statistics, 1815–1950* (HMSO, 1953)

4 *Parliamentary Papers*

Royal Commission on the Natural Resources, Trade and Legislation of certain
  portions of His Majesty's Dominions, First Interim Report (1912–13),
  Cd 6515
Memorandum on Preferential Tariffs in their application to India, presented
  by the India Office to the Colonial Conference in 1907 (XXIII). Papers laid
  before the Colonial Conference of 1907, Cd 3524

B. PUBLISHED SOURCES

1 *Newspapers, Periodicals and Campaign Guides*

The Empire Review
The Imperial Colonist
Monthly Notes on Tariff Reform
Navy League Annual
Navy League Journal/The Navy
The Royal Colonial Institute Year Book (edited by J.R. Boose)
Tariff Reformer and Empire Monthly
Tariff Reform Speakers' Handbook
The Times
United Empire
War Notes. For members of the Tariff Reform League

2 *Diaries, Memoirs, Speeches and Biographies*

Amery, L., *My Political Life. Vol. I: England before the Storm, 1896–1914* and *Vol. II: War and Peace, 1914–1929* (1953).

Asquith, H.H., *Trade and the Empire. Mr Chamberlain's Proposals examined in Four Speeches and a Prefatory Note* (1903).

Boose, J.R., *Memory Serving. Being Reminiscences of Fifty Years of the Royal Colonial Institute* (1928).

Brooke-Hunt, V., *A Woman's Memories of the War* (1901).

Blumfeld, R.D., *RDB's Diary 1887–1914* (1930).

—— *All in a Lifetime* (1931).

—— *The Press in My Time* (1933).

Borden, H.H., *Robert Laird Borden: His Memoirs*, 2 vols (Toronto, 1969).

Borden, R.L., *Canadian Constitutional Studies. The Marfleet Lectures, University of Toronto, October 1921* (Oxford, 1922).

Boyd, C.W. (ed.), *Mr. Chamberlain's Speeches*, 2 vols (1914).

Brittain, H., *Pilgrims and Pioneers* (1946).

Clifford, J., *God's Greater Britain. Letters and Addresses by John Clifford* (1899).

Curzon, G.N., *The Place of India in the Empire. Address delivered before the Philosophical Institute of Edinburgh, October 19th, 1909* (1909).

Dark, S., *The Life of Sir Arthur Pearson* (1922).

Fairbridge, K.O., *The Autobiography of Kingsley Fairbridge* (1927).

Garvin, J.L. (ed.), *Compatriots Club Lectures. First Series* (1905).

Garvin, J.L. and Amery, J., *The Life of Joseph Chamberlain*, 6 vols (1932–69).

Garvin, K., *J.L. Garvin. A Memoir* (1948).

Hardman, T.H., *A Parliament of the Press. The First Imperial Press Conference, 1909. With a Preface by the Earl of Rosebery* (1909).

Hewins, W.A.S., *The Apologia of an Imperialist: Forty Years of Empire Policy*, 2 vols (1929).

Hughes, W.M., *The Splendid Adventure* (1929).

Leal, W., *D.C. Lamb. A Memoir* (1912).

Lloyd George, D., *War Memoirs*, 2 vols (1938).

Milner, A., *The Nation and the Empire* (1913).

Page Croft, H., *My Life of Strife* (1949).

Earl of Ronaldshay, *The Life of Lord Curzon*, 3 vols (1928).

Ross, P.D., *Retrospects of a Newspaper Person* (Toronto, 1931).

Lord Rosebery, *Miscellanies. Literary and Historical*, Vol. II (1921).

Spender, J.A., *Life, Journalism and Politics* (1927).

Spenser Wilkinson, H., *Thirty-Five Years, 1874–1909* (1933).

3 *Contemporary Literature*

Amery, L., *The Fundamental Fallacies of Free Trade. Four Addresses on the Logical Groundwork of the Free Trade Theory* (1908, popular edn).

—— *Union and Strength. A Series of Papers on Imperial Questions* (1912).

Bellairs, C., *A New System of Preference* (1912).

Clarke, G.S. and Thursfield, J.R., *The Navy and the Nation, or Naval Warfare and Imperial Defence* (1897).

Clifford, J., *Brotherhood and the War in South Africa* (1900).

Earl of Cromer, *Ancient and Modern Imperialism* (1910).

Dilke, C.W., *Greater Britain: A Record of Travel in English-speaking Countries during 1866 and 1867* (1868) and *Problems of Greater Britain* (1890).

—— and Spenser Wilkinson, H., *Imperial Defence* (1892).

Froude, J.A., *Oceana or England and her Colonies* (1886).

Hobson, J.A., *Imperialism: A Study* (3rd revised edn, 1938).

Hurd, A., *The British Fleet. Is it Sufficient and Efficient?* (1901).

—— *The Command of the Sea. Some Problems of Imperial Defence considered in the light of the German Navy Act of 1912* (1912).

Jebb, R., *Studies in Colonial Nationalism* (1905).

—— *The Britannic Question* (1913).

Jones, K., *Fleet Street and Downing Street* (1919).

Kidd, B., *Social Evolution* (1895).

Lethbridge, R., *India and Fiscal Policy* (1903).

—— *India and Imperial Preference* (1907).

Low, S., *A Vision of India* (1906).

Milner, A., *Constructive Imperialism: Five Speeches* (1908).

Newspapers of Greater Britain associated with the Empire Press Union (1918).

Parkin, G.R., *Imperial Federation* (1892).

—— *The Problem of National Unity* (1892).

Pearson, C.H., *National Life and Character. A Forecast* (1893).

Seeley, J.R., *The Expansion of England* (edited and introduced by J. Gross; reprint, Chicago, 1971).

Thursfield, J.R., *The Navy and the Nation or Naval Warfare and Imperial Defence* (1897).

—— *Nelson and Other Naval Studies* (1909).

Webb, S., *Twentieth Century Politics: A Policy of National Efficiency*, Fabian Society Tract, no. 108 (1901).

—— *Fabianism and the Fiscal Question. An Alternative Policy*, Fabian Society Tract, no. 116 (1904).

Wyatt, H.S. and Horton-Smith, L., *The Truth about the Navy* (1909).

C. SECONDARY SOURCES

1 Books

Ayerst, D., *Garvin of the* Observer (1985).

Baines, D., *Migration in a Mature Economy. Emigration from England and Wales, 1861–1900* (Cambridge, 1985).

—— *Emigration from Europe, 1861–1900* (Cambridge, 1991).

Beeler, J., *British Naval Policy in the Gladstone–Disraeli Era, 1866–80* (Stanford, CA, 1997).

Blewett, N., *The Peers, the Parties and the People. The General Elections of 1910* (1972).

Brown, B.H., *The Tariff Reform Movement in Great Britain* (New York, 1943).

Burton, A., *Burdens of History. British Feminists, Indian Women and Imperial Culture, 1865–1915* (Chapel Hill, NC, 1994).

—— *At the Heart of Empire. Indians and the Colonial Encounter in Late-Victorian Britain* (1998).

Butler, J.R.M., *Lord Lothian (Philip Kerr) 1882–1940* (1960).

Cain, P.J. and Hopkins, A.G., *British Imperialism. Vol. I: Innovation and Expansion, 1688–1914* and *Vol. II: British Imperialism: Crisis and Deconstruction, 1914–1990* (Harlow, 1993).

Coetzee, F., *For Party or Country. Nationalism and the Dilemmas of Popular Conservatism in Edwardian England* (Oxford, 1990).

Constantine, S. (ed.), *Emigrants and Empire. British Settlement in the Dominions between the Wars* (Manchester, 1990).

Dark, S., *The Lambeth Conferences: Their History and Their Significance* (1930).

Darwin, J., *Britain, Egypt and the Middle East: Imperial Policy in the Aftermath of War, 1918–22* (1981).

Davis, L.E. and Huttenback, R.A., *Mammon and the Pursuit of Empire: The Political Economy of British Imperialism, 1860–1912* (Cambridge, 1986).

Eldrige, C.C., *England's Mission. Imperial Ideas in the Age of Gladstone and Disraeli, 1868–1880* (1973).

Fedorowich, K., *Unfit for Heroes. Reconstruction and Soldier Settlement in the Empire between the Wars* (Manchester, 1995).

Fitzhardinge, L.F., *The Little Digger, 1914–52. William Morris Hughes. A Political Biography* (1979).

Friedberg, A.L., *Britain and the Weary Titan. Britain and the Experience of Relative Decline, 1895–1914* (Princeton, NJ, 1988).

Gallagher, J., *The Decline, Revival and Fall of the British Empire. The Ford Lectures and Other Essays*, edited by Anil Seal (Cambridge, 1982).

Gilmour, D., *Curzon* (1994).

Gollin, A.M., *Proconsul in Politics. A Study of Lord Milner in Opposition and Power* (1964).

Gordon, D.C., *The Dominion Partnership in Imperial Defence, 1870–1914* (1965).

Grayson, R., *Austen Chamberlain and the Commitment to Europe. British Foreign Policy 1924–29* (1997).

Green, E.H.H., *The Crisis of Conservatism. The Politics, Economics and Ideology of the British Conservative Party, 1880–1914* (1995).

Grigg, J., *The Young Lloyd George* (1973).

Hadley, M.L. and Sarty, R., *Tin-Pots and Pirate Ships: Canadian Naval Forces and German Sea Raiders, 1880–1918* (Montreal, 1991).

Halpern, D., *The Mediterranean Naval Situation, 1908–14* (Cambridge, MA, 1971).

Hammerton, A.J., *Emigrant Gentlewomen. Genteel Poverty and Female Emancipation, 1830–1914* (1979).

Hancock, W.K., *Smuts. The Sanguine Years, 1870–1919* (Cambridge, 1962).

Hendrick, H., *Child Welfare. England, 1872–1989* (1994).

Holland, R., *Britain and the Commonwealth Alliance, 1918–39* (1981).

Hutcheson, J.A., *Leopold Maxse and The National Review, 1893–1914. Right-wing Politics and Journalism in the Edwardian Era* (1989).

Jeffrey, K., *The British Army and the Crisis of Empire, 1918–22* (Manchester, 1984).

Kennedy, P., *The Rise and Fall of British Naval Mastery* (1976).

Kinnear, M., *The Fall of Lloyd George: The Political Crisis of 1922* (1973).

Koebner, R. and Schmidt, H.D., *Imperialism. The Story and Significance of a Political Word, 1840–1960* (Cambridge, 1964).

Koss, S., *The Rise and Fall of the Political Press. Vol. I: The Nineteenth Century* (1981) and *Vol. II: The Twentieth Century* (1984).

Mackenzie, J.M., *Propaganda and Empire. The Manipulation of British Public Opinion, 1880–1960* (Manchester, 1986).

—— (ed.), *Imperialism and Popular Culture* (Manchester, 1986).

Mangan, J.A., *The Cultural Bond. Sport, Empire and Society* (1992).

Marder, A.J., *The Anatomy of Sea Power: A History of British Naval Policy in the Pre-Dreadnought Era, 1880–1895* (1964).

—— *From Dreadnought to Scapa Flow: The Royal Navy in the Fisher Era, 1904–19* (Oxford, 1978).

Marrison, A.J., *British Business and Protection, 1903–32* (Oxford, 1996).

Matthew, H.C.G., *The Liberal Imperialists. The Ideas and Politics of a Post-Gladstonian Elite* (Oxford, 1973).

Neidpath, J., *The Singapore Naval Base and the Defence of Britain's Eastern Empire, 1919–41* (Oxford, 1981).

d'Ombrain, N., *War Machinery and High Policy: Defence Administration in Peacetime Britain, 1902–14* (1973).

Parr, J., *Labouring Children. British Immigrant Apprentices to Canada, 1869–1924* (1980).

Phillips, G.D., *The Diehards. Aristocratic Society and Politics in Edwardian England* (1979).

Porter, B., *The Lion's Share. A Short History of British Imperialism, 1850–1983* (2nd edn, Harlow, 1984).

—— *Britain, Europe and the World, 1850–1982: Delusions of Grandeur* (1983).

Pugh, M., *The Tories and the People, 1880–1935* (Oxford, 1985).

Reese, T.R., *The History of the Royal Commonwealth Society* (Oxford, 1968).

Robbins, K., *Nineteenth Century Britain. Integration and Diversity* (Oxford, 1995).

Sanders, M.L. and Taylor, P., *British Propaganda during the First World War, 1914–18* (1982).

Sandiford, K.A., *Cricket and the Victorians* (1994).

Scally, R.J., *The Origins of the Lloyd George Coalition: The Politics of Social Imperialism* (Princeton, NJ, 1975).

Schurman, D.M., *The Education of a Navy. The Development of British Naval Strategic Thought, 1867–1914* (1965).

Self, R., *Tories and Tariffs. The Conservative Party and the Politics of Tariff Reform, 1922–32* (1986).

Semmel, B., *Imperialism and Social Reform. English Social Imperial Thought, 1895–1914* (1960).

Startt, J.D., *Journalists for Empire. The Imperial Debate in the Edwardian Stately Press, 1903–13* (Westport, CT, 1991).

Sumida, J.T., *In Defence of Naval Supremacy: Finance, Technology and British Naval Policy, 1889–1914* (1989).

Tomes, J., *Balfour and Foreign Policy. The International Thought of a Conservative Statesman* (Cambridge, 1997).

Trollope, J., *Britannia's Daughters. Women of the British Empire* (1983).

Turner, J., *Lloyd George's Secretariat* (Cambridge, 1980).

Vernon, J., *Politics and the People: A Study in English Political Culture, c. 1815–1867* (Cambridge, 1993).

Wagner, G., *Children of the Empire* (1982).

Wigley, P.G., *Canada and the Transition to Commonwealth. British–Canadian Relations, 1917–26* (Cambridge, 1977).

Williams, R., *Defending the Empire. The Conservative Party and Britain's Defence Policy, 1899–1915* (1991)

2 Articles

Blakeley, B.L., 'Women and Imperialism: The Colonial Office and Female Emigration to South Africa, 1901–10', *Albion* (1981).

Bush, J., ' "The Right Sort of Woman". Female Emigrators and Emigration to the British Empire, 1890–1910', *Women's History Review* (1994).

Brown, K.D., 'The Trade Union Tariff Reform Association, 1904–13', *JBS* (1970).

Cain, P.J., 'The Economic Philosophy of Constructive Imperialism', in Navari, C. (ed.), *British Politics and the Spirit of the Age* (Keele, 1996).

Colley, L., 'Britishness and Otherness', *JBS* (1992).

Constantine, S., 'Empire Migration and Social Reform, 1880–1950', in Pooley, C.G. and Whyte, I.D. (eds), *Migrants, Emigrants and Immigrants. A Social History of Migration* (1991).

Cook, G.L., 'Sir Robert Borden, Lloyd George and British Military Policy, 1917–18', *HJ* (1971).

Darwin, J., 'The Fear of Falling. British Politics and Imperial Decline since 1900', *TRHS*, 5th series (1986).

Dubow, S., 'Colonial Nationalism, the Milner Kindergarten and the Rise of "South Africanism", 1902–10', *HWJ* (1997).

Garside, W.R., 'Party Politics, Political Economy and British Protectionism, 1919–32', *History* (1998).

Gibbs, N.H., 'The Origins of Imperial Defence', in Hattendorf, J.B. and Jordan, R.S. (eds), *Maritime Strategy and the Balance of Power. Britain and America in the Twentieth Century* (Basingstoke, 1989).

Harrison, B., 'A Different World for Women: Nineteenth-Century Women Campaigners', *TCBH* (1992).

Hawkins, A., ' "Parliamentary Government" and Victorian Political Parties, *c*. 1830–80', *EHR* (1989).

Lambert, N., 'British Naval Policy, 1913–14: Financial Limitation and Strategic Revolution', *JMH* (1995).

—— 'Economy or Empire? The Fleet Unit Concept and the Quest for Collective Security in the Pacific, 1909–14', in Neilson, K. and Kennedy, G. (eds), *Far Flung Lines. Studies in Imperial Defence in Honour of Donald Mackenzie Schurman* (1997).

Mackenzie, J.M., 'Essay and Reflection: On Scotland and the Empire', *IHR* (1993).

—— 'Empire and National Identities: The case of Scotland', *TRHS* (1998).

Marks, S., 'History, the Nation and the Empire: Sniping from the Periphery', *HW* (1990).

Marshall, P.J., 'Imperial Britain', *JICH* (1995).

—— 'Imperial Britain', in Marshall (ed.), *The Cambridge Illustrated History of the British Empire* (Cambridge, 1996).

McKercher, B.J.C., 'The Politics of Naval Arms Limitation in Britain in the 1920s', in Goldstein, E. and Maurer, J. (eds), *The Washington Conference, 1921–22. Naval Rivalry, East Asian Stability and the Road to Pearl Harbor* (1993).

Mehrotra, S.R., 'Imperial Federation and India, 1868–1917', *JCPS* (1961).

—— 'On the use of the term "Commonwealth" ', *JCPS* (1963).

Offer, A., 'The British Empire, 1870–1914: A Waste of Money?', *EcHR* (1993).

Saul, S.B., 'The Economic Significance of Constructive Imperialism', *JEH* (1957).

Stearn, R.T., 'War Correspondents and Colonial War, *c*. 1870–1914', in Mackenzie, J.M. (ed.), *Popular Imperialism and the Military, 1850–1950* (Manchester, 1992).

Summers, A., 'The Character of Edwardian Nationalism: Three Popular Leagues', in Kennedy, P. and Nicholls, A. (eds), *Nationalist and Racialist Movements in Britain and Germany before 1914* (Oxford, 1981).

Thompson, A.S., 'The Language of Imperialism and the Meanings of Empire: Imperial Discourse in British Politics, 1895–1914', *JBS* (1997).

—— 'Tariff Reform: An Imperial Strategy, 1903–13', *HJ* (1997).

—— 'Imperial Ideology in Edwardian Britain', in Bosco, A. and May, A. (eds), *The Round Table, the Empire/Commonwealth and British Foreign Policy* (1997).

Van-Helten, J.J. and Williams, K., ' "The Crying Need of South Africa": The Emigration of British Single Women to the Transvaal, 1901–10', *JSAS* (1983).

Waites, B., 'Peoples of the Underdeveloped World', in Cecil, H. and Liddle, P. (eds), *Facing Armageddon. The First World War Experienced* (1996).

Williams, R., 'Arthur Balfour, Sir John Fisher and the Politics of Naval Reform', *BIHR* (1987).

Wilson, K., 'Empire of Virtue. The Imperial Project and Hanoverian Culture, *c*. 1720–1785', in Stone, L. (ed.), *An Imperial State at War. Britain from 1689 to 1815* (1994).

3 Unpublished Theses

May, A.C., 'The Round Table, 1910–1966', University of Oxford D.Phil (1995).

Murphy, R., 'Walter Long and the Conservative Party, 1905–21', University of Bristol PhD (1984).

Thompson, A.S., 'Thinking Imperially? Imperial Pressure Groups and the Idea of Empire in Late-Victorian and Edwardian Britain', University of Oxford D.Phil (1994).

Williams, K.I., 'The British State, Social Imperialism and Emigration from Britain, 1900–22: The Ideology and Antecedents of the Empire Settlement Act', University of London PhD (1985).

Index